Institutional Diversity in American Postsecondary Education

A Volume in
Identity & Practice in Higher Education-Student Affairs

Series Editors

Pietro A. Sasso
Delaware State University

Shelley Price-Williams
University of Northern Iowa

Identity & Practice in
Higher Education-Student Affairs

Pietro A. Sasso and Shelley Price-Williams, Series Editors

Institutional Diversity in American Postsecondary Education (2024)
edited by Tiffany J. Davis, Shelley Price-Williams, and Pietro A. Sasso

Affirming Identity, Advancing Belonging, and
Amplifying Voice in Sororities and Fraternities (2024)
edited by Pietro A. Sasso, Mónica Lee Miranda, and J. Patrick Biddix

Latinx College Students: Innovations in Mental Health, Advocacy, and
Social Justice Programs (2023)
edited by José Miguel Maldonado and Adrianne L. Johnson

Stir What You've Got: Insights From a College President (2023)
by William T. Greer Jr.

Stir What You've Got: Insights From a College President (2023)
by William T. Greer Jr.

Identity in Supervision:
Understanding Who Works for You and
Who You Work for in Higher Education (2023)
edited by Roger "Mitch" Nasser Jr.

Still Working While Black:
The Untold Stories of Student Affairs Practitioners (2023)
edited by Antione D. Tomlin

Working While Black:
The Untold Stories of Student Affairs Practitioners (2022)
edited by Antione D. Tomlin

Institutional Diversity in American Postsecondary Education

Editors

Tiffany J. Davis
University of Houston

Shelley Price-Williams
University of Northern Iowa

Pietro A. Sasso
Delaware State University

INFORMATION AGE PUBLISHING, INC.
Charlotte, NC • www.infoagepub.com

Library of Congress Cataloging-in-Publication Data

CIP record for this book is available from the Library of Congress
http://www.loc.gov

ISBNs: 979-8-88730-613-1 (Paperback)

979-8-88730-614-8 (Hardcover)

979-8-88730-615-5 (ebook)

Copyright © 2024 Information Age Publishing Inc.

All rights reserved. No part of this publication may be reproduced, stored in
a retrieval system, or transmitted, in any form or by any means, electronic,
mechanical, photocopying, microfilming, recording or otherwise, without written
permission from the publisher.

Printed in the United States of America

CONTENTS

Scholar Foreword
Eboni M. Zamani-Gallaher .... *ix*

Editorial Foreword
Pietro Sasso, Shelley Price-Williams, and Tiffany J. Davis.....................*xi*

SECTION I: INSTITUTIONAL SPECTRUMS

1. Views From the Ivy Tower: Exploring Prestige, Privilege, and Perseverance Within American Ivy League Universities
   Ayana T. Hardaway, Brandy M. Jones, Sharron Scott, and Janelle L. West... *5*

2. Research Universities
   Ginny Jones Boss *19*

3. Land-Grant Institutions
   Ashley B. Clayton and Victoria C. Lloyd *33*

4. Small Colleges and Universities
   Carolyn H. Livingston and Christa J. Porter.. *47*

5. Rural Colleges & Universities: The Overlooked Champions of Higher Education
   Sabrina A. Klein and Andrew Koricich... *59*

6. Urban Serving Institutions: Serving Students, Serving Cities
   Yolanda M. Barnes and Tiffany J. Davis *71*

vi CONTENTS

SECTION II: EQUITY-ORIENTED INSTITUTIONS

7. Literacy and Liberation: Historically Black Colleges and
Universities and Culturally Relevant Praxis
Jennifer M. Johnson and Stephanie J. Tisdale 85

8. America's Most Adaptable Institutions: Community Colleges
Vincent D. Carales and Erin E. Doran 97

9. Native American Serving and Tribal Colleges
*Tara Leigh Sands, Terry Chavis, April Brannon Yazza,
and Roger Davis, Jr.* 109

10. Hispanic-Serving Institutions: Levers of Latina/o/x/e Uplift
Stephanie Aguilar-Smith 119

11. Asian American and Native American Pacific Islander-Serving
Institutions (AANAPISI) as Critical Sites for Asian American,
Native Hawaiian, and Pacific Islander (AA&NHPI) Students
in Higher Education
*Mike Hoa Nguyen, Demeturie Toso-Lafaele Gogue,
Kristine Jan Cruz Espinoza, Becket C. Duncan,
Rikka J. Venturanza, and Dong M. Dinh* 131

12. Serving Students With Disabilities: Institutions and Programs
Casey Yocum and Aaron Hughey 145

SECTION III: SPECIAL MISSION COLLEGES
AND UNIVERSITIES

13. Art and Design Institutions
Nicholas E. Negrete and Yoi Tanaka 161

14. Men's Colleges in the United States: A Tale of Three Cities
Terrell L. Strayhorn 177

15. U.S. Women Colleges and Universities
Carrie Kortegast 193

16. Faith-Based Higher Education in the United States: The
History and Present Status of Religiously Associated Institutions
Dennis E. Gregory and Kim E. Bullington 209

Contents vii

17. Military and Maritime Colleges and Universities
Julie Shank, Eric T. Olson, Emily Fisher Gray,
Tamara S. McKenna, David Taliaferro, and David J. Mollahan *223*

18. Occupational and Vocational Institutions
Kimberly R. Davis *239*

About the Authors..*249*

SCHOLAR FOREWORD

Eboni M. Zamani-Gallaher
University of Pittsburgh

It was during my adolescent years that I first took notice of the variation in the higher education landscape. During this time, it was impressed upon me that I should be college-bound. During this period, I was made aware of special population institutions such as women's colleges and historically Black colleges and universities (HBCUs) such Spelman College and Howard University through Ada S. McKinley Community Services on Chicago's Southside that encouraged first-generation students like me to attend college to foster educational and economic mobility to empower our communities. Now, 30+ years later, I have come full circle as a higher education scholar conversant with the nuances, challenges, and opportunities across different institutional types that comprise the U.S. postsecondary education system.

The collection of work in the text, *Institutional Diversity in American Postsecondary Education* features notable voices from the field that offer subject matter expertise that spans the spectrum of postsecondary institutions. Hence, the editors/authors provide both breadth and depth relative to a variety of types, with each chapter highlighting a different type of educational setting and experience for a diverse array of collegians. Edited by Drs. Tiffany J. Davis (University of Houston), Pietro A. Sasso (Delaware State University) and Shelley Price Williams (University of Northern Iowa), the book foregrounds the importance of context as well as the microenvironments that reside within such distinctive collegiate spaces. This text

---

Institutional Diversity in American Postsecondary Education, pp. ix–x
Copyright © 2024 by Information Age Publishing
www.infoagepub.com
All rights of reproduction in any form reserved.

blends theory and practice with contributing authors both celebrating and problematizing postsecondary education that is expansive, yet siloed. As you immerse yourself in this volume, critically consider the necessity of these unique academic spaces. It is in having this institutional spectrum that students from various backgrounds and walks of life may experience cultural congruence and have a person-environment fit. Chapters detailing a cross-section of institutional types are included: from small colleges to large land-grant institutions and from Ivy league and research universities to rural colleges, community colleges, and minority-serving institutions. In addition, the book features thoughtful contributions on disability access institutions, vocational schools, art and design institutions, military colleges, single-sex colleges, and religiously associated.

Among the many salient aspects of institutional types that are prominent in the text, other key areas that the book leans into are identity and intersectionality. The chapters contextualize the academic setting while also calling attention to how colleges are important spaces for the exploration and affirmation of identity. As youth and adult learners access postsecondary education, they do not enter the doorsills of their respective institutions absent of reconciling with aspects of self and how they identify individually as well as members of society outside of campus. Therefore, this book also provides things to consider to readers on how institutional and individuals' identity intersect and blend to create unique college-going experiences for every person.

In summary, higher education features a wide variety of postsecondary institutions, each providing something different for students to consider in light of their interests, aspirations, and in pursuit of their professional and personal goals. The multi-layered and complex nature of institutional identity and mission is especially important when considering student identity and the important matters of diversity, equity, inclusion, and belonging. College can be a transformative time for many students. For those wanting to explore current ideas and challenge old held beliefs regarding how valuable special population colleges are or whether there is too much variation of institution type in higher education, this book will be engaging. It is essential to question the foundations of, and experiences within, American higher education that often leads both institutions and individuals being positioned in the margins, particularly students already marginalized, decentered, and deemed as not mattering. In short, the editors/authors have provided a collection that reflects understanding and advocacy for the intersections of identity. From the institutional pedigreed elite ivies to resource dependent institutions, *Institutional Diversity in American Postsecondary Education* is also a treatise for recognizing the ways in which privilege intersects with identities (i.e., identities of the schools and the students).

EDITORIAL FOREWORD

Pietro Sasso, Shelley Price-Williams, and Tiffany J. Davis

Collectively, the editors have worked at more than 10 institutional types in faculty and higher education administration contexts. However, we continued to question why a text did not exist that explored the different institutional types, especially when there is an increased scholarly emphasis on "servingness" (student success) related to Minority Serving Institutions (MSIs) or other university formats. Many scholars describe the academic discipline of the study of postsecondary education as a low-consensus field. However, what has emerged within the last decade are *institutional scholars* or those faculty or researchers who focus their scholarly inquiry entirely on institutional types such as rural institution, regional public comprehensives, or Hispanic Serving Institutions. This crystallized the distinctiveness of higher education institutions and pushed for equitable greater support and resources for different student communities and formats of institutions. As editors, we believe we sourced some of the emerging and established institutional scholars in our academic field. We anticipate that this could be adopted as a seminal text within student affairs and higher education graduate preparation programs. Each chapter prompts reader reflection and/or class discussion or engagement. We encourage readers and university professors selecting this text for their courses to inspire specific courses about institutional types to hopefully inspire the next generation of institutional scholars.

Institutional Diversity in American Postsecondary Education, pp. xi–xix
Copyright © 2024 by Information Age Publishing
www.infoagepub.com
All rights of reproduction in any form reserved.

OUR ASSUMPTIONS

The relationship between higher education institutions is one that is rooted within the social contract, which has eroded. Society expects higher education to serve as what Clark Kerr terms the *multiversity* and higher education expects that society will properly provide endless resources for its insatiable and voracious appetite in both *branding* and prestige. This relationship altered the perception of higher education as a mature industry. Colleges and universities transformed themselves from insular pockets of learning and knowledge transfer to vehicles of economic entrepreneurship. No longer do colleges and universities operate in a vacuum, but they are now subject to free-market laws of supply and demand. They are subject to these same laws of capitalism because they have begun to engage in market-like behaviors through entrepreneurial initiatives and competition among themselves.

Stewards of colleges and universities have begun acting as entrepreneurs through attempts to generate ideas into revenue. They are seeking to generate revenue from other significant roles: research and service functions. This is happening through several methods. They are investing increasing amounts of venture capital in hopes of generating research into income to diversify their own revenue streams. It is the anticipation of an institution that this investment of capital will lead to patents which generate high returns. They are also investing in faculty curriculum and instruction which can be copyrighted and then marketed. Private-public partnerships through corporate sponsorships and research contracts are also ways colleges and universities are generating revenue. The goals of such partnerships are meant to facilitate the same outcome of others: to increase revenue. Beyond the entrepreneurial initiatives of venture capital, corporate sponsorships, and product marketing of faculty scholarship, higher education institutions are competing among themselves. They have diversified their external typologies to broadcast institutional differences to make themselves appear distinctive.

Colleges and universities now have begun a kind of arms race or *edifice complex*. They want to be the best; they want to be the "next" new Yale or Harvard. In doing so, they are vying for institutional prestige, which is the key factor that drives their competition. In doing so, colleges are willing to invest their resources in services and amenities to attract the best students, faculty, and researchers. Colleges and universities have engaged in extravagant spending to compete. They are building new residence halls, constructing fantastic student unions, and establishing state-of-the-art scientific labs to attract the best and brightest students, faculty, and researchers. Colleges and universities feel that to attract the best students, they have to raise the ceiling, but not the floor. They feel they can still serve their educational mission of accessibility for all prospective individuals, while attracting the best and the brightest. This head-long vie for prestige gives them a competitive edge in which they may gain greater market share in specific research areas, student interests, and other sought-after advantages which are needed to further generate revenue. This shift to a more entrepreneurial and capitalistic college or university is caused by the erosion of funding from the state government.

Higher education institutions have chosen to engage in market behaviors because of decreases in proportional state aid. To survive, they must diversify their revenue streams and locate alternative sources of funding. Higher education institutions have been very selective and careful about what they have chosen to invest in when locating alternative funding sources. This circumstance underscores the notion that most colleges are investing in their quest for prestige. If all colleges are investing their resources in prestige, they are establishing a precedent—colleges and universities are investing their own resources and human capital in a reputation. As colleges spend their diversified revenue streams and what little state appropriations they get in the *college arms race*, they endanger their reputation and, more importantly, their sustainability.

Although a college can invest and find new revenue streams, can it do the same with students? Colleges have sought to invest in students to establish prestige and stay competitive by offering more and more. In fact, colleges are not competing for affordability; they are competing for prestige. This is the heart of the change in higher education. However, colleges and universities need to be careful how much, if any, return they will get on their investment.

Meanwhile, the collegiate conflict of right versus privilege has facilitated access to higher education. This more open-door policy has facilitated the propagation of a new type of student, one that is not radical but more professionally minded. The American events of the 1960s were related to the fact that both young students and faculty realized that the new cultural capital acquired in education would not guarantee social mobility and economic success.

\More than a mere *power struggle* between the different aforementioned stakeholders, the student movements of the 1960s may well have symbolized a movement of privilege. At the time, students who fought against privilege ironically opened up an ethos of privilege in higher education and society. After this period, the campus became the social space where the *new outsiders*, that is, the working classes would emerge. The university changed its role from provider of elitist culture and high-brow character to that of the *certifier* of middle-class America in search of privilege.

The trend toward consumerism in higher education is antithetical to life of the mind and a well-rounded liberal arts education. This evolution of the core purpose of the college into a university industry made possible new attitudes about authority, social and geographic mobility, merit, and success that have come to characterize contemporary American society. This movement became central to middle-class habits of thought and action that a majority of current U.S. citizens have taken for granted. This text will seek to revivify our understanding of the American institutional diversity, with a critical lens toward equitable student success and professional contexts.

BACKGROUND AND CONTEXT

Inasmuch as postsecondary education has become a nearly expected right, it has begun to unravel from its initial, primary ethos. The historical significance of higher education was to provide societal and individual good in the pursuit of a life of the mind through the *artes liberales* approach. Universities have a foundational mission centered on undergraduate education and collegiality between the student as the learner and the faculty member as the professor. However, they seem far removed from that status in the modern age.

Contemporary colleges and universities are a far cry from what they originally were. Higher education of yesterday held true to its primary role, that is, to create new knowledge, disseminate past knowledge, and then transmit it to each generation. That function has changed over time. When our society was primarily agrarian, these same colleges catered to a different population. They were originally for elite, privileged males. If they did attend a college, their purpose was mainly to become a doctor, statesman, theologian, or a clergyman. The curriculum usually included Latin and English classical studies, which were usually complemented by courses in astronomy and metaphysics. These early colleges offered little else besides a faculty in residence, academic classes, and a dormitory. These circumstances established higher education as a privilege. However, the American Civil War and the continuation of *manifest destiny* across the country created new educational demands that extant private universities could not meet. Therefore, in 1862, President Lincoln signed the Morrill Act, which established 102 land-grant institutions to meet the growing technical and agricultural demands of the increasing U.S. population. This act established the "social contract" between the public and the various state colleges.

This unwritten social contract is more hypothetical and metaphorical in its existence. It states that all would invest in the advancement of postsecondary education via large-scale learning communities that would create the next generation of educated persons. Students would then reinvest their knowledge in the state and local communities to generate new economic opportunities. This social contract continued to work for decades, and thousands of students were afforded the benefits of reasonably priced tuition. Many colleges were able to then attract bright, young minds from across the United States and from abroad. The state colleges and their supporting governmental agencies continued to uphold the social contract as enrollment swelled during the Great Depression. Students enrolled in colleges and universities to weather the economic downturn. The G.I. Bill further invigorated this social contract after World War II when it sent thousands of veterans to colleges. Soon after, colleges became the pathway to the middle class and a vehicle for social mobility. Equal access for all citizens, at least in theory, was the calling card much later. This established college as an expected right.

The federal government, under President Johnson's *Great Society,* passed the Higher Education Act and Civil Rights Act during the 1960s, which created grants and equal opportunity respectively. These grants, or tuition waivers, were offered to low-income families. This afforded many under-represented identities the chance to attend college, but their presence was not supported on campus. Higher education was seen as a platform for equal access for all individuals, regardless of socioeconomic status. Through college, many have advanced themselves and created better lives for their families and communities. However, this social contract in which everyone invests their money through their individual tax contribution is failing, thus dramatically transforming higher education.

Higher education is so much of an expected right that undergraduate students have become mass consumers. Colleges and universities have sold their services and educational opportunity to students as part of this expected right under pressures to meet their bottom-line, therefore further enabling the consumerism of higher education. Accordingly, higher education has evolved from a privilege to a right into simply a product. This has given rise to academic capitalism as the colleges and universities have become increasingly entrepreneurial to cope with decreased state allocations. In the face of increasing student consumerism and academic capitalism, higher education continues to cope with difficult times.

This change marks a transformation as current colleges take on a radically different primary function, that is, academic capitalism. Furthermore, this dramatic shift has established an existential moment in the emerging historical narrative of higher education in that this new primary function and purpose is being questioned.

Since 2016, more than 80 non-profit higher education institutions have closed or merged. The density of these appears in the Northeast and Midwest amid demographic shifts and tend to be private residential colleges or special-mission institutions such as arts or seminaries. These mergers include institutions such as Bloomfield College being absorbed by

Montclair State University or University of the Sciences collapsing into St. Joseph's University. Holy Names University and Cazenovia College made announcements in the 2022–2023 academic year to close.

Additionally, state systems have consolidated state-supported institutions in Georgia, Maine, Pennsylvania, and Texas. For example, Stephen F. Austin State University is affiliating with the University of Texas system after being one of only two remaining independent state universities which follows other similar regional public universities in the state affiliating with others such as Texas Tech or Texas A&M. In Pennsylvania, the PA State System of Higher Education (PASSHE) system represents the other public, state-assisted institutions outside of the Penn State University system and they merged many of their institutions into two new universities as part of a planned system redesign process. These storied institutions included California, Clarion, and Edinboro forming Penn West University as well as Bloomsburg, Lock Haven, and Mansfield, becoming Commonwealth University. Each of these campuses retains some signature programs, but many administrative functions, such as campus oversight, were centralized. These are no longer distinctive, independent colleges. Higher education is again in another period of contraction following what Thelin (2017) posits as the *College Arms Race* during the early part of the 21st century when there was a building boom on college campuses and expansion of online learning infrastructure. Thelin also noted that higher education transitioned from *bucks for brains* to *bucks for bricks* to demonstrate the changes in the ways higher education prioritized spending its fiscal resources. This is a component of the larger *edifice complex* facing higher education in which institutions have expanded their campuses and amenities to attract new students or in their quests for prestige.

This is not the first-time higher education has experienced contraction across its national, loosely coupled system. After the Civil War, many professional and vocational colleges closed as the first Morrill Land Grant was instituted. Many institutions also temporarily suspended operations during the Great Depression or lowered their academic level from junior college to college preparatory high schools. What this suggests is that historically higher education has expanded and contracted over time, but it remains resilient and flexible to the needs of traditional-age undergraduate students or adult learners. What has allowed higher education to remain resilient and respond to shifting demographics and other learner or research needs is its complex, loosely coupled network of colleges that span a dizzying variety of forms.

These range from residential liberal arts such as the Union College, military college such as the U.S. Naval Academy, or special-mission institutions such as Fashion Institute of Technology. These include institutions such as junior or community colleges as well as a larger *multiversity* such as the University of Michigan in settings that include urban, rural, suburban, and online. There are even still single-gender institutions such as Spellman College, Sweetbriar College, or Mount Holyoke College for women or Hampden–Sydney, Moorehouse Colleges, Wabash College for men. There are additionally hundreds of sacred religious institutions ranging from Brigham Young University to Georgetown University. Each category should have its own business card detailing its different aims. Even if placing a specific school inside this framework gives some guidance, it serves as a reminder that American higher education is complex and varied—a point that is reinforced by the framework.

This institutional diversity is a distinguishing feature of American higher education. In fact, Thelin (2017) articulated this "diversity of choice" as a strength, outlining the marketplace of higher education in which different types of colleges exist across a spectrum of missions, institutional sagas, and histories. Within this marketplace is a bewildering and disorienting catalog of different institutional types and classifications that exist within a conglomerate of rankings and ratings that are ordered by *U.S. News & World Report* and Petersons. Since 1984, *U.S. News and World Report* has proliferated its ratings and rankings of American universities and academic programs. Such rankings are often connected to a larger quest for prestige and primarily facilitated by these private-sector publications, but are juxtaposed to the higher education industry-created Carnegie Classification system.

The Carnegie Classification originated in 1973 and now is under the stewardship of the Center for Postsecondary Research at Indiana University. It includes more than 2,800 four-year degree and 1,700 two-year degree institutions. The Carnegie Classification system was created as an approach to differentiate the more than 4,000 institutions by size, mission, and scope for research and policy analysis. However, the continued reclassification of the system in 2005, 2010, and the addition of new categories in 2018, such as the doctoral/professional (Research III category), has advanced the call attention to and emphasize the importance of the considerable institutional diversity of U.S. higher education. It is revised to accommodate the differentiation in institutional missions amidst the mission creep of land-grants or state flagships into Clark Kerr's concept of the multiversity or the advancement of regional public universities into lower-tier research institutions as they add more graduate or doctoral programs. Additionally, institutions beyond Historically Black Colleges and Universities (HBCU) have taken on secondary descriptors about the populations they serve to become federally designated which include Minority Serving Institutions (MSIs) with servingness subtypes of Asian American Native American Pacific Islander-Serving Institutions (ANNAPISIs), Alaska Native and Native Hawaiian Serving Institutions (ANNHs), Historically Black

Colleges & Universities (HBCUs), Hispanic Serving institutions (HSIs), Native American-Serving Non-Tribal Institutions (NASNTIs), Predominantly Black Institutions (PBIs), Tribal Colleges and Universities (TCUs), and MSI Community Colleges (MSICC).

No taxonomy by itself can provide a classification that is not superficial. For instance, while public four-year colleges enroll the greatest number of students, they are not the biggest number of institutions. This is because these institutions often have large student populations. However, these typologies do not fully describe or conceptualize the organizational, administrative, culture, or student experiences of each of these typologies. Furthermore, they often overlook the nuance of special mission institutions and the role and impact of Minority Serving Institutions (MSIs). This lack of recognition often facilitates continued invisibility for different institutional types and the diverse student populations they may educate and support. Therefore, this edited text seeks to be a compendium resource to fill this gap for readers to understand more about institutional diversity in American higher education.

ORGANIZATION OF TEXT

We have organized the text by grouping institutional types into clusters: (a) institutional spectrums; (b) equity-oriented institutions; and (c) special mission colleges and universities. The institutional spectrum section includes those that are primarily distinguished by geographic location and size. Section I contains chapters on urban, research, land-grant (state flagships), small colleges, rural, and Ivy League institutions. Section II contains chapters about equity-oriented institutions who primarily serve historically excluded populations whose primary role is to promote access and expand opportunities for marginalized and disenfranchised student populations, including minority-serving institutions and community colleges. This section includes chapters on HBCUs, community colleges, Native American Serving, Hispanic Serving, Asian American Native American Pacific Islander-Serving, and Disability. Section III explores special mission institutions with narrow, historical foci that support distinctive curricula. These include art, men's colleges, women's colleges, faith-based, military, and vocational institutions. Each section contains a lead-in as a primer or framing for each of the sections to guide the reader.

CHAPTER FRAMING

Each chapter is self-contained and independent, much like our national loosely coupled system of higher education. Each chapter also features standard headings and ends with questions to prompt reflection, which provides continuity and cohesion for this text. What is distinctive about this text is the focus on organizational culture in describing what it is like to specifically work in administrative positions at these institutions. There is also a specific section dedicated to access equity and student success to elucidate the servingness of each institutional type.

The *History* section discusses the historical foundations and evolution of the institutional type to consider how their historical evolution connects to its contemporary positionality within the higher education landscape. The *Organization Structure and Culture* identifies the traditional organization or administrative structure of these institutions and highlights the various potential institutional culture(s) that may exist across the institutional type related to academic affairs, student success/affairs, and enrollment management. *Student Success & Populations* describes the demographics and experiences of students with an emphasis on educational equity, access, and student success. *Professional Context* explores what it is like to work at the specific institutional type and its working conditions/experiences which serves as "voices from the field" to better describe the requisite skills, knowledge, or dispositions that are essential for working within this institutional type. *Future Considerations and Directions* include contemporary, critical, or emerging issues and trends and provides critique or directionality for the continued sustainability of these institutions and how they can better contribute to educational equity and access. The final section is *Discussion Questions,* in which each chapter features a set of questions to prompt discussion and critical thinking.

REFERENCE

Thelin, J. R. (2017). *American higher education: Issues and institutions.* Routledge.

SECTION I

INSTITUTIONAL SPECTRUMS

Intentionally positioned at the beginning of the book, the section on "Institutional Spectrums" details foundational institutions of higher education that began with the ivy league and spans across the demographic landscape of the United States. This historical expansion of institutional types provides a continuum of access, ranging from citizens located in urban populations to academic deserts and regional locales. The chapters in this section form the early frame of higher education.

As the first chapter in the text, Hardaway et al. "Views From the Tower" provides a historical overview of this early institutional type known for its prestige, selective admissions, faculty, and rigor. The Ivies are wealthy institutions with healthy retention and graduation rates. Although the institutions hold great prominence in the history of higher education, an intentional focus on diversity, equity, and inclusion is more recent. Hardaway et al. note, "Students privileged to attend ivy league institutions benefit from a host of irrefutable advantages, all of which transfer to social elitism." There is no question this institutional type will continue to hold a premier place in higher education; yet, this sector is challenged to halt the reproduction of inequality.

Boss, in Chapter 2, positions research universities as the "predominant institutional type" in the United States. Cultivated in part by government legislation in the late 1800s, research universities mirrored a shift in educational purpose to generate new knowledge and advance society. This altered the relationship between faculty and students and generated early semblances of what we now know as student affairs. Boss characterizes

---

Institutional Diversity in American Postsecondary Education, pp. 1–3
Copyright © 2024 by Information Age Publishing
www.infoagepub.com
All rights of reproduction in any form reserved.

2 SECTION I: INSTITUTIONAL SPECTRUMS

research universities as "complex and dense organizational structures with large enrollments." Moreover, the focus on prestige and economic logics inadvertently results in challenges to access by historically underserved groups. A challenge, Boss specifies, is for research universities to prioritize access and support student success, while maintaining a focus on research excellence.

The focus in Chapter 3 is on land-grant institutions. Clayton and Lloyd note this institutional type as instrumental in the access to higher education by women, religious minorities, and Students of Color. Established through governmental action and considered one of the most influential polices in history, the land-grant institution was born. Yet, the authors emphasize the detrimental impact to numerous Indigenous tribes. Land-grant institutions, half of which are Historically Black Colleges and Universities and Tribal Colleges and Universities, serve over half of all college students in the United States. Clayton and Lloyd point to a need for visibility and state, "while the land-grant institution is still alive and well, not enough individuals are knowledgeable about its history and relevance."

In Chapter 4, Livingston and Porter focus on the small college and university that holds fewer than 5,000 students, and in the 19th century prepared clergy and leaders for local communities. These institutions helped "young men make the transition from rural farms to complex urban occupations." Later in history, women, Students of Color, and persons with disabilities found access through this sector of higher education. The authors indicate its values, personalized relationships, and organic change as unique characteristics that distinguish this type of institution. A challenge, Livingston and Porter note, is for small colleges to be externally focused as much as it is internally.

Klein and Koricich introduce the rural college and university in Chapter 5. The authors define this institutional type as one that is unique due to its physical location in rural areas that evolved from normal and denominational schools and governmental action. Rural colleges and universities provide broad access to what is often a land-based education desert or an online education desert. Klein and Koricich remarked, "these rural institutions provide a distinctive access point to higher education" and there is "still much to be learned about the students who attend." More importantly in this work, the authors unveil the harm of inaccurate narratives about rurality overall on rural institutions, students, and the surrounding regions.

Finally, in Chapter 6, Barnes and Davis magnify the value of the urban-serving institution (USI) and its critical role in extending access to higher education to historically underserved populations to include low-income, racial/ethnic minority, and first-generation students. Birthed during the last century in tandem with population growth in urban settings, the authors emphasize the need to understand how these "anchor" institutions came to be situated demographically and the associated complexities in mission. Barnes and Davis state, "USIs reflect the demographics of the community in which they reside." This sustainability of USIs is critical and reliant on leaders to safeguard the institution's core purpose.

This section distills what might be considered the historical foundation of higher education in the United States. What may be gleaned from the six respective chapters is that no sector of higher education is immune from internal and external challenges. Grounded in history and governmental action for the benefit of the citizenry, these foundational types continue to evolve and change. Each institution's role in advancing equitable access is premier, while striding closely to its mission. Lastly, small colleges and universities and rural institutions must promote publicized external value to their institutional stakeholders for future sustainability.

CHAPTER 1

VIEWS FROM THE IVY TOWER

Exploring Prestige, Privilege, and Perseverance Within American Ivy League Universities

Ayana T. Hardaway
Stanford University

Brandy M. Jones
University of Michigan

Sharron Scott
Temple University

Janelle L. West
Thrive Scholars

The Ivy League was originally grouped together as an athletic conference and the term formally became official through the formation of the National Collegiate Athletic Association (NCAA) Division I athletic conference in 1954 (Leitch, 1978). Over time, as these athletic teams began to attract more funding, the demands for admissions and academic excellence became the standard. Ivy League institutions are known for matriculating some of the world's most renowned leaders and individuals including United States presidents, executive branch cabinet members, Supreme Court Justices, Pulitzer Prize recipients, Nobel Laureates, politicians, prime

---

Institutional Diversity in American Postsecondary Education, pp. 5–17
Copyright © 2024 by Information Age Publishing
www.infoagepub.com
All rights of reproduction in any form reserved.

6 A. T. HARDAWAY ET AL.

ministers, scientists, philosophers, artists, entertainers, and athletes (Thelin, 2004). In the following chapter, we discuss institutional characteristics of Ivy League institutions through the following sections: organization structure and culture, student populations and experiences, professional context, conclusion, and reflection questions.

HISTORY

Among the first colleges and universities in America, Ivy League institutions laid the foundation for the development of higher education within the United States and are known for their prestige, highly selective admissions process, award-winning faculty, and academic rigor (Marine, 2015). Founded in New England, New York, and Pennsylvania during the 17th and 18th centuries, Ivy League universities, also known as the Ancient Eight and the Ivies, are comprised of the following institutions: Brown University, Columbia University, Cornell University, Dartmouth College, Harvard University, Princeton University, University of Pennsylvania, and Yale University. Seven of the eight schools were founded before the Revolutionary War, during the U.S. colonial period (Desmond, 2011). Cornell University is the exception, which was founded in 1865 (see Table 1.1).

Table 1.1

The Ancient Eight

Institution	Year Founded	Location
Harvard University	1636	Cambridge, Massachusetts
Yale University	1701	New Haven, Connecticut
University of Pennsylvania	1740	Philadelphia, Pennsylvania
Princeton University	1746	Princeton, New Jersey
Columbia University	1754	New York, New York
Brown University	1764	Providence, Rhode Island
Dartmouth College	1769	Hanover, New Hampshire
Cornell University	1865	Ithaca, New York

ORGANIZATIONAL STRUCTURE AND CULTURE

As private research universities, Ivy League institutions are recipients of some of the largest financial endowments in the world, along with millions of dollars in research funding annually, offering ample resources for financial aid, research endeavors, and academic programs which fuel their prestige (American Council on Education, 2012). For example, in 2021, Harvard's endowment soared to $53.2 billion dollars, reaching its largest sum in history and for any educational institution in the world (Ma & Simauchi, 2021). As highly selective institutions, Ivy League schools are also known for their extremely low acceptance rates. Despite having some of the highest recorded application rates in 2021, on average, all eight schools reported having acceptance rates below 10% for the class of 2025 (Top Tier Admissions, 2022). Ranking among the top 17 universities in the 2022 *U.S. News and World National University Report*, all eight Ivy League institutions serve as members of the Association of American Universities, one of the most prestigious alliances of American research institutions of higher education (Association of American Universities, n.d.).

Student Life and Academics

As Ivy League is often equated to elite, it has been important to maintain this integrity, or at least the perception thereof. To do so, the Council of Ivy Group Presidents, composed of the current sitting Presidents, set academic, admission, staffing, financial, and athletic standards (Ivy Council, n.d.). Recent statistics show that due to their relatively small size in comparison to state and public universities, Ivy League institutions have small student-to-staff ratios, with Columbia having the smallest ratio of 4.6 students to one instructor (Duffin, 2021). Academics are rigorous, as to be expected among these elite institutions; however, as of 2020, full-time student retention rates averaged 75%, with an average of 86% 4-year graduation rate as of 2021 (Duffin, 2021).

Diversity, Equity, Inclusion, and Culture

More recently, Ivy League institutions have placed more financial resources and efforts toward addressing issues of diversity, equity, and inclusion because of racial tension, campus protests, and students demanding more equitable conditions for underrepresented students on their campus (Friedersdorf, 2015; Hernandez et al., 2015). For example, Brown allocated $100 million to address issues of diversity amid student protests. Even more recently, Harvard President Larry Bacow released the *Report of the Committee on Harvard & the Legacy of Slavery*, a University-wide effort in collaboration with the Harvard Radcliffe Institute and guided by a committee of faculty members drawn from every Harvard school, and announced that Harvard will commit $100 million in research funding to

8 A. T. HARDAWAY ET AL.

reckon with the institutional ties to slavery (Radcliffe Institute for Advanced Study at Harvard University, 2022). Dean Tomiko Brown-Nagin, Chair of the Presidential Committee stated, "We cannot dismantle what we do not understand, and we cannot understand the contemporary injustice we face unless we reckon honestly with our history" (Harvard University, 2022, para. 3). The report details the institutional benefits gained from slavery and the university's role in perpetuating racial inequality.

STUDENT SUCCESS AND POPULATIONS

Recent enrollment data from the National Center for Education Statistics (NCES) report that during the 2020–2021 academic year, a total of 156,851 undergraduate and graduate students were enrolled within Ivy League institutions: 63,012 undergraduate and 83,839 graduate students (NCES, n.d.). Among Ivy League institutions, overall enrollment rates range from approximately 6,100 in the case of Dartmouth, to over 20,000 in the case of Columbia, Cornell, Harvard, and Penn in both undergraduate and graduate programs (NCES, n.d.). Over the last 20 years, Ivy League universities have adopted a variety of online education courses and degree programs. As of 2020–2021, 99,834 students have enrolled online exclusively at Ivy League institutions.

Students privileged to attend Ivy League institutions benefit from a host of irrefutable advantages, all of which transfer to social elitism in American society. In other words, "Elite colleges may be few in number but their influence on the lives of individual students and on American society as a whole is outsized" (Jack, 2019, p. 7). One example of this privilege can be seen in the establishment of the Ivy Council in 1990. The council, consisting of student government leaders from each of the eight Ivy League institutions, is an incubator for business and political leadership (Ivy Council, n.d.). Those who have benefitted and succeeded as a result of attending Ivy League institutions have historically been associated with American upper-class White Anglo-Saxon men. Data shows that more students come from families in the top 1% of the income distribution (14.5%) than the bottom half of the income distribution (13.5%; Chetty et al., 2017). Furthermore, while Ivy League institutions have started offering considerable financial aid packages to middle- and lower-income students to help increase class and socioeconomic diversity, student enrollment data suggest that those occupying less affluent households remain low (Chetty et al., 2017). Although the benefits of matriculating at an Ivy League institution are well documented within the higher education discourse, including graduates experiencing greater financial and social gains, and securing favorable employment opportunities, American Ivy League universities have also received scrutiny for their reputation around educational equity and access for underrepresented students (Zimmerman, 2019).

Enrollment Data by Race and Gender

Given America's complicated history with race and the inherent social caste system, it comes as no surprise that, for much of their existence, America's Ivy League institutions were the exclusive terrain of White males (Bradley, 2018; Wilkerson, 2020). Although White women eventually joined the ivy ranks, Hodges (2021) argues that post-civil rights movement, Ivy League institutions made little success recruiting students of color. Affirmative action policies resulted in an increase, albeit minimal, of Black students on its premier campuses. However, Wilkerson (2020) informs, "But while Affirmative Action grew out of the civil rights movement fought by the lowest-caste people and their White allies, decades of analyzes show that it is White women, and thus White families, rather than African Americans, who became the prime beneficiaries of a plan intended to redress centuries of injustice against the lowest-caste people" (p. 193). Since 1994, Black students have only made up only 7% to 8% of Ivy League campuses. As of 2017, Black students within the Ivy League make up 9% of freshmen and only 15% of college-age Americans (Ashkenas et al., 2017). More recently, arguments have been made in 2019 and 2020 against Yale and Harvard for engaging in racist discriminatory admissions practices against Asian-American candidates (Shortell & Romine, 2020). Consequently, contemporary educational equity and access issues continue to plague America's top-rated institutions of higher learning.

Experiences of Underrepresented Students

Although seemingly a rite of passage for America's wealthy elite, the presence, and experiences of underrepresented students on Ivy League campuses is ambiguous at best. When students of color make it to the Ivy League, the question of what constitutes campus diversity increasingly bears scrutiny. Scott et al. (2021) coined the term "dubious Diversity" (p. 82) as a salient finding in their investigation exploring how race and class shaped the college choice process and collegiate experiences of Black undergraduate students attending Ivy League institutions. The researchers found an underrepresentation of Black native students and an overrepresentation of Black immigrant or Black international undergraduates on Ivy League campuses. Study findings reveal that respondents perceived their university recruitment efforts as linked to perceptions of socioeconomic status, reporting that "If anything, I think they're making more of an effort with African students given that a lot of them are wealthier" (Scott et al., 2021, p. 83).

Massey et al. (2007) reported that the overrepresentation of Black immigrants on Ivy League campuses results in heated debates about the degree to which Black immigrants benefit from affirmative action as opposed to Black natives for whom the policies were originally intended. Equally important, the researchers found that Black natives and Black immigrants report having different ethnic identities. Thus, the question of "Who is Black on America's Ivy League campuses?" has recently emerged within the higher education discourse.

Race and Gender Issues

Issues of racism and gender discrimination continue to be a challenge at America's most prestigious institutions. Bradley (2018) argued that Black Ivy League students have always been marginalized and that their race sets them apart resulting in isolation and alienation. Scholars have also argued that Latino and Black students attending Ivy League institutions reported feeling like *outsiders* and found the classroom environment, interactions with faculty, and course curriculum to be oppressive; impacting their sense of belonging and ability to socially integrate into their campus (Jaimes, 2020; Johnson, 2017; Johnson et al., 2022, Hardaway et al., 2022; Pérez, 2016; Williams & Jones, 2019). Furthermore, Pan and Reyes (2020) reported that Latino students experience tokenism inside and outside of the classroom and felt like their admittance served as a visual manifestation of diversity efforts. In their rhetorical analysis, Cole and Harper (2017) found that some Black students report racist campus incidents, while others do not. Reported or not, from a success perspective, Johnson et al. (2022) informed, "With the high retention rates of Black students at Ivy League institutions, these students may choose to endure these conditions rather than depart" (p. 10).

Ivy, Black, and Female

Guinier et al. (1997) explored women's experiences within an Ivy League institution and found that within the classroom, White men receive more positive feedback and are encouraged to speak more often, and for longer periods of time than other minoritized groups and White women. Additionally, Williams and Jones (2019) evaluated the experiences of Black women student leaders in doctoral programs at an Ivy League institution in the Mid-Atlantic and found that women experienced feelings of isolation, relied heavily on the communities that reflected their own identities, and created their own spaces to talk through their realities with racism on campus.

While sitting in her confirmation hearing, Harvard alumnae and Supreme Court Justice Judge Ketanji Brown Jackson, the first Black woman to serve as a justice in the 232-year history of the Court, was asked about the advice she would give to young people. She recounted how difficult her transition was when she first arrived on Harvard University's campus. She shared:

> The first semester I was really homesick. I was really questioning; do I belong here? Can I make it in this environment? And I was walking through the yard in the evening and a Black woman I did not know was passing me on the sidewalk and she looked at me and I guess she knew how I was feeling, and she leaned over as we crossed and said, "persevere" ... I would tell them to persevere. (Swoyer, 2022, para. 2)

Improving Ivy

Given the complexity of these dynamics, it remains critical for American Ivy League universities to explore the experiences of all students enrolled within their institutions. Now, more than ever, it is imperative for Ivy League institutions to take institutional accountability by acknowledging their role in promoting and reproducing campus racism, by contributing to the educational equity and access for all students attending their institutions. First, one must recognize that students of color often persevere through collegiate environments that can leave them feeling unwelcome and othered. Johnson et al. (2022) offered recommendations for Ivy League institutions including: "ensuring a campus landscape free from exposure to racist statues and monuments; implementation of bias training for all faculty, staff, and students; and execute swift, deterrent action when racialized incidents are observed or reported" (p. 10). Efforts to make curricula more representative of minoritized populations will also address the lack of inclusion reported by students of color attending the Ivies, by increasing their sense of belonging and making them feel validated. As a result, these students can better integrate academically and develop intellectually within these institutions.

PROFESSIONAL CONTEXT

Based on reputation, prestige, funding, and ample resources, Ivy League institutions attract faculty and scholars who are well-renowned experts within their field. As a result, these institutions are likely to be as equally selective in recruiting highly motivated staff and administrators to support their students, faculty, and operations. Although data on the professional experiences within Ivy League institutions are limited, we explore the importance of diversifying faculty, staff, and administration within this institution type.

Diversification among Senior Leadership, Faculty, and Staff

Following an influx in racialized incidents toward minoritized students by campus police officers and White peers, Ivy League institutions have recently been criticized by scholars for their lack of accountability in adequately addressing issues of diversity, equity, and inclusion as well as their role in reproducing White privilege and White power structures in America (Gasman et al., 2015; Hernandez et al., 2015; Wilder, 2013). Despite institutional efforts made to diversify student populations through more equitable admissions practices within the Ivy League, when considering minoritized faculty, staff, and administrators, Gasman et al. (2015) noted that:

> Senior leadership, both administrators and faculty, continues to be exceedingly White ... [while] the positions of university senior leadership have remained relatively exempt from the urgency for diversity, maintaining the White power structure that has remained in place for centuries in the case of ivy league institutions. (p. 5)

Within this institutional type, some Ivy League institutions have made strides in becoming more diverse within its leadership. Up until the late 20th century, all eight of the Ivy League schools were led primarily by White male presidents (Alderman, 2007). Between 2001 and 2012, Dr. Ruth Simmons became not only the first Black woman to lead Brown University but also the first Black president of any Ivy League institution. Similarly, by 2011, up to three other Ivy League schools were led by women presidents (Harvard, Princeton, and the University of Pennsylvania). Since the end of Dr. Simmon's tenure at Brown in 2012, there has not been another Black man or woman to lead an Ivy League institution. Furthermore, since 2013, data reveal deficiencies in the racial diversity of the senior leadership staff at all eight of the Ivy League institutions (Gasman et al., 2015).

Faculty and Staff

There is a dearth of literature on the experiences of underrepresented faculty and staff at Ivy League institutions. In general, faculty of color are grossly underrepresented within the professoriate. According to NCES data, in the fall of 2020, nearly three-quarters of full-time faculty were White; 39% were White males and 35% were White females. The next largest racial/ethnic group was Asian/Pacific Islander faculty; 7% Asian/Pacific Islander males and 5% Asian/Pacific Islander females. Black and Hispanic faculty followed; with 4% reflecting Black females, and 3% reflecting Black males, Hispanic males, and Hispanic females. Lastly, American Indian/Alaska Native and individuals of two or more races each made up 1% or less of full-time faculty (NCES, 2022).

At Ivy League schools, where research has a larger emphasis on faculty promotion, underrepresented faculty may struggle to meet the needs of their faculty appointment given their other obligations often bestowed upon them by colleagues and department leadership. For example, Davis and Maldonado (2017) found that Black women administrators are perceived to take on gendered roles based on stereotypes about their inherent domestic responsibilities and often face barriers that men are not expected to grapple with in the academy. These scholars also found that leveraging White male sponsorship for career advancement and learning how to "play the game" (p. 58) or strategically navigate the politics of the academy, have been helpful in ensuring continued career growth. Within the Ivy League, these tools for career growth are especially relevant given the dominance of the White power structure at these institutions. Furthermore, the lack of diversity in higher education adversely impacts the experiences of underrepresented students (Rankin & Reason, 2005).

Faculty of color are not only underrepresented within the academy, but administrative leaders of color are also often underrepresented within institutions of higher education. Despite the growing number of students of color at colleges and universities, there is still a substantial lack of diversity among those in senior-level positions (president, vice presidents, provost, deans). Elite institutions tend to perpetuate and reinforce the White power structure despite the documented benefits of having diverse leadership and the changing landscape of higher education (Gasman et al., 2015).

FUTURE CONSIDERATION AND DIRECTIONS

The legacy and reputation of Ivy League schools are irrefutable and these institutions will continue to be viewed among the most prestigious universities in the world. The extant literature reinforces the imperative need to diversify recruitment efforts on ivy campuses. We agree with scholars who maintain that institutions must prioritize "diversifying across the board including senior leadership to meet the needs of their current and future student body as well as their future alumni, which will hold the keys, in part, to financial stability of these institutions" (Gasman et al., 2015, p. 5). As student populations continue to become more racially diverse, it is incumbent upon the Ivies to hire more diverse senior leadership and minoritized faculty as scholars. Beyond the prestige, Ivy League institutions will continue to be the world's most revered and sought-out institutions. However, until all Ivy League universities reckon with their complicated histories with racism in this country and acknowledge their campuses as sites for reproducing inequality as experienced by their minoritized students, faculty, and staff, real, impactful, and transformational change cannot take place. As global leaders in higher education and exemplars for knowledge production, these institutions must be the vanguard of equity, inclusion, and anti-racism.

REFLECTION QUESTIONS

1. How might demographic markers such as gender, race, class, etc., shape the collegiate experiences for students of color attending Ivy League institutions?
2. How can Ivy League institutions assess and evaluate the effectiveness of their recruitment efforts for retaining minoritized senior leadership, faculty, and administrators?
3. In what ways can Ivy League institutions actively demonstrate a milieu that is welcoming, inclusive, and responsive to high-achieving, low-SES students during the enrollment and recruitment process?
4. How can these institutions transform themselves to value the contributions of these populations and view their presence as a central driver of institutional excellence?
5. How does including the experiences of minoritized student populations (re)shape the conversation and perceptions about student success within Ivy League educational settings?

REFERENCES

Alderman, J. (2007). Ivy league's female presidents gather. *The Boston Globe*. http://www.boston.com/news/education/higher/articles/2007/05/03/ivy_leagues_female_presidents_gather/

American Council on Education (ACE). (2012). *The American college president* (2012 ed.). American Council on Education, Center for Policy Analysis.

Ashkenas, J., Park, H., & Pearce, A. (2017, August 24). Even with affirmative action, Blacks and Hispanics are more underrepresented at top colleges than 35 years ago. *The New York Times*. https://www.nytimes.com/interactive/2017/08/24/us/affirmative-action.html

Association of American Universities (AAU). (n.d.) *Our members.* https://www.aau.edu/who-we-are/our-members

Bradley, S., M. (2018). *Upending the ivory tower: Civil rights, Black power, and the Ivy League.* NYU Press.

Chetty, R., Friedman, J. N., Saez, E., Turner, N., & Yagan, D. (2017). *Mobility report cards: The role of colleges in intergenerational mobility* (No. w23618). National Bureau of Economic Research.

Cole, E. R., & Harper, S. R. (2017). Race and rhetoric: An analysis of college presidents' statements on campus racial incidents. *Journal of Diversity in Higher Education, 10*(4), 318.

Davis, D. R., & Maldonado, C. (2015). Shattering the glass ceiling: The leadership development of African American women in higher education. *Advancing Women in Leadership Journal, 35,* 48–64. https://doi.org/10.21423/awlj-v35.a125

Desmond, J. C. (2011). Ivy halls and ivy walls: The continuing legacy of the Ivy League. *American Studies, 34,* 203–231.

Duffin, E. (2021, October 25). *Topic: The Ivy League.* Statista. https://www.statista.com/topics/4970/the-ivy-league/#dossierKeyfigures

Friedersdorf, C. (2015). Brown University's $100 million inclusivity plan. *The Atlantic.* https://www.theatlantic.com/politics/archive/2015/11/brown-universitys-100-million-plan-to-be-more-inclusive/416886//

Gasman, M., Abiola, U., & Travers, C. (2015). Diversity and senior leadership at elite institutions of higher education. *Journal of Diversity in Higher Education, 8*(1), 1–14.

Guinier, L. (1997). *Becoming gentlemen: Women, law school, and institutional change.* Beacon Press.

Hardaway, A., Scott, S., & Johnson, J. (2022). Beyond bothered: Exploring identity, stressors, and challenges of Black women ivy collegians. *The Journal of African American Women and Girls in Education.* https://doi.org/10.21423/jaawge-v2i2a114

Harvard University. (2022). *Harvard and the legacy of slavery.* Harvard and the Legacy of Slavery. https://www.harvard.edu/president/news/2022/harvard-and-the-legacy-of-slavery/

Hernandez, B. N., Munoz, P., & Zumba, S. (2015). Letter to the editor: A letter on behalf of the Cornell Latinx Delegation. *Cornell Daily Sun.* https://cornellsun.com/2015/11/17/letter-to-the-editor-a-letter-on-behalf-of-the-cornell-latinx-delegation/

Hodges, S. (2021) *Black students make space for themselves in the Ivy league.* The Monitor. http://www.nabjmonitor.com/2021/black-students-make-space-for-themselves-in-the-ivy-league/

Ivy Council. (n.d.). Retrieved October 14, 2022, from https://www.ivycouncil.org/about

Jack, A. A. (2019). The privileged poor: How elite colleges are failing disadvantaged students. *Harvard University Press.* https://doi.org/10 .4159/9780674239647

Jaimes, F. J. (2020). *An examination of latino male undergraduate students' experiences integrating academically & socially at Ivy League institutions* [Doctoral dissertation, Northeastern University]. ProQuest Dissertations Publishing.

Johnson, J. M. (2017). Choosing elites: Experiences of working-class Black undergraduate women at an Ivy league university. In L. D. Patton Davis & N. Croom (Eds.), *Critical perspectives on Black women and college success.* (pp. 158–169). Routledge.

Johnson, J., Scott, S., Phillips, T., Rush, A. (2022). Ivy Issues: An exploration of Black students' racialized interactions on Ivy League campuses. *Journal of Diversity in Higher Education.* Advanced Online Publication. https://doi.org/10.1037/dhe0000406

Leitch, A. (1978). *A Princeton companion.* Princeton University Press.

Ma, V., & Simauchi, K. (2021, October 15). Harvard's endowment soars to $53.2 billion, reports 33.6% returns. *The Harvard Crimson.* https://www.thecrimson.com/article/2021/10/15/endowment-returns-soar-2021/

Marine, S. (2015). Combating sexual violence in the Ivy league: Reflections on politics, pain, and progress. In S. C. Wooten & R. W. Mitchell (Eds.), *The crisis of campus sexual violence* (pp. 55–73). Routledge.

Massey, D. S., Mooney, M., & Torres, K. C. (2007). Black immigrants and Black natives attending selective colleges and universities in the United States. *American Journal of Education, 113*(2), 243–271.

National Center for Education Statistics. (2022). Characteristics of postsecondary faculty. *Condition of Education.* U.S. Department of Education, Institute of Education Sciences. Retrieved from https://nces.ed.gov/programs/coe/indicator/csc

Pan, Y. Y. D., & Reyes, D. V. (2021). The norm among the exceptional? Experiences of Latino students in elite institutions. *Sociological Inquiry, 91*(1), 207–230. https://doi.org/10.1111/soin.12354

Pérez, D., II, (2016). Over the ivy wall: Latino male achievers nurturing community cultural wealth at a highly selective, predominantly White institution. In V. B. Sáenz, L. Ponjuán, & J. López Figueroa (Eds.), *Ensuring the success of Latino males in higher education: A national imperative* (pp. 130–146). Stylus.

Radcliffe Institute for Advanced Study at Harvard University. (2022). *Harvard & the legacy of slavery.* https://www.radcliffe.harvard.edu/?page=8

Rankin, S. R., & Reason, R. D. (2005). Differing perceptions: How students of color and white students perceive campus climate for underrepresented groups. *Journal of College Student Development 46*(1), 43–61. https://doi.org/10.1353/csd.2005.0008

Scott, S., Johnson, J., Hardaway, A., & Galloway, T. (2021). Investigating ivy: Black undergraduate students at selective universities. *Journal of Postsecondary Student Success, 1*(2), 72–90. https://doi.org/10.33009/fsop_jpss128468

Shortell, D., & Romine, T. (2020, August 13). *Justice Department accuses Yale of discriminating against Asian American and white applicants.* CNN. https://www.cnn.com/2020/08/13/politics/justice-department-yale-discrimination/index.html

Swoyer, A. (2022, March 23). Ketanji Brown Jackson gets emotional, tells youth to 'persevere'. *The Washington Times.* https://www.washingtontimes.com/news/2022/mar/23/ketanji-brown-jackson-gets-emotional-tells-youth-p/

Thelin, J. (2004). *A history of American higher education.* Johns Hopkins Press.

Top Tier Admissions. (2022). *Admission Statistics for the Class of 2025*. 2025 Ivy League & College Admission Statistics. https://toptieradmissions.com/counseling/college/2025-ivy-league-admission-statistics/

Wilder, C. (2013). *Ebony and ivy: Race, slavery, and the troubled history of America's universities*. Bloomsburg Press.

Wilkerson, I. (2020). *Caste: The origins of our discontents*. Random House.

Williams, J. L., & Jones, B. (2019). *Black and Ivy: How Black female student leaders create community and inclusion at an Ivy League institution* [Unpublished manuscript]. Samuel DeWitt Proctor Institute for Leadership, Equity, & Justice.

Zimmerman, S. D. (2019). Elite colleges and upward mobility to top jobs and top incomes. *The American Economic Review, 109*(1), 1–47. https://doi.org/10.1257/aer.20171019

CHAPTER 2

RESEARCH UNIVERSITIES

Ginny Jones Boss
University of Georgia

Research universities remain the predominant postsecondary institutional type in U.S. higher education. Though research universities only make up approximately 9.6% of all U.S. postsecondary educational institution types, they account for over a third of all student enrollments, produce the lion's share of global scholarship and research, and train most of the faculty for all U.S. institutions (Checkoway, 2001; The Carnegie Classification of Institutions of Higher Education [Carnegie], n.d.). Research universities are defined as: "institutions that awarded at least 20 research/scholarship doctoral degrees and had at least $5 million in total research expenditures (as reported through the National Science Foundation (NSF) Higher Education Research & Development Survey [HERD])" (Carnegie, n.d., para. 3). As of 2018, the Carnegie Foundation (n.d.) classified three types of research universities: (1) R1: Doctoral Universities—Very high research activity; (2) R2: Doctoral Universities—High research activity; and (3) D/PU: Doctoral/Professional Universities. The Carnegie classification system is not intended to be a ranking system. However, both internal and external constituents of U.S. postsecondary education use the Carnegie classification and other ranking systems to determine prestige (Berger et al., 2012; Zerquera, 2019). Research universities, which are listed first on Carnegie's website, are considered by many to be the most prestigious universities, with R1s at the pinnacle (Zerquera, 2019). The outsized student enrollments and intellectual influence of research universities further signal their

---

Institutional Diversity in American Postsecondary Education, pp. 19–32
Copyright © 2024 by Information Age Publishing
www.infoagepub.com
All rights of reproduction in any form reserved.

20 G. J. BOSS

prominence in the U.S. higher educational landscape. In this chapter, I explore (a) the historical evolution of research universities that resulted in their prominence, (b) the organizational and administrative structures of research universities, (c) the state of student success among various student populations at research universities, and (d) the professional context of academic and student affairs employees at research universities. I conclude this chapter with contemporary, critical, or emerging issues and trends related to research universities.

HISTORY

The distinctive nature of U.S. research universities can be traced back to increased government involvement with higher education in the late 19th century. Most notably, the establishment of public universities through the 1862 and 1890 Morrill Acts brought increasing access to higher education to student populations who had been historically excluded (Berger et al., 2012). Checkoway (2001) explained that research universities aimed to prepare civic-minded individuals; however, in the late 19th century, a shift to the German model resulted in greater emphasis on research and expertise. With the German model came a change in faculty roles away from the holistic care of students toward a focus on research and outsourcing of student care to Deans of Women and Deans of Men, whose roles have shifted and expanded into what is contemporarily known as student affairs professionals (Hevel, 2016). Today, few research universities have maintained a civic mission but have become more focused on economic goals and policies (Checkoway, 2001; Taylor, 2020; Warshaw & Upton, 2020).

Kirwan (2010) described three significant waves of change, connecting government involvement with the establishment of research universities, which occurred: (a) after the Second World War [WWII], (b) during the space race, and (c) during the information age. During the first wave, post-WWII U.S. industry was booming, leading to partnerships between the government and research universities. Kirwan explained, "in 1950 the National Science Foundation was established, further cementing the federal government's role in the research function of our universities" (p. 102). During the second wave, President Dwight D. Eisenhower signed the National Defense Education Act into law in 1957 to support the educational development of American citizens toward advancing the United States' position in the space race against the Russians. This legislation increased STEM education for higher education and affordability to bolster student enrollment numbers. During the third wave, the Bayh-Doyle Act was passed, allowing universities to claim intellectual property over their research (Kirwan, 2010). Amendments and revisions to this act allowed universities to transfer patents of their basic research to external constituents. As Kirwan explained, these transfers allowed industry partners to transform the basic research of universities into applied research, leading to "the development of life-altering—and life-saving—breakthroughs" (p. 103) and other innovations.

Around the same time as the Bayh-Doyle Act in 1980, student success became a major focus for universities. This new interest in student success, which included a focus on retention, graduation, and competitive enrollment, happened during the same time that student retention and graduation became added measures in *U.S. News and World Report*'s rankings of the best colleges (Berger et al., 2012). As Berger et al. (2012) explained, "campuses around the country have become increasingly concerned about retention rates as a source of prestige that can be converted into other kinds of symbolic, material, and human resources—particularly in the competition for more and better students" (p. 15). With this renewed interest also came the study of retention, which led to the wide adoption of enrollment management at U.S. universities. *Enrollment management* is a systematic approach in which university leaders use research on college students to bolster student enrollment and retention (Berger et al., 2012). Trends in enrollment management have moved to focus on retention efforts across group differences and the:

> Interactive influence between organizational contexts and the individual and collective characteristics of students; particular attention is given to how the dominant traditional organizational patterns have affected access and retention for students from underrepresented groups—including students of color and those with lower socioeconomic status. (Berger et al., 2012, p. 31)

These trends have also resulted in an increase in academic and student affairs administrative professionals and an outcry from many constituents of the administrative bloat (Lee et al., 2021).

ORGANIZATION STRUCTURE AND CULTURE

Research universities are complex and dense organizational structures with large student enrollments, multiple levels of learning (undergraduate, graduate, and professional), multi- and interdisciplinary endeavors, professional and research institutes, and an assemblage of faculty and administrative professionals (Hirt & Robbins, 2016; Taylor, 2020; Warshaw & Upton, 2020). Several scholars have employed institutional logics to examine the practices, values, beliefs, and assumptions that influence the structures and behaviors of postsecondary institutions (Taylor, 2020;

Warshaw & Upton, 2020). Taylor (2020) named three different institutional logics of research universities: (a) civic logics, (b) activist logics, and (c) economic logics. Taylor described *civic logics* as those that position universities with a civic mission and view higher education as a public good, and *activist logics* as those fueled by key constituents' advocacy efforts. Although civic, activist, and other logics exist at research universities, Taylor argued that economic logics predominate in research universities. *Economic logics* involves "the emergence of economic ideals and values (neoliberalism), market-like academic environments (marketization), and market-driven behaviors (academic capitalism)" (p. 1073). Taylor drew on a broad literature base to describe how economic logics lead to competition, entrepreneurialism, the prioritization of efficiency, and the "dispossession of individuals and entities that diverge from economic logics" (p. 1073) within universities.

Institutional missions provide much insight into the logics of research universities and drive their organizational and administrative structures (Taylor, 2020; Warshaw & Upton, 2020). As Hirt and Robbins (2016) explained, "Mission statements of research and doctoral institutions reflect both this density and a sense of elitism. Nearly all discuss their tripartite mission of teaching, research, and service, but research is clearly the crown jewel" (p. 31). Zerquera (2019) made a similar argument about *prestige-seeking*, research universities' investments in attaining and maintaining positive public perception and national rankings. University leaders focus on faculty engagements, research endeavors, athletics, program offerings, or admissions processes, with the ultimate goal of increasing revenues and attracting competitive faculty and student bodies. These prestige-seeking behaviors often lead to a slow shift of university missions, resulting in meaningful changes to organizational and administrative structure and practice, also known as *mission creep* (Zerquera, 2019). Zerquera (2019) explained that R2 and D/PU institutions are particularly prone to mission creep as they aspire to R1 status.

Many important constituent groups are employed at research universities: custodians, facility managers, information technology specialists, office and administrative support staff, faculty, and academic and student affairs administrative professionals. It is beyond the scope of this chapter to discuss the intricacies and essential contributions of all of these groups. Instead, the remainder of this chapter will focus on the two groups that most *directly* impact student success and are most prone to the effects of mission creep: administrative professionals and faculty. Administrative professionals are non-faculty academic and student affairs administrators and upper-level administrators who may hold dual faculty and administrative titles (e.g., department chairs, deans, provosts). To varying degrees, each group is concerned with enrollment management and student outcomes

(Berger et al., 2012). Academic affairs administrators and those in dual faculty-administrator roles report to a provost in many research universities. These professionals are often more focused on data-driven areas of student success, such as admissions, financial aid, registration, institutional research, and curriculum development. Whereas student affairs administrators typically report to a vice president of student affairs and are concerned with supporting student learning and development within the cocurricular campus environment (Hirt & Collins, 2004). Faculty work can be classified in many ways; however, economic logics has created a stratified faculty system between tenure-track/tenured faculty and full- and part-time non-tenure-track faculty. Robertson (2020) argued that universities with complex missions require unbundling the historical role of faculty (teaching, research, and service) so that non-tenure-track faculty members focus more on teaching and tenure-track/tenured faculty focus more on research. In recent years, many research universities have increased the number of contingent appointments relative to permanent appointments due to the cost savings and the control this practice provides university leadership (Robertson, 2020). Robertson explained that this unbundling presents research universities with the challenge of finding balance in their missions as institutions address student success and access while striving for research preeminence. Specifically, he stated that research universities face threats in four critical areas of their institutional mission: (a) breadth and quantity of scholarship, (b) research doctoral education, (c) faculty governance, and (d) reputations and rankings by drastically reducing the number of permanent full-time faculty and making them a minority relative to contingent full-time faculty.

Research universities' prestige-seeking and creeping missions can be traced back to the economic logics described by Taylor (2020). The behavior of university leaders due to these logics have had negative impacts on faculty and staff satisfaction and retention as well as student success and access goals (Drake et al., 2019; Hirt & Collins, 2004; Taylor, 2020; Levin et al., 2013; Ostrove et al., 2021; Robertson et al., 2020). Through their research, Warshaw and Upton (2020) found that some research universities were employing hybrid institutional logics, blending civic and economic logics by "bend[ing] market mentalities and initiatives to bolster their public mission and social goals" (p. 1300). The universities in their study purposefully and publicly distanced themselves from capitalist values, opting instead to find alternative funding structures to pursue civic missions. Yet, like universities operating predominantly from economic logics, the hybrid logics of the research universities in Warshaw and Upton's (2020) study also came at a cost to student success.

STUDENT SUCCESS AND POPULATIONS

More than one-third of all U.S. college students are enrolled at research universities, making research universities the highest enrolling institutional type in the Carnegie (n.d.) classification system. As of 2020, research universities enrolled 5,204,588 undergraduate students and 2,091,692 graduate students (National Center for Education Statistics [NCES], 2020). Among those enrolled in undergraduate education, 55% were identified by NCES (2020) as women and 45% as men. Among graduate students, 59% were identified by NCES (2020) as women and 41% as men. Across both groups was a range of racial/ethnic categorization, with white students representing the majority of students at each level (see Table 2.1).

Research universities' investment in economic logics presents increasing challenges to access and student success, especially among underrepresented groups (Batyrshina et al., 2021; Berger et al., 2012; Wade, 2019; Zerquera, 2019). Wade (2019) reported that some colleges only admit undergraduate students with the highest admissions test scores in the fall semester and only admit students with lower admissions test scores during the spring semester because those students are not counted in rankings data. Zerquera (2019) examined the potential relationship between prestige-seeking and access for undergraduate Black and Latinx students at urban-serving research universities. She found that some prestige-seeking behaviors led to lower enrollments for Black students, such as increased SAT scores. She also found that an increase in graduate student enrollment led to lower undergraduate enrollment for Black and Latinx students. Alternatively, Zerquera found other prestige-seeking behaviors, such as the presence of graduate degree programs and offerings of remedial services, led to increased enrollments for Latinx students. Paradoxically, due to mission creep, offerings of remedial services are being discontinued at many research universities (Zerquera, 2019).

Economic logics are not the only challenge to access for underrepresented groups. Even in research universities that employ hybrid logics, access can be decreased for in-state students and Pell-eligible students to maximize tuition dollars in support of public good endeavors (Warshaw & Upton, 2020). Underrepresented students who gain access to research universities may face several challenges to their sense of belonging and subsequently their retention to the university (Batyrshina et al., 2019). Warshaw and Upton (2020) argued that, despite the access challenges some institutions have by employing hybrid logics, other models exist where both access and civic engagement are increased. Kwon et al. (2020) also found that co-curricular activities were instrumental in student success skill-building among women of all races and students of color. Their findings suggest that student clubs and organizations may be numerous enough and/or

Table 2.1

Percentage of Student Enrollment by Level of Student and Race/Ethnicity: Fall 2020

Level of student	American Indian or Alaska Native	Asian	Black or African American	Hispanic or Latino	Native Hawaiian or Other Pacific Islander	White	Two or more races	Race/ethnicity unknown	Nonresident alien
Undergraduate	< 1%	8.8%	9.6%	16%	< 1%	52%	4.4%	3.6%	4.7%
Graduate	.36%	7.1%	10%	10%	.14%	48%	2.8%	5.8%	15%

heterogeneous enough that students from a wide variety of backgrounds can find a place in them and gain experiences that may be valuable in the workforce and civic life. Kwon et al. argued that cocurricular activities "provide an important balance to the environment of classrooms where competition for grades can be a dominating influence" (p. 105). Research universities' access and retention are particularly germane given their role in the undergraduate-graduate-to-faculty pipeline.

One of the unique characteristics of research universities, in terms of student success and populations, is their large population of graduate students and substantial influence on the pipeline of faculty and faculty career choice (Levin et al., 2013). Levin et al. (2013) investigated the institutional practices and behaviors that shape graduate students of color's career decisions. They found that representation within faculty demographics made a meaningful difference in orientations of graduate students of Color to faculty and their belief about their belongingness in a faculty career. Similarly, they found belongingness in their programs inspired or dulled desire for faculty life. Relatedly, Ostrove et al. (2011) argued that social class might play a significant role in pursuing and becoming a graduate student and ultimately pursuing faculty career paths, as academic self-concept and sense of belonging of graduate students with low socioeconomic status were lower than their peers. Their lower academic self-concept influenced how much they believed they could be successful as a faculty member at a research university (Ostrove et al., 2011).

Graduate and undergraduate students from underrepresented groups are negatively impacted by a lack of representation among faculty and staff at most research universities. Given the faculty and administrative pipeline is greatly affected by economic logics, this issue becomes a self-destructive loop in universities' quest for prestige; economic logics reduce the talent pool of faculty and administrative staff, particularly among underrepresented groups in which representation and mentoring are essential components for thriving and retention. Yet, the pipeline is not the only issue affected by economic logics; these logics also shape the working environments of administrative professionals and faculty at research universities.

PROFESSIONAL CONTEXT

The working environment in a research university presents many challenges and rewards for administrative professionals and faculty. Due to space limitations and in response to the theme of this book on unequal access, this section of the chapter is dedicated to describing the working experiences of the two sub-constituent groups, student affairs administrators (Taylor,

2020) and non-tenure-track faculty (Drake et al., 2019), who are most likely and often to be dispossessed, discouraged, defunded, and devalued due to economic logics.

Student Affairs Professionals

Student affairs administrators in research universities are likely to have more administrative responsibilities than those working in other Carnegie (n.d.) classifications, necessitating a deeper understanding of structural and policy functions (Hirt & Collins, 2004; Hirt & Robbins, 2016). Moreover, they must be prepared for the challenges and opportunities they may face if they do not subscribe to economic logics. Using the Nature of Professional Life Survey, Hirt and Collins (2004) investigated the nature of work, relationships, rewards, and campus student affairs administrators experienced in their professional lives. They found that, compared to their other institutional counterparts, student affairs professionals were more likely to: (a) rate their institutions' undergraduate teaching mission as significantly less important, (b) work with graduate and professional students in specialized fields, (c) have robust benefits packages, and (d) have opportunities for advancement. Relatedly, they found these professionals were less likely to: (a) know and collaborate with other student affairs professionals, (b) spend significant time in direct service to students, and (c) have input into decisions made in their offices. They also suggested that, given the intense focus on the research mission of research universities, student affairs professionals at these institutions may be required to engage in and put great emphasis on the assessment of their student success efforts. Taylor (2020) found that research universities' increased focus on quantitative data-driven methods for addressing student success led to the silencing and diminishment of the work by institutional actors who did not buy into economic logics, with the bulk of the negative impacts on student affairs professionals and students. This increased focus can result in the (re)allocation of resources to support the collection of quantitative data and interventions, leaving minimal resources for constituents doing other student success work.

Non-Tenure Track Faculty

Non-tenure-track faculty in research universities are likely to have heavy teaching and administrative responsibilities in environments in which both are undervalued (Boss et al., 2021b; Drake et al., 2019; Kezar et al., 2019; Robertson, 2020; Waltman et al., 2012). Yet, non-tenure-track faculty play

28   G. J. BOSS

key roles in student success efforts, teaching the lion's share of undergraduate gateway classes (Kezar et al., 2019; Robertson, 2020). Waltman et al. (2012) conducted a study of non-tenure-track faculty at research universities and found they experience an immense sense of job satisfaction from teaching, mentoring, and supporting students as well as having flexibility for their personal lives. Waltman et al. also found that having a lack of job security, opportunities for advancement, and respect and inclusion were sources of great job dissatisfaction for non-tenure-track faculty. Relatedly, in their study on faculty agency among full-time non-tenure-track faculty at research universities, Drake et al. (2019) found faculty's "agency varied widely based on how well established they were—a function of longevity and collegial respect" (p. 1655). Longevity afforded full-time non-tenure-track faculty agency in their classrooms, but they remained excluded from faculty governance and decisions about the broader curriculum. The resultant effect was that the non-tenure-track faculty felt devalued and invisible within their organizational structure.

Student affairs administrators and non-tenure-track faculty have large attrition rates. Their working conditions, particularly under economic logics, are isolating and disempowering (Boss & Bravo, 2021; Boss et al., 2021b; Drake et al., 2019; Kezar et al., 2019; Robertson, 2020; Taylor, 2020). Although both groups find ways to exercise tremendous agency in their small realms of influence (Drake et al., 2019; Taylor, 2020), their efforts are undermined and undercut by policies and practices that forefront market values over civic ones. These effects are exacerbated when a closer look reveals higher concentrations of women of all races and women of color in particular within both groups (Boss et al., 2021a; Boss et al., 2021b). About the reliance on data-driven decision making, Taylor (2020) argued the effects were most negative for underrepresented student populations whose nuanced experiences cannot be captured in the data. A similar argument can be made for student affairs professionals and non-tenure-track faculty who may provide crucial support to those students and serve as representation and possibility models for them. The devaluation of qualitative data representing students' experiences and outcomes coupled with the shifting power dynamic away from academic freedom with the erosion of shared governance signals poor long-term effects for research universities.

FUTURE CONSIDERATIONS AND DIRECTIONS

Because research universities are a mainstay of U.S. postsecondary education, the future of student success at these types of institutions necessitates a different momentum than what is currently in place. I offer future directions and considerations by first starting with a question and leveraging the writings of several scholars in response to that question. Taylor (2020) asked, "If those tasked with delivering and supporting student success efforts are themselves dispossessed, discouraged, defunded, and devalued, what does this mean for students' success?" (p. 1093). Though not answering this question directly, several scholars have argued that research universities must learn to operate in the "both/and," if they hope to increase access, build sustainability of student success efforts, and establish or maintain research preeminence. Robertson (2020) discussed this work as living in the generative paradox, while Warshaw and Upton (2020) offered a similar term of hybrid institutional logics. In the following paragraph, I introduce interdisciplinarity as the vehicle for establishing hybrid institutional logics and validating the expertise, value, and necessity of all constituents within research universities.

If U.S. research universities want to meet the complex challenges of the world and ensure an educated and innovative citizenry, they must do so "through a reengineering of [their] operations and a refocusing of [their] mission and priorities" (Kirwan, 2010, p. 109). I join many scholars who have proposed interdisciplinarity as the way forward (Barringer, 2020; Boss et al., 2021a; Holley, 2009; hooks, 1994). *Interdisciplinarity* involves integrating the best elements of individual disciplinary insights and methods to generate a more comprehensive and nuanced approach to problem-solving. The foundation for an interdisciplinary infrastructure is already available to many research universities. Governmental agencies offer sizable grants for interdisciplinary research, and more universities are beginning to make interdisciplinary research a part of their mission (Barringer et al., 2020). Yet, interdisciplinary research is not enough; research universities have to invest in hybrid logics and interdivisional work. At the start of the millennium, Checkoway (2001) asserted there was declining interest among students and faculty for civic engagement. However, Generation Z has been heralded as one of the most politically and socially engaged generational cohorts (Seemiller & Grace, 2016). These students, who make up most of the research university population, are primed to be change agents in social life and industry. The right collegiate environment can equip them with the knowledge and tools to actualize it. Integrating specialized knowledge across academic disciplines and student affairs professionals' knowledge of student learning and development alongside empowering integrated teaching among non-tenure-track faculty can help actualize the promise of hybrid logics.

The landscape of research universities has changed over time from civic-minded missions to those focused on research and industry. Although these changes have driven important innovation, they have also come at a great cost to accessibility, affordability, and equity for particular groups of students, staff, and faculty. External drivers and economic logics have resulted in the creeping missions of research universities, where greater emphasis is placed on outcomes over process. For student success purposes, this shift in focus has resulted in more stringent admission criteria, fewer offerings of remedial and other support services, and increased hiring of non-tenure-track faculty. A growing body of literature has responded to these threats to student success efforts by advocating for hybrid logics in research universities. Hybrid logics have the potential to increase student support and drive innovation. Moreover, increased engagement of inter-disciplinarity not only creates more support conditions for hybrid logics it also necessitates great involvement of a variety of a variety of stakeholders across these institutions.

DISCUSSION QUESTIONS

1. Choose a research university and examine its mission statement and most recent strategic plan. Based on these two documents, what institutional logics seem to drive the operating practices of that institution?
2. What challenges and opportunities might research universities face in investing in more civic-minded missions?
3. How should research universities balance teaching and research needs with respect to funding and innovation?

REFERENCES

Barringer, S. N., Leahey, E., & Salazar, K. (2020). What catalyzes research universities to commit to interdisciplinary research? *Research in Higher Education, 61*(6), 679–705.

Batyrshina, A. N., Anistranski, J. A., & Bradford Brown, B. (2021). How does ethnic identity relate to adjustment for minoritized students? A two-site comparison of large public universities. *Journal of College Student Retention: Research, Theory & Practice, 0*(0). https://doi.org/10.1177/15210251211022

Berger, J. B., Ramírez, G. B., & Lyons, S. C. (2012). Past to present: A historical look at retention. In A. Seidman (Ed.), *College student retention: Formula for student success* (2nd ed., pp. 1–30). American Council on Education.

Boss, G. J., & Bravo, N. (2021). (En)counterspaces: An analysis of working conditions for student affairs professionals of Color in an un-Ideal world. In M. W. Sallee (Ed.), *Creating sustainable careers in student affairs: What ideal worker norms get wrong and how to make it right* (pp. 201–217). Stylus.

Boss, G. J., Porter, C. J., & Davis, T. J. (2021a). Co-conspirators and community care: Toward theorizing a post-COVID-19 academy. *Journal of the Professoriate, 12*(1), 30–54.

Boss, G. J., Porter, C. J., Davis, T. J., & Moore, C. M. (2021b). Who cares?: (Re) visioning labor justice for Black women contingent faculty. *Journal of African American Women and Girls in Education, 1*(1), 80–94.

Checkoway, B. (2001). Renewing the civic mission of the American research university. *The Journal of Higher Education, 72*(2), 125–147. http://doi.org/10.2307/2649319

Drake, A., Struve, L., Meghani, S.A., & Bukoski, B. (2019). Invisible labor, visible change: Non-tenure-track faculty agency in a research university. *The Review of Higher Education 42*(4), 1635–1664. http://doi.org/10.1353/rhe.2019.0078

Hevel, M. (2016). Toward a history of student affairs: A synthesis of research, 1996–2015. *Journal of College Student Development, 57*(7), 844–862.

Hirt, J. B., & Collins, D. (2004). Work, relationships, and rewards in student affairs: Differences by institutional Type. *College Student Affairs Journal, 24*(1), 4–19.

Hirt, J. & Robbins, C. (2016). The importance of institutional mission. In G. McClellan, J. Stringer, and Associates (Eds.), *The handbook of student affairs administration* (pp. 25–47). Jossey-Bass.

Holley, K. A. (2009). Interdisciplinary strategies as transformative change in higher education. *Innovative Higher Education, 34*(5), 331–344.

hooks, b. (1994). *Teaching to transgress: Education as the practice of freedom.* Routledge.

Kezar, A., DePaola, T., & Scott, D. (2019). *The gig academy: Mapping labor in the neo-liberal university.* Johns Hopkins University Press.

Kirwan, W. E. (2010). The 21st century: The century of the American research university. *Innovative Higher Education, 35*(2), 101–111. https://10.1007/s10755-009-9132-1

Kwon, R., Brint, S., Curwin, K., & Cantwell, A. (2020). Co-curricular learning at research universities: Results from the SERU survey. *Journal of Student Affairs Research and Practice, 57*(1), 90–112.

Lee, E., Somers, P., Taylor, Z., & Fry, J. (2021). Academic professionals: The changing face of teaching, research, and service in the American research university. *Policy Futures in Education, 0*(0), 1–19. https://doi.org/10.1177/14782103211031500

Levin, J. S., Jaeger, A. J., & Haley, K. J. (2013). Graduate student dissonance: Graduate students of color in a U.S. research university. *Journal of Diversity in Higher Education, 6*(4), 231–244. https://10.1037/a0034568

National Center for Education Statistics. (2020). *Postsecondary education.* https://nces.ed.gov/programs/coe/indicator/cha

Ostrove, J. M., Stewart, A. J., & Curtin, N. L. (2011). Social class and belonging: Implications for graduate students' career aspirations. *The Journal of Higher Education, 82*(6), 748–774.

Robertson, D. L. (2020). Student success, research preeminence, and unintended consequences at public metropolitan research universities. *Innovative Higher Education, 45*(1), 35–49.

Seemiller, C., & Grace, M. (2016). *Generation Z goes to college.* Jossey-Bass.

Taylor, L. D., Jr. (2020). Neoliberal consequence: Data-driven decision making and the subversion of student success efforts. *The Review of Higher Education 43*(4), 1069–1097. http://doi.org/10.1353/rhe.2020.0031

The Carnegie Classification of Institutions of Higher Education. (2018). *Basic classification description*. Retrieved September 22, 2021, from https://carnegieclassifications.iu.edu/classification_descriptions/basic.php

Wade, N. L. (2019). Measuring, manipulating, and predicting student success: A 10-year assessment of Carnegie R1 doctoral universities between 2004 and 2013. *Journal of College Student Retention: Research, Theory & Practice, 21*(1), 119–141. https://doi.org/10.1177/1521025119831456

Waltman, J., Bergom, I., Hollenshead, C., Miller, J., & August, L. (2012). Factors contributing to job satisfaction and dissatisfaction among non-tenure-track faculty. *The Journal of Higher Education, 83*(3), 411–434.

Warshaw, J. B., & Upton, S. (2020). Hybrid logics in the resource strategies of U.S. public research universities. *Journal of Further and Higher Education, 44*(9), 1289–1303.

Zerquera, D. D. (2019). The problem with the prestige pursuit: The effects of striving on access for Black and Latino students at urban-serving research universities. *The Review of Higher Education 42*(5), 393–424. http://doi.org/10.1353/rhe.2019.0057

CHAPTER 3

LAND-GRANT INSTITUTIONS

Ashley B. Clayton
Louisiana State University

Victoria C. Lloyd
Louisiana Department of Education

The establishment of higher education in the United States began in the 1600s, but many of these early institutions excluded certain student populations. Specifically, the first colleges primarily enrolled White men and were closed to women, religious minorities, and Students of Color (Daun-Barnett et al., 2014). It would be 200 years before Justin Smith Morrill sponsored legislation to reflect the need for broadly accessible agricultural and technical education (Association of Public and Land-Grant Universities [APLU], 2012). In the mid-1800s, the focus shifted to providing more access to higher education for individuals who could not afford to attend private colleges. The establishment of land-grant institutions was the first nationwide effort to provide access to public higher education in the United States. Land-grant universities were founded with a trifold focus: research, teaching, and service.

The first Morrill Act of 1862 established a land-grant university in each state and was one of the most influential policies in the history of access to American higher education (APLU, 2012). The second Morrill Act of 1890 established Historically Black Colleges and Universities (HBCUs) with the land-grant designation. Finally, the third Morrill Act of 1994 gave land-grant status to numerous Tribal Colleges and Universities (TCUs). Today,

---

Institutional Diversity in American Postsecondary Education, pp. 33–46
Copyright © 2024 by Information Age Publishing
www.infoagepub.com
All rights of reproduction in any form reserved.

there are a total of 112 land-grant universities in the United States, located in all 50 states, Washington D.C., and six territories (see Appendix). Specifically, there were 58 institutions established by the 1862 legislation (52%), 19 HBCU land-grant institutions established by the 1890 legislation (17%), and 35 TCUs who were given land-grant status beginning in 1994 (31%). This chapter provides an overview of the history of land-grant universities, organizational structure, student populations, professional context, future considerations, and reflection questions.

HISTORY

In 1857, Vermont Senator Justin Morrill, first introduced the bill to establish a land-grant university in each state and territory (APLU, 2012). These institutions would all have a focus on Agriculture and Mechanic Arts (commonly known as A&M). It was an uphill battle establishing these institutions; the first several versions of the bill were rejected. In 1858, the Committee on Public Lands voted against the bill. Morrill reintroduced the bill in 1859 when it was successfully passed by Congress but vetoed by President James Buchanan. Two years later, Morrill re-introduced the bill again with two major modifications: (1) Each state would receive 30,000 acres to fund their institution's endowment (i.e., the meaning of land-grant), and (2) each institution was required to teach military tactics. With these modifications, the First Morrill Act of 1862 was passed by Congress and signed into law by President Abraham Lincoln on July 2, 1862.

Although the 1862 land-grant universities were established with a focus on "access," many of these institutions still had race-based admissions and denied Students of Color. The recognition of this inequity led to the passing of the Second Morrill Act of 1890. Each 1862 land-grant university had to either (1) eliminate race-based admission or (2) share their land-grant designation with another institution in their state that was open to all races/ethnicities. Federal funding was revoked if they failed to satisfy either condition (Abramson et al., 2014; APLU, 2012). In 1862, the second Morrill Act established 17 Historically Black Colleges and Universities (HBCUs) referred to as 1890 land-grant institutions, providing access to primarily Black students (APLU, 2012; Gavazzi & Gee, 2018). There are now 19 HBCU land-grant universities, which are primarily located in the southern region of the United States, where the 1862 institutions historically resisted integration admissions policies.

In 1994, the Equity in Educational Land-Grant Status Act became the third land-grant act, which designated numerous Tribal Colleges and Universities (TCUs) as land-grant institutions (National Institute of Food and Agriculture [NIFA], 2015). Initially, there were 29 TCUs designated with the land-grant status through the third Morrill Act of 1994. The passage of the new act provided a onetime endowment of $23 million to be divided amongst the 1994 land-grant institutions, and subsequent funding was allocated based on the total student count (Shreve, 2019). This legislation resulted in the current designation of 35 land-grant TCUs, which are primarily located in the Midwest and Northwest regions of the country.

ORGANIZATION STRUCTURE AND CULTURE

In addition to the three Morrill Acts, several other major acts contributed to the evolution and mission of land-grant universities (Abramson et al., 2014). The Hatch Act of 1887 established funding "to conduct agricultural research programs at State Agricultural Experiment Stations in the 50 states, the District of Columbia, and the U.S. insular areas" (National Institute of Food and Agriculture [NIFA], n.d., para. 1). Its financial appropriations vary from year to year. The Smith-Lever Act of 1914 established the Cooperative-Extension Services system, with the goal of translating knowledge from research labs to the people, to engage with the community and distribute knowledge. The Evans-Allen Act supports agricultural research on 1890 land-grants. Funding is required to be at least 15% of the Hatch Act for each associated 1862 land-grant. The National Agricultural Research, Extension, and Teaching Policy Act of 1977 provides federal funds to support agricultural extension programs for 1890 land-grants. Funding is awarded through a combination of formula funding, non-competitive, and competitive grants (see https://fas.org/sgp/crs/misc/R45897.pdf).

While land-grant universities are some of the most established colleges in the country, their founding was detrimental to numerous Indigenous tribes. Many incorrectly assume that the land that the colleges are built on was "granted" to them. However, states were given acres of land (primarily in the Midwest) that they could sell to fund their institutions. Roughly 11,000,000 acres of land were stolen from approximately 250 native tribes by the federal government to create land-grant universities (Gavazzi, 2020). The land given to the states to open these schools is often referred to as federally owned or uninhabited public land (Gavazzi & Gee, 2018; Nash, 2019). This land was obtained by unfair deals, forced removal, or in some cases extermination of the communities (Gavazzi, 2020; Nash, 2019). Records of these transactions are still on university ledgers. There has been little in the way of reparations to the tribal communities that were impacted, even when considering the 1994 tribal land-grant institutions, there was only $23,000,000 given across 5 years to be shared by 29 universities (APLU, 2012). For more information on the land that was stolen to fund land-grant universities, visit this interactive map: https://www.landgrabu.org/.

The design and operation of early institutions of higher learning in the United States, including land-grant universities, depended on the efforts and labor of enslaved Black individuals not only for their construction, but also their daily operation. "In the daily routine of a college there was a lot of work to be done, and enslaved people often performed the most labor-intensive tasks" (Wilder, 2013, p. 134). This oppressive history is often glossed over when discussing early higher education. Notably, the segregated and racist history of postsecondary education is what ultimately led to the second Morrill Land-Grant Act, as the 1890 schools were funded and founded because the 1862 universities did not want to admit Black students (APLU, 2012).

The three types of land-grant universities (1862, 1890, and 1994) each have access to different resources with specific populations of focus leading to varying institutional priorities. There are several designations available to land-grant colleges and universities, ranging from research output to community engagement for which land-grant universities can strive.

Organizational Structures

The majority of land-grant institutions are public, with three notable exceptions (Cornell University, Massachusetts Institute of Technology, and Tuskegee University; see Appendix; Carnegie, n.d.). Research output, a core value of the land-grant mission, informs the Carnegie Classification that each U.S. postsecondary school receives. The R1 or Very High Research Activity Carnegie Classification indicates that a school granted at least 20 research/scholarship doctoral degrees and spent at least $5 million on research expenditures. In 2022, there are 146 R1 institutions in the United States, 44 of which are land-grants. All 44 of the R1 land-grants are 1862 universities (Carnegie, n.d.). Institutions that distinguish themselves as leaders in research and graduate education may be invited to membership in the Association of American Universities [AAU] (n.d.). There are currently 64 AAU schools in the United States and two in Canada. Of the 66 institutions, 17 are land-grant universities. New members can be invited by producing research that exceeds current members, and by the same token, members can lose their place by reducing their research outputs.

The Association of Public and Land-Grant Universities (APLU) is an organization dedicated to supporting public and land-grant universities in the United States, Canada, and Mexico through research, policy, and advocacy (APLU, 2012). APLU serves 244 institutions, including 75 land-grant institutions. Service is also a crucial aspect of the land-grant mission, leading many institutions to actively engage in community outreach. The elective Community Engagement Carnegie classification is a designation that can only be achieved by completing a self-survey and application. As of 2022, there are 351 institutions that have earned this classification, 38 (two from 1890 and 36 from 1862) of which are land-grant universities (Carnegie, n.d.).

Extension

Agriculture is central to the extension and service mission of a land-grant institution. Universities assist farmers in crop and business development, as well as teach young people the importance of raising, showing, and selling livestock. Extension educators employed by land-grant universities live in the community they serve (Stoecker, 2014). Extension services act as the bridge between the research universities conduct and the community they serve.

The National Institute of Food and Agriculture (NIFA), housed within the U.S. Department of Agriculture (USDA), sets national outreach objectives and partially funds state operations. Many faculty members with extension appointments are considered extension specialists. They often have joint appointments (research and/or teaching), as well as extension role-research-based programs and technical support to regional and county extension staff. Each land-grant institution has a cooperative extension program that benefits the citizens of that state (Stoecker, 2014). Research conducted by the university is made accessible and available to the community through Cooperative Extension programs.

STUDENT SUCCESS AND POPULATIONS

Land-grant universities serve close to 1.7 million students in the United States (Congressional Research Service, 2021). While over half of land-grant institutions are Predominantly White Institutions (PWIs), nearly half are designated at HBCUs or TCUs. Further, eight of the 1862 land-grants are designated Hispanic-Serving Institutions (HSIs), indicating that at least 25% of their student population identifies as Hispanic. Sixty percent of college students attend land-grant universities, more than any other type of college in the nation (Glossner, 2012, as cited in Page et al., 2014). The original target population for land-grant universities was undergraduates, and although these institutions have expanded to serve graduate education, the primary focus remains on undergraduate students (Page et al., 2014).

The original mission of the land-grant university was to educate and serve the sons and daughters of toil (i.e., working-class families). In modern practice, however, land-grants have become increasingly selective with ever-shrinking admission rates. This trend has sparked anger in alumni and college access advocates alike (Gavazzi & Gee, 2018). "If we are to retain our standing as the 'people's universities,' we had best be perceived as being an open and inclusive place for all those people" (Gavazzi & Gee, 2018, p. 25). This generation of students is more intentional about college choice than those before. They actively seek out land-grants to better expand their worldview with a focus on community engagement. Prospective students are completing significant amounts of community service, and they are seeking service opportunities in college. Thus, it is more important than ever to focus on improving access to land-grants. "If students are not able to enroll, then they are not able to learn" (Penn et al., 2014, p. 110).

PROFESSIONAL CONTEXT

In many institutional contexts, faculty and staff are very aware of the institutional type and mission of the school at which they are employed. For example, most individuals at community colleges and HBCUs are likely very aware of their missions and histories. For faculty and staff working at land-grant universities; however, many have little knowledge of this. Arguably, the faculty and staff who are the most aware of the land-grant designation are those who work in the agriculture colleges and divisions of the campus. Most of the faculty in agriculture intentionally attended land-grant universities and are keenly aware of agriculture extension and research stations, which are two pillars of land-grant universities. The 1890 HBCU land-grants highlight their historical founding and are more intentional about education on the history and mission compared to their 1862 peers.

While many faculty and staff are unfortunately less aware of the land-grant mission, they often are aware of other aspects of the land-grant. First, many of the 1862 land-grant universities are classified as Carnegie R1: Very High Research Activity. Only 146 universities in the country have this designation and many universities strive to get R1 status, which is reevaluated approximately every 5 years (Carnegie, n.d.). Notably, 76% (44 of 58) of 1862 land-grant universities are designated as R1 and the remaining are R2. Therefore, these institutions all have a strong focus on research and faculty are highly engaged in research activities, including publishing and grant writing.

Faculty and staff who work at the 1890 HBCU land-grant universities are at some of the most recognized HBCUs in the country. For example, North Carolina A&T University and Florida A&M University are consistently ranked as the top public HBCUs. These two institutions in particular have very high student enrollments. HBCUs have a rich history, which coupled with the land-grant mission, makes the 1890 land-grant institutions unique. Housed within the APLU is the Council of 1890 institutions, and they work together to advocate and support the 19 HBCU land-grants (see https://www.aplu.org/members/councils/1890-universities/council-of-1890s-institutions.html).

The 1994 land-grant institutions are all Tribal Colleges and Universities. Many faculty and staff at these institutions are likely part of the tribal communities. These institutions existed long before they were designated as land-grant universities. "This new land-grant system would teach in a cultural context that empowered students by drawing on the strength of their peoples' history, indigenous knowledge, and traditions" (United States Department of Agriculture, 2015, p. 3). These institutions received funding from NIFA to fund research, extension, and education programs to help recruit more Native American students into the fields of food and agricultural sciences. The 1994 land-grant universities have had a commitment to agriculture long before their 1994 designation, but with this official designation comes more federal funding and support.

Arguably, some faculty are intentionally employed at a land-grant university, but most are there more coincidentally or because of one of the other designations (e.g., R1, HBCU, TCU). Gavazzi and Gee (2018) argued, "When faculty members feel connected to the land-grant mission, they are going to think about how their scholarship engages with the communities that they are serving" (p. 123). Yet, faculty are often aligned more with their academic discipline and not necessarily the institution where they are employed (Ruben et al., 2017). If faculty are able to learn more about the history and mission of land-grant universities, it is possible they can have more buy-in to the institutional context.

FUTURE CONSIDERATIONS AND DIRECTIONS

While the land-grant mission is still alive and well, not enough individuals are knowledgeable about its history and relevance today. We offer future considerations for higher education administrators, faculty, research, and practitioners. We encourage all stakeholders to have a better understanding of the history and mission of land-grants, and then align their leadership, work, and service to this unique institutional context.

Suggestions for Leadership

Leaders of land-grant universities have a great opportunity to not only make the land-grant mission more visible, but to actually implement policies and practices aligned with the land-grant mission. First, many land-grants institutions have several other designations, which might be promoted more. One example is that many 1862 land-grant universities are also the state's "flagship" institution, which does not have a consistent definition but is often viewed as the most well-known, prominent public university in the state. This designation has recently come under scrutiny as it is ambiguous and more of a symbol of elitism, but really has no meaning (Cantwell & Byrd, 2021). "Labeling an institution as a flagship sends a message about whom and what is valued in American higher education: specifically, name brands and the allure of status" (Cantwell & Byrd, 2021, para. 15). Many land-grant universities tout the shallow "flagship" status and rarely promote the more salient "land-grant" designation. In states where the 1862 land-grant is not the "flagship" university, the land-grant status is often more salient in their messaging and mission statements. For 1890 and 1994 land-grant universities that have a historical mission to serve Black/African American students and Native American students, the land-grant mission might be less salient. We encourage all leaders of land-grant universities to have a deep understanding of the history and mission, and intentionally address this in missions, strategic plans, promotion and tenure requirements, engagement with the local community, and extension broadly.

Suggestions for Faculty

Arguably, faculty and staff who are most aware and knowledgeable about the land-grant mission are those in the agriculture disciplines. The extension function at land-grant universities is key to fulfilling the research-to-practice mission. We encourage faculty in other disciplines to take on *extension* in their respective fields. Often there is a disconnect between institutions and local communities, and this is not how land-grant universities were designed to operate. Faculty at land-grant universities should think strategically about how they can connect their research and teaching to the local community and the state where they work. Land-grant universities were not designed to be prestigious silos separated from their communities, but instead to be partners with the community and share knowledge. The agriculture extension model is one that all faculty can embrace as they work to *extend* their research and teaching to improve the lives of the local citizens. For example, faculty can find innovative ways to incorporate community engagement pedagogies into their courses, such as designating courses as service-learning. Lastly, universities need to think about how to teach current students about the history and mission of land-grant universities. This can be accomplished through a standalone course, or more practically through a lesson in a first-year seminar course that reaches all students.

Suggestions for Research

While land-grant universities have been the focus of scholarships, much of this work focuses on the 1862 institutions, which are majority PWIs. Less scholarship is focused on 1890 HBCU land-grant universities and 1994 land-grant Tribal Colleges and Universities. We find that 1890 land-grants have more of an awareness of their land-grant designation, which is salient in many mission statements, and in their involvement on the APLU Council of 1890 Institutions. However, more work is needed to look at the funding structures of the1890 land-grants, which often face funding inequities compared to the 1862 institutions. Further, the 1994 TCUs have relatively new designations and research is needed to examine finances, Indigenous student experiences, and the role of agriculture in tribal communities.

Our hope is that the mission of land-grant universities is more salient in institutional service to communities, and that land-grant leaders promote their unique mission. Leaders need to think critically about how to continue to fulfill the access mission that land-grants were founded on, while not letting prestige and elitism always take priority. Land-grant universities were the first major step that the United States took toward investing in public higher education and making education more accessible. It is important that leaders, faculty, staff, and students all understand this history and are thoughtful about extending the work of land-grants into the communities they were designed to serve.

REFLECTION QUESTIONS

1. Land-grant universities were founded with a focus on access to public education. However, many of the 1862 have high admissions standards and tout their high rankings. Do you think that there is a way to honor the historical access mission, while still pursuing rankings/prestige?
2. How can more students and faculty learn about the founding and history of land-grant universities?
3. Consider the history of many land-grant universities using stolen Native American land to fund their endowments. How should land-grant universities acknowledge and address this past wrong?

42   A. B. CLAYTON and V. C. LLOYD

4. Consider the resistance of many 1862 land-grants to integrate, which led to the historical founding of 1890 HBCU land-grants. How should 1862 PWI land-grants acknowledge this history and work with their 1890 HBCU land-grant in their state?

5. Do you feel that your personal mission is aligned with the land-grant mission?

REFERENCES

Abramson, C. I., Damron, W. S., Dicks, M., Sherwood, & P. M. A. (2014). History and mission. In Sternberg, R. J. (Ed). *The modern land-grant university* (pp. 3–13). Purdue University Press.

Association of American Universities [AAU]. (n.d.) *Membership policy.* Association of American Universities. https://www.aau.edu/who-we-are/membership-policy

Association of Public and Land-Grant Universities [APLU]. (2012). *The land-grant tradition.* http://www.aplu.org/library/the-land-grant-tradition/file

Cantwell, B., & Byrd, C. (2021, April 28). *The flagship folly.* The Chronicle of Education. https://www.chronicle.com/article/the-flagship-folly

Carnegie. (n.d.) *Carnegie classification of institutions of higher education.* Carnegie. https://carnegieclassifications.iu.edu/index.php

Congressional Research Service. (2021). *1890 Land-grant universities: Background and selected issues.* United States Government. https://crsreports.congress.gov/product/pdf/IF/IF11847

Daun-Barnett, N., Behrend, C., & Bezek, C. (2014). *College counseling for admissions professionals: Improving access and retention.* Routledge.

Gavazzi, S. M., & Gee, E. G. (2018). *Land-grant universities for the future: Higher education for the public good.* Johns Hopkins University Press.

National Institute of Food and Agriculture [NIFA]. (n.d.). *The Hatch Act of 1887.* https://www.nifa.usda.gov/grants/programs/capacity-grants/hatch-act-1887

National Institute of Food and Agriculture [NIFA]. (2015). *The First 20 Years of the 1994 Land-Grant Institutions Standing on Tradition | Embracing the Future.* National Institute of Food and Agriculture.

Page, M. C., Bailey, L. E., Lin, H., Jacobs, S. C., & Bruner, B. (2014). Teaching and learning. In Sternberg, R. J. (2014). *The modern land-grant university.* Purdue University Press.

Penn, J. D., Hathcoat, J. D., & Kim, S. (2014). Undergraduate Academic Experience. In Sternberg, R. J. (2014). *The modern land-grant university.* Purdue University Press.

Ruben, B. D., De Lisi, R., & Gigliotti, R. A. (2017). *A guide for leaders in higher education: Core concepts, competencies, and tools.* Stylus.

Sandmann, L. R., & Plater, W. M. (2009). Leading the engaged institution. In L. R. Sandmann et al. (Eds.), *New directions for higher education* (pp. 13–24). Wiley Periodicals.

Shreve, B. (2019). Joe McDonald on the passage of the 1994 land-grant. *Journal of American Indian Higher Education, 30*(3).

Stoecker, R. (2014). Extension and higher education service-learning: Toward a community development service-learning model. *Journal of Higher Education Outreach and Engagement, 18*(1), 15–42.

Thelin, J. R. (2019). *A History of American Higher Education* (3rd ed.). Johns Hopkins University Press.

Wilder, C. S. (2013). *Ebony & ivy: Race, slavery, and the troubled history of America's* Universities. Bloomsbury Publishing.

APPENDIX

1862 Land-Grant Institutions (58)

American Samoa Community College*

Auburn University	University of Connecticut
Clemson University	University of Delaware
College of Micronesia, Kolonia*	University of Florida
Colorado State University	University of Georgia
Cornell University+	University of Guam*
Iowa State University	University of Hawaii
Kansas State University	University of Idaho
Louisiana State University	University of Illinois
Massachusetts Institute of Technology+	University of Kentucky
Michigan State University	University of Maine
Mississippi State University	University of Maryland
Montana State University	University of Massachusetts
New Mexico State University	University of Minnesota
North Carolina State University	University of Missouri System
North Dakota State University	University of Nebraska System
Northern Marianas College*	University of Nevada
Ohio State University	University of New Hampshire
Oklahoma State University	University of Puerto Rico*
Oregon State University	University of Rhode Island

Pennsylvania State University

Purdue University

Rutgers University

South Dakota State University

Texas A&M University

University of Alaska

University of Arizona

University of Arkansas

University of California System

University of Tennessee

University of the District of Columbia*

University of the Virgin Islands*

University of Vermont

University of Wisconsin

University of Wyoming

Utah State University

Virginia Tech

Washington State University

West Virginia University

+ Private College

*U.S. Territory or Washington D.C.

1890 Land-Grant Institutions (19)

Alabama A&M University

Alcorn State University

Central State University

Delaware State University

Florida A&M University

Fort Valley State University

Kentucky State University

Langston University

Lincoln University

North Carolina A&T State University

Prairie View A&M University

South Carolina State University

1994 Land-Grant Institutions (35)

Aaniiih Nakoda College–MT

Bay Mills Community College–MI

Blackfeet Community College–MT

Cankdeska Cikana Community College -ND

Chief Dull Knife College–MT

College of Menominee Nation–WI

College of Muscogee Nation–OK

Diné College–AZ

Fond du Lac Tribal and Community College–MN

Fort Peck Community College–MT

Haskell Indian Nations University–KS

Ilisagvik College–AK

Land-Grant Institutions   45

Southern University System

Tennessee State University

Tuskegee University+

University of Arkansas at Pine Bluff

University of Maryland Eastern Shore

Virginia State University

West Virginia State University

+ Private College

Institute of American Indian Arts–NM

Keweenaw Bay Ojibwa Community College–MI

Lac Courte Oreilles Ojibwa Community College–WI

Leech Lake Tribal College–MN

Little Big Horn College–MT

Little Priest Tribal College–NE

Navajo Technical University–NM

Nebraska Indian Community College–NE

Northwest Indian College–WA

Nueta Hidatsa Sahnish College -ND

Oglala Lakota College–SD

Red Lake Nation College–MN

Saginaw Chippewa Tribal College–MI

Salish Kootenai College–MT

Sinte Gleska University–SD

Sisseton Wahpeton College–SD

Sitting Bull College–ND

Southwestern Indian Polytechnic Institute –NM

Stone Child CollegevMT

Tohono O'odham Community CollegevAZ

Turtle Mountain Community CollegevND

United Tribes Technical College–ND

White Earth Tribal and Community College–MN

CHAPTER 4

SMALL COLLEGES AND UNIVERSITIES

Carolyn H. Livingston
Carleton College

Christa J. Porter
Kent State University

The first type of institution established in America was the baccalaureate college (Hirt, 2009) whose early purpose was to train students for the ministry and educate civic leaders. Baccalaureate colleges had small enrollments, and it was not until 1860 did Harvard graduate more than a hundred students from a single class (Lucas, 1994). Consistent with the American colonial aspiration to follow English academic precedents as closely as possible, early colleges were mostly residential institutions (Thelin, 2019). Whereas no college enjoyed sufficient resources to reproduce elaborate quadrangular enclosures after the fashion of Oxford or Cambridge, the tendency was to house students together in a residential dormitory of one sort or another whenever possible (Lucas, 1994).

From 1638 to 1819, only 49 institutions of higher education existed; 40 of them were private (Goldin & Katz, 1999). The next 80 years saw a great expansion with more than 400 institutions established with speculation that the peak in the founding of colleges and universities might be attributed to the Morrill Acts of 1862 and 1890 (Goldin & Katz, 1999). The number of colleges swelled as the country expanded, and over time, baccalaureate

---

Institutional Diversity in American Postsecondary Education, pp. 47–57
Copyright © 2024 by Information Age Publishing
www.infoagepub.com
All rights of reproduction in any form reserved.

colleges took one of two paths (Hirt, 2009). Some moved away from their religious roots and evolved into secular colleges. Many increased their academic offerings and student enrollment to become master's colleges and universities, or research and doctoral-granting universities.

Baccalaureate colleges or small colleges continued to help young men make the transition from rural farms to complex urban occupations. In addition, these small colleges especially promoted upward mobility by preparing ministers and thereby provided towns across the country with a core of community leaders (Katz, 1983). Many of these small colleges tried to meet the demands of their constituencies through curricular flexibility and innovation through low tuition made possible by support from various national denominational organizations (Katz, 1983). It was the small institutions that, in conjunction with contemporary professional forces, moved students from old to new cultures and environments (Burke, 1982). In other words, the training local leaders received at small colleges shaped their ability to influence change, social mobility, and cultural values. In this chapter, we magnify specific student populations served by small colleges and universities. We also provide additional information on the organizational structure and culture of this institutional type and professional context and end with reflection questions.

HISTORY

So-called female seminaries (or women's colleges and universities) were new additions to the growing roster of collegiate institutions that appeared in the first half of the 19th century (Lucas, 1994; Renn, 2014). Women's colleges proliferated in states where there was high resistance to coeducation—primarily states in the east, with private education for men and fewer in the west with the rapid expansion of public institutions (Hurtado, 2003; Rudolph, 1965). In 1836, Wesleyan became the first women's college in the world and over the next several decades, other women's colleges opened, including Barnard, Vassar, Bryn Mawr, Smith, and Wellesley (Carleton, 2021). Coeducation was virtually unheard of until Oberlin College opened its portals to women as well as men in 1837 (Oberlin, n.d.). In 1862, Oberlin awarded a degree to Mary Jane Patterson, making her the first Black woman to earn a bachelor's (Carleton, 2021).

Black Students at Small Colleges

Oberlin also freely admitted Black people and, like other small colleges such as Middlebury College (Vermont), Amherst College (Massachusetts), and Bowdoin College (Maine); they were some of the early pioneers of Black college graduates at predominantly white institutions (Pilgrim, 2010). By 1900, Oberlin had produced one-third of all African American college graduates in the United States and at the start of the Civil War, Oberlin enrolled more Black students than any other American institution of higher education (Pilgrim, 2010).

Between 1860 and 1900, historically excluded constituencies such as women, Black, and Native American students gained some access to higher education (Thelin, 2003). Avery College (Pittsburgh, PA), Miner Academy (Washington, DC), Wilberforce (Ohio), and Lincoln University (Pennsylvania) were among the first Black colleges to begin operations (Lucas, 1994). Today, more than 100 historically Black colleges and universities (HBCUs) exist in the United States, with most of them being small colleges and universities. Specifically, Spelman College (Atlanta, GA) and Bennett College (Greensboro, NC) are the only two private HBCUs liberal arts colleges serving women-identified students while Morehouse College (Atlanta, GA) serves male-identifying students.

Special Mission Colleges

Although some small colleges were admitting Black students, other campus (and national) leaders were similarly developing missions to meet the needs of students with varying disabilities and those wanting to investigate human relationships. Since 1864, when President Abraham Lincoln signed legislation authorizing the establishment of a college for deaf and hard-of-hearing students in Washington, DC, Gallaudet University remains the world's only university dedicated strategically to this mission (Gallaudet, n.d.). Approximately 99% of courses at Gallaudet have an online component, and virtually all students take at least one course using an online learning system. All 1,500 students must study abroad.

Since 1969, the College of the Atlantic in Maine has been the first college in the United States to focus exclusively on the relationship between humans and the environment. Through an ecological perspective, students are provided opportunities to integrate knowledge from various academic disciplines and examine the relationships between people and their national communities. In addition to nearly 350 students designing their own major in human ecology, more than half of the students at the college have international experience (College of the Atlantic, n.d.). Beacon College, founded in 1989, is the first college in the nation accredited to award bachelor's degrees exclusively to students with learning disabilities. Beacon College's sole mission is to support the educational goals of students who

50   C. H. LIVINGSTON and C. J. PORTER

learn differently while teaching empowering strategies for life for nearly 500 students (Beacon College, n.d.).

Throughout the preceding sections, we provide a historical overview of small colleges and universities and their unique role in influencing demographic and cultural change in higher education. From training ministers and shaping communities to increasing access for students of color, women, and students with disabilities, small college and university missions continue to respond to the challenges and transformation of higher education. In the next sections, we highlight working at small colleges and universities, the work of student success, and populations.

ORGANIZATION STRUCTURE AND CULTURE

The historical foundation of the small college has led to its contemporary positionality within higher education. For this chapter, we specifically refer to Carnegie's classification for small colleges and universities; those with full-time enrollment fewer than 5,000 (Carnegie, n.d.). Full-time enrollment numbers, however, only offer a snapshot of the broader story and culture of small colleges and universities.

American colleges and universities are like snowflakes, with structures that appear like the casual observer, though in fact no two have been found to be exactly alike (Carpenter-Hubin & Snover, 2013). The large university usually follows an ideology that is much more specialized in quantification and adaptation to societal needs. In contrast, each small college and university is different—their mission, origins, student population served, and academic specialties. There is no typical small college, but there are some general characteristics that tend to distinguish it from a large university (Young, 1986). The small college is characterized by synergy and values education, personalized relationships, and organic change.

Even the most seasoned college and university administrators often ask themselves, "What holds this place together? Is it mission, values, bureaucratic procedures, or strong personalities? How does this place run and what does it expect from its leaders?" (Tierney, 1988, p. 3). At small colleges and universities, these answers are easier to find. Working at a small college or university necessitates collegiality, connection, and collaboration. The small college or university allows—indeed requires—one to develop relationships across campus to effectively accomplish one's goals (Oblander, 2006). The depth of the relationships that exist between colleagues often extends beyond the workday. Many small colleges and universities are in smaller/rural towns where oftentimes colleagues can socialize together on the weekends at sporting activities, civic engagement work, evening lectures, and other university programs.

Due to the size of smaller colleges, the professional expectation is to get to know nearly all of one's colleagues, and the functional silos, if they exist, are more porous. Fewer divisions exist between faculty and staff that are often in place at larger institutions. For example, a collaborative learning and teaching center discussion on *Supporting Students' Religious and Spiritual Identities* hosted by a professor of politics and the Chaplain's office is common and expected at the small college. A weekly convocation lecture series that brings fresh insights and perspectives from experts in a variety of fields to stimulate thought and conversation on a wide range of subjects is par for the course (Carleton College, n.d.).

In the small college, where relationships and personal attention to students are often the mantra, staffing is critical. Because of smaller class sizes in many small colleges, faculty know the students they teach (Oblander, 2006) as well as the staff who support the academic mission of the college. Furthermore, staffing levels at small colleges and universities are rather lean compared to larger colleges and universities. A relatively new practitioner can assume significant responsibility early in their career due to the flat organizational structure that frequently exists in the small college environment (Oblander, 2006). It is not unheard of to have one-person offices with a director and student employees. This lean workforce, however, creates challenges with staff departures and vacancies. Staff departures and vacancies seem to create an even larger disruption than they might otherwise at larger institutions, where there is more capacity to absorb the additional labor, at least temporarily.

STUDENT SUCCESS AND POPULATIONS

Small colleges and universities have created a distinctive niche in opportunities for higher education; they are primarily residential and serve mostly undergraduate students. Akin to the variation among small colleges and universities, the population of students enrolled at small colleges and universities is similarly diverse. Demographic shifts due to local, national, and international socio-historical trends, legislation, and employment needs impact who enrolls in higher education (Bastedo et al., 2016; Wilder, 2014).

Factors such as regional birth rates, national (and local) immigration policies, and marketability/competition (for employment) impact shifting college student demographics. Potential and current students are accessing higher education differently than before (e.g., online/distance learning vs solely in person) and seeking out institutions that can meet and support their respective needs (Grawe, 2018). Similarly, to avoid large amounts of debt, students are choosing in-state institutions and electing (when possible) to live at home (Seemiller & Grace, 2019).

Grawe (2018) asserted "everyone in higher education agrees that dramatic shifts in demand lie ahead, but few seem to understand their situation with the clarity required for decisive action" (p. 5). Marcy (2020) furthered this sentiment by stating:

> The pressure for small colleges is particularly pertinent, for on the one hand, the environment of independent colleges makes them particularly well-positioned to respond to an increasingly diverse student body; small classes and integrated support systems can be especially effective.... On the other hand, many small colleges were created for, and still primarily serve, middle- and upper-class White students. (p. 3)

Some small college and university administrators are recruiting and subsequently admitting increased numbers of students who identify as low-income, or are undocumented, first-generation, students of color, international, and students with disabilities (Marcy, 2020). Through formal partnerships, such as with the Posse Foundation (n.d.) and Questbridge (n.d.), some small colleges and universities are responding strategically to demographic shifts by reimagining and supporting the needs of potential and current students. Additional formal partnerships exist with the Schuler Foundation (n.d.) and the American Talent Initiative (n.d.) to diversify the student body. We highlight examples of successful practices in response to student needs in the next section.

PROFESSIONAL CONTEXT

It is common, particularly in larger student affairs units, for core functions such as budget management, personnel decisions, and day-to-day management tasks to occur in a decentralized environment where each unit head, in effect, serves as the senior student affairs officer. On smaller campuses, decentralization is less common (Dungy, 2003). Administrators and staff members across units and status assume various responsibilities within their respective positions and are often knowledgeable of processes affecting their stakeholders. For example, the Associate Dean of Students will serve as Class Dean for first-year students while also serving as a co-facilitator of a class on civil discourse. Similarly, the Director of Student Activities may co-chair a working group highlighting the opportunities and challenges for low-income and first-generation students. Furthermore, this organizational interconnectedness assists the small college and university in meeting the dynamic needs of a diverse student body.

Some administrators and staff working within student (and academic) affairs divisions at small colleges and universities have gained graduate preparation in the field of higher education and student affairs. Others are equipped with various levels of expertise and administrative experience relevant to serving student and institutional needs. In addition to ongoing professional development and training within small college and university departments, national organizational spaces serve to promote understanding of missions and successful practices (i.e., ACPA-College Student Educators International or NASPA-Student Affairs Administrators in Higher Education). Within NASPA (n.d.) for example, the small colleges and universities division serves as a smaller community within a larger, national association, wherein campus leaders, staff, and administrators can share strategies and ideas to best meet the needs of students and respective campuses enrolling less than 5,000 students (i.e., budget and enrollment concerns, innovation, and shifting demographics).

Examples of Successful Responses to Student Needs

Small college and university leaders possess both a responsibility and opportunity to respond to students' diverse needs. Due to smaller enrollment numbers, opportunities for intentional relationship-building across and alongside stakeholders often becomes a reality for students and those working on their behalf. Efforts to prioritize student success and engagement have included the implementation of identity-based groups, proactive and intentional social support models, and student participation in college-wide shared governance structures (e.g., Pomona College, a private liberal arts college in Claremont, CA; Carleton College, a private liberal arts college in Northfield, MN). Spelman College, one of two historically Black colleges and universities for women, "deliberately crafted, high-touch practices that promoted success for Black women from their entry point through graduation" (Winkle-Wagner et al., 2019, p. 654). Spelman College alumnae highlighted how administrators focused on their identities as assets, as opposed to deficits, to support their success. Supportive environments and relationships among students, faculty, and staff at HBCUs can serve as an example for predominantly white small colleges and universities, particularly to promote and increase academic achievement, occupational aspirations, and identity development for students of Color (McCoy et al., 2017; Watt, 2006).

Co-curricular and curricular support through faculty-led student cohorts, learning communities, and advising models to have strengthened students' academic connection to campus as well as to their respective discipline (e.g., John Carroll University, a private liberal arts Jesuit institution in Cleveland, OH; New Mexico Highlands University, a public Hispanic-serving institution in Las Vegas, NM). Internship and career support services have enhanced students' marketability and provided experiential learning experiences (e.g., College of William and Mary, a public liberal arts college in Williamsburg, VA; University of Minnesota Morris, a public liberal arts college in Morris, MN).

Innovation (or creatively responding to student needs) is ever-present at small colleges and universities through financially supporting students and enhancing multi-campus partnerships. Not all small colleges and universities are in the same fiscal position. Yet, small colleges' drive for innovation in meeting student needs (particularly in times of crises) is responsive and interdisciplinary. For example, Trinity Washington University (a private Catholic school for women in Washington DC) increased enrollment by providing sustained financial support to students of color and revising the curriculum. Kalamazoo College (a private liberal arts college in Kalamazoo, MI) collaborated with Western Michigan University (a large institution in the same city) by utilizing doctoral interns to provide counseling services and in return, students completed clinical supervision hours on-site. Despite examples of successful practices, institutional leaders, faculty, and staff should continually assess students' feelings of belonging within their respective disciplines (e.g., STEM classes) and the broader campus community whether a predominantly white institution or a minority-serving institution (Mobley & Johnson, 2015; Porter, 2022). The small college and university community may consist of a small(er) enrollment number, but the impact and influence of those working on campus have long-term implications for student success and engagement.

FUTURE CONSIDERATIONS AND DIRECTIONS

As microcosms of society, institutions have experienced tensions across socio-historical and political lines as well as a pressing need to (re)examine responses to crises such as a global pandemic. In some cases, tension has included forms of violence and vicarious trauma for students, staff, and faculty who are historically marginalized (e.g., due to increased and more visible incidents of racial injustice). Potential and current students want to know their campus leadership, faculty, and staff are able and willing to support their ability to live, learn, and grow within their college environments. Future considerations include small college and university leaders (a) reconciling how and to what extent their respective institution perpetuates the historical marginalization of certain groups of students (see Cole, 2020; Wilder, 2014); (b) proactively responding to the ever-changing needs of students at small colleges (e.g., moving from equality to equity and inclusion in both policy and practice; see Pope et al., 2019; Stewart, 2017); and (c) maximizing intentional relationships with varying stakeholders to advance strategic institutional goals.

Small colleges and universities are central to the history of higher education. These institutions have increased social mobility for those who were generally excluded and among the early recipients of enrollment spaces in higher education. And, while their enrollments remain less than 5,000 students, they continue to have many distinct and compelling strengths. Whether private, public, special mission, minority-serving, or originally created as single-sex institutions, those working within small colleges and universities will continue to strategically respond to students' evolving needs.

REFLECTION QUESTIONS

1. Discuss strategies to respond to students' ever-changing needs (particularly students who are historically marginalized). How have the socio-historical context and political climate influenced institutional leaders' abilities to serve and support students within a small college community and university context?
2. What potential opportunities and threats exist at small colleges and universities within the broader context of higher education?
3. What must institutional leaders, staff, and faculty proactively address and/or consider when creating, advancing, or sustaining equitable practices and policies?
4. In what ways, if any, will professional expectations change in the upcoming years? How can graduate programs prepare the next generation of leaders to address these changing professional expectations?
5. How might professional associations partner with small colleges and universities to increase the dearth of research on student success programs and services?

REFERENCES

American Talent Initiative. (n.d.). https://americantalentinitiative.org/
Bastedo, M. N., Altbach, P. G., & Gumport, P. J. (Eds.) (2016). *American higher education in the 21st century: Social, political, and economic challenges* (4th ed.). John Hopkins University Press.
Beacon College (n.d.). https://www.beaconcollege.edu/
Burke, C. (1982). *American collegiate populations: A test of the traditional view.* New York University Press.
Carleton College. (n.d.). https://www.carleton.edu/convocations/about/

Carleton, G. (2021, March 15). *A history of women in higher education*. https://www.bestcolleges.com/news/2021/03/21/history-women-higher-education/

Carnegie Classification of Institutions of Higher Education (n.d.). https://carnegieclassifications.iu.edu/classification_descriptions/size_setting.php

Carpenter-Hubin, J., & Snover, L. (2013). Key leadership positions and performance expectations. In P. J. Schloss & K. M. Cragg (Eds.), *Organization and administration in higher education* (pp. 27–49). Routledge.

Cole, E. R. (2020). *The campus color line: College presidents and the struggle for Black freedom*. Princeton University Press.

College of the Atlantic (n.d.). https://www.coa.edu/

Dungy, G. J. (2003). Organization and functions of student affairs. In S. R. Komives, D. B. Woodward, Jr., & Associates (Eds.). *Student services: A handbook for the profession* (4th ed.) (pp. 339–357). Jossey-Bass.

Gallaudet (n.d.). https://www.gallaudet.edu/

Goldin, C., & Katz, L. F. (1999). The shaping of higher education: The formative years in the United States, 1890 to 1940. *Journal of Economic Perspectives, 13*(1), 37–62.

Grawe, N. D. (2018). *Demographics and the demand for higher education*. Johns Hopkins University Press.

Hirt, J. B. (2009). The importance of institutional mission. In G.S. McClellan, J. Stringer, & Associates. (Eds), *The handbook of student affairs administration* (3rd ed.) (pp. 21–44). Jossey-Bass.

Hurtado, S. (2003). Institutional diversity in American higher education. In S. R. Komives, D. B. Woodward, Jr. & Associates (Eds.), *Student services: A handbook for the profession* (4th ed.), (pp. 23–44). Jossey-Bass.

Katz, M. B. (1983). The role of American colleges in the nineteenth century [Review of *American Collegiate Populations: A Test of the Traditional View; The Organization of American Culture: Private Institutions, Elites, and the Origins of American Nationality*, by C. B. Burke & P. D. Hall]. *History of Education Quarterly, 23*(2), 215–223. https://doi.org/10.2307/368160

Lucas, C. J. (1994). *American higher education: A history*. St. Martin's Press.

Marcy, M. B. (2020). *The small college imperative: Models for sustainable futures*. Stylus.

McCoy, D. L., Luedke, C. L., & Winkle-Wagner, R. (2017). Encouraged or "Weeded out" in the STEM disciplines: Students' perspectives on faculty interactions within a predominantly White and a historically Black institution. *Journal of College Student Development, 58*(5), 657–673.

Mobley, S. D., Jr., & Johnson, J. M. (2015). The role of HBCUs in addressing the unique needs of LGBT students. *New Directions for Higher Education, 170*, 79–89. https://doi.org/10.1002/he.20133

NASPA. (n.d.). https://www.naspa.org/division/small-colleges-and-universities-division

Oberlin. (n.d.). https://www.oberlin.edu/about-oberlin/oberlin-history

Oblander, D. A. (2006). Student affairs staffing in the small college. *New Directions for Students Services, 116*, 31–44.

Pilgrim, D. (2010). The first college to admit blacks. *Ferris State University*. https://www.ferris.edu/HTMLS/news/jimcrow/question/2010/june.htm

QuestBridge. (n.d.). https://www.questbridge.org/

Renn, K. A. (2014). *Women's colleges and universities in a global context.* Johns Hopkins University Press.

Rudolph, F. (1965). *The American college and university: A history.* Knopf.

Pope, R. L., Reynolds, A. L., & Mueller, J. A. (2019). *Multicultural competence in student affairs: Advancing social justice and inclusion* (2nd ed.). Jossey-Bass.

Porter, C. J. (2022). (Re)Imagining belonging: Black women want more than survival in predominantly White institutions. *Journal of College Student Development, 63*(1), 106–110. https://doi.org/10.1353/csd.2022.0002

Posse Foundation. (n.d.). https://www.possefoundation.org/

Schuler Education Foundation. (n.d.). https://schulereducationfoundation.org/schuler-access-initiative

Seemiller, C., & Grace, M. (2019). *Generation Z: A century in the making.* Routledge.

Stewart, D.-L. (2017). Language of appeasement. *Inside Higher Ed.* https://www.insidehighered.com/views/2017/03/30/colleges-need-language-shift-not-one-you-think-essay

Thelin, J. R. (2003). Historical overview of American higher education. In S. R. Komives, D. B. Woodward, Jr., & Associates (Eds.). *Student services: A handbook for the profession* (4th ed.), (pp. 3–22). Jossey-Bass.

Thelin, J. R. (2019). *A history of American higher education* (3rd ed). John Hopkins University Press.

Tierney, W. G. (1988). Organizational culture in higher education: Defining the essentials. *The Journal of Higher Education, 59*(1), 2–21. https://doi.org/10.2307/1981868

Watt, S. K. (2006). Racial identity attitudes, womanist identity attitudes, and self-esteem in African American college women attending historically Black single-sex and coeducational institutions. *Journal of College Student Development, 47*(3), 319–334.

Wilder, C. S. (2014). *Ebony and ivy: Race, slavery, and the troubled histories of America's universities.* Bloomsbury.

Winkle-Wagner, R., Forbes, J. M., Rogers, S., Reavis, T. B. (2019). A cultural of success: Black alumnae discussions of the assets-based approach at Spelman College. *The Journal of Higher Education, 91*(5), 653–673. https://doi.org/10.1080/00221546.2019.1654965

Young, R. (1986). The small college point of view: An ideology of student affairs. *Journal of College Student Personnel, 27*, 4–18.

CHAPTER 5

RURAL COLLEGES AND UNIVERSITIES

The Overlooked Champions of Higher Education

Sabrina A. Klein
MDRC

Andrew Koricich
Appalachian State University

Rural colleges and universities are often misunderstood and undervalued institutions of higher education. Historically, there has been a lack of focus and examination of rural institutions and rural students. This paucity of empirical research on rurality has created many difficulties in defining rural institutions, rural communities, and rural students. The purpose of this chapter is to provide an introduction to rural colleges and universities in the United States. To better understand what a rural college is, it is important to note the differences between rural-located institutions and rural-serving institutions. The former is fairly straightforward, in that, these are institutions located in areas officially classified as rural in some state or federal typology, though a given definition of rurality would cause the set of rural-located institutions to vary, resulting in some institutions being wrongly omitted. On the other hand, rural-serving institutions are those that serve rural students and communities in important ways but may

Institutional Diversity in American Postsecondary Education, pp. 59–70
Copyright © 2024 by Information Age Publishing
www.infoagepub.com
All rights of reproduction in any form reserved.

59

or may not be located in places officially classified as rural. For example, as land-grant universities have grown significantly in size and complexity, they have had a corresponding urbanizing effect on their surrounding community. So, although many would no longer be seen as rural-located, their service to rural communities remains an important aspect of their activities.

In an effort to center the rural context, specifically, this chapter will focus on public and private institutions located *in* rural areas, not institutions that *serve* predominantly rural areas, but may themselves be located in non-rural places. This chapter begins with a brief historical background of rural institutions and discusses the different institutional types located in rural areas. Next, an overview of student success and populations present at rural colleges and universities is presented, followed by a contextualization of professional experiences within rural institutions. Lastly, the authors offer considerations and directions for future research, policy, and practice, as well as supply questions to foster discussion and reflection.

HISTORY

Rural colleges and universities have been shaped by many different policies and historical events, which have shaped these institutions into what we see today. A large percentage of institutions located in rural areas are broad-access institutions that include Master's Universities, Baccalaureate Colleges, and Associates Colleges (Koricich et al., 2020). These broad-access institutions can be traced back to normal schools, or teachers' colleges, and denominational colleges (Koricich & Fryar, 2021). Normal schools, which were prevalent in the late 19th century through the mid-20th century, mostly provided education for future teachers and awarded teaching credentials (Thelin, 2019). At this time in history, women made up much of the population at normal schools, as teaching was seen as a profession to be held by a woman (Thelin, 2019). During the rapid expansion of postsecondary education following the conclusion of World War II, most normal schools evolved into the comprehensive universities currently known (Koricich & Fryar, 2021; Thelin, 2019).

Denominational colleges are another type of institution that shaped the identity and trajectory of current rural colleges and universities. These institutions were created in partnership with different religious organizations, such as Methodist, Presbyterian, and Baptist, as the colonization of Indigenous lands continued westward (Thelin, 2019). The nature of denominational colleges was to serve their local constituents, which embedded the colleges into the community. Their service to the local population varied from transforming curriculum that addressed local and institutional needs, such as shifting from a curriculum focused on classics to a more comprehensive one, to admitting students who were not in the denomination (Thelin, 2019). Those denominational colleges that remained in rural spaces have become integral to providing access to higher education for rural students (Koricich & Fryer, 2021), and have evolved over time to continue serving their local communities. Broad-access institutions and comprehensive universities have not only been influenced by teacher training and liberal education provided by normal schools and denominational colleges, but also by the Morrill Land Grant Acts which influenced the evolution of focus on agriculture and engineering.

Passed in 1862 and 1890, the Morrill Land Grant Acts were a legislative intervention from the federal government that granted states large sums of Indigenous land, taken either by exploitative treaties or outright theft. This land could then be sold with the proceeds funding institutions of higher education that focused on agriculture and the mechanical arts alongside traditional liberal arts subjects (Thelin, 2019). Some states established new institutions through the proceeds of these land sales, whereas others identified existing colleges as the beneficiaries. There are several instances of land-grant funds being reassigned to different institutions when the original beneficiary failed to offer the required subject areas, and the conclusion of the Civil War resulted in the establishment of Black land-grant institutions in states where racial segregation was still legal. Because the granted lands were primarily west of the Mississippi River, the Morrill Acts also had the effect of motivating further westward colonization and development that resulted in the establishment of new rural communities in need of colleges, a need that was commonly met by the denominational colleges noted above (Thelin, 2019).

More than 50 years after the Second Morrill Act in 1890, Congress enacted the Servicemen's Readjustment Act of 1944, also known as the G.I. Bill, in response to the social and economic needs of service members who were returning from World War II. The educational benefits of the G.I. Bill caused enrollment to surge at land-grant institutions and comprehensive universities that were formerly normal schools or denominational colleges (Thelin, 2019). Particularly in rural areas, these institutions were not only access points to viable degrees and certificates in fields of rural importance, such as agriculture, teaching and the liberal arts, but often were the only means through which rural students, military veterans and otherwise, had access to higher education (Thelin, 2019). More recently, this phenomenon of an area or community having few or no nearby post-secondary institutions came to be known as an education desert (Hillman & Weichman, 2016). Rural areas are more likely than non-rural areas to be in an education desert (Hillman & Weichman, 2016), which represents an important structural barrier for these communities. When considering education deserts, we cannot see these merely as a result of the organic development of institutions over the last 250 years but must also consider how the implicit and explicit decisions states made about where to build institutions of higher education have shaped the experiences and challenges faced by rural colleges and universities today.

ORGANIZATION STRUCTURE AND CULTURE

There are a variety of institutional types in rural areas: public and private, non-profit and for-profit, and broad-access and selective institutions. For the purposes of the chapter, public and private, not-for-profit, four-year institutions will be the focus. Further, a broad access institution is one that admits 80% or more of applicants who apply (Crisp et al., 2018). Using the Carnegie Classification system to identify some of the range of institutional types in rural spaces, which include Doctoral Universities, Masters's Colleges and Universities, Baccalaureate Colleges, Baccalaureate/Associates Colleges, and Special Focus Four-Year Institutions. Doctoral Universities account for the least number of institutions in rural areas, while Master's Colleges and Universities account for the most institutions (Koricich & Fryar, 2021; Koricich et al., 2020). Among four-year institutions, Koricich et al. (2020) found that doctoral institutions are more likely located in non-rural areas, whereas baccalaureate and master's institutions that likely have a regional-focused mission serve predominately rural areas. Therefore, baccalaureate and master's institutions, along with their community college partners, provide pivotal access not only to higher education but to bachelor's and advanced degrees and credentials for rural areas. Of rural broad access institutions, the majority are public institutions; however, there are a significant number of private, not-for-profit institutions located in rural areas, such as Dakota Wesleyan University in South Dakota. Dakota Wesleyan University is a private, Methodist-affiliated institution located in a rural area, with approximately 800 students in attendance. This institution also holds conferences centering on rurality and raises awareness about regional issues and points of interest.

Beyond utilizing the Carnegie Classification system to discuss variances in institutional types in rural areas, there are also rural colleges and universities that hold different designations, including federal designations for Historically Black Colleges and Universities (HBCUs), Tribal Colleges & Universities (TCUs), and Native American Serving Non-Tribal Institutions. HBCUs are those institutions that were established prior to 1964 and were created with–and continue to hold–the mission of educating Black Americans (U.S. Department of Education, n.d.a). Although not all HBCUs are located in rural areas, a number of these institutions are, which underscores their important role in serving not only Black communities, but rural ones as well. For example, Alcorn State University in Lorman, Mississippi, is the oldest historically Black land-grant institution in the United States and is embedded in a rural region with many partnerships and programs with a rural emphasis. Regarding TCUs, there are 34 such institutions in the United States, which are mostly located in the Midwest and Southwest, and 31 are in rural areas (U.S. Department of Education, n.d.b). In addition to TCUs, Native American Serving Non-Tribal Institutions are another key institutional designation that serves Native students and communities, and 88% are rural located (McClure et al., 2021). An example of one such institution is the University of North Carolina at Pembroke, which serves Native American students and Students of Color, and offers rural-specific majors such as a bachelor's degree in nursing, with a concentration in rural case management.

These institutional types all play a crucial role in serving a diverse and evolving rural population. Rural colleges and universities provide a great deal beyond granting degrees and credentials, including acting as important centers and drivers of community development, economic development, cultural hubs, and public-health cultivators (Koricich et al., 2020; McClure et al., 2021; Orphan & McClure, 2019). Although these designations and classifications help instruct us about the mission and foundations of these institutions, there is much to be learned about rural colleges and universities from an institutional lens to better understand rural higher education in this country.

STUDENT SUCCESS AND POPULATIONS

In the United States, there are many commonly held misconceptions about rural places and rural people. Overall, there is scant empirical data collected on students who attend rural colleges and universities, particularly data that is disaggregated by institutional type. Some examination has been conducted on students at rural broad access institutions and community colleges, but the majority of research historically examines rural students at large. Examining the body of work on rural students, predominantly K–12, aids in bettering an understanding of the students who attend rural colleges and universities. Given that a majority of students attend a postsecondary institution within 100 miles of their home (Hillman & Weichman, 2016), it is likely that many students who attend rural colleges and universities are from rural areas and small towns.

Rural students, when compared to their nonrural peers are more likely to graduate from high school (Irvin et al., 2011), but less likely to obtain a postsecondary degree (Koricich et al., 2018) even though they aspire to obtain one (Tieken, 2016). Some of this disparity is explained by the fact that many rural students live in an education desert (Hillman & Weichman, 2016) and many also live in an online education desert (Rosenboom & Blagg, 2018), with limited access to broadband internet. Many rural students attend community colleges, to which they are more likely to be in commuting distance, however, are less likely to obtain a bachelor's degree given the lack of tangible access to 4-year institutions (McDonough et al., 2010). For rural students, this means that these rural institutions provide a distinctive access point to higher education, particularly for first-generation and underrepresented students (Means et al., 2016).

Although rural institutions are less racially diverse than their nonrural counterparts, they do serve a diverse student population. Koricich and Fryar (2021) found in their examination of rural broad access institutions that White students make up a higher percentage of the student population, and fewer Latinx, Asian, and Black students enrolled. However, Koricich and Fryar (2021) did find that rural broad-access institutions enroll higher percentages of American Indian students than nonrural institutions. Because many rural institutions are near or serve Tribal nations, their role is virtually important. Native and Indigenous students are twice as likely to attend a rural institution than their peers (McClure et al., 2021). Although rural institutions are likely to enroll many rural students from their region, rural institutions do also serve nonrural students who relocate to attend the institution. Koricich and Fryar (2021) found that rural broad-access institutions enroll a higher percentage of out-of-state students than their nonrural counterparts, though this could be associated with students who live near state borders.

Each region served by a rural institution has unique needs and challenges and thus needs to provide unique academic and cocurricular opportunities for students. In 2019 alone, rural public institutions awarded over 120,000 bachelor's degrees, 25,000 master's degrees, and 17,000 associate degrees and certifications (McClure et al., 2021). Rural institutions offer different types of degrees and credentials that are unique to their institutional type and local industries (McClure et al., 2021; Orphan & McClure, 2019). For example, a report by the Alliance for Research on Regional Colleges (ARRC) in 2021, found that rural institutions awarded degrees predominately in education, health professions, business, hospitality, tourism, and natural resource management (McClure et al., 2021). This report also revealed that "rural public colleges produced 16,248 degrees in health professions and related programs, including 9,662 nursing degrees, addressing critical workforce shortages in this area" (p. 6). Other degrees awarded in 2019 include 6,573 degrees in homeland security, law enforcement, firefighting, and related protective services, 13,067 teaching certificates, and 5,261 degrees in parks, recreation, leisure, and fitness management (McClure et al., 2021). These numbers demonstrate how rural colleges and universities help students receive degrees and credentials that prepare them to meet local workforce needs and shortages.

There is still much to be learned about the students who attend rural institutions. Data are typically not collected to track the success of rural students at colleges and universities, and more specifically are data not collected about rural students at rural colleges and universities. This issue partially stems from an inconsistent definition of a rural student, rural institution, and rural-serving institution at the state and federal levels. Further, most data collected at both the federal and state levels about student degree completion do not consider place as a factor, and therefore empirical studies that utilize these data are limited.

PROFESSIONAL CONTEXT

There are unique benefits and challenges for those who are employed by a rural institution. To better understand those benefits and challenges at the individual level, it is essential to understand the distinctive experiences and challenges at the institutional level. First, compared to non-rural institutions, rural institutions (including rural community colleges) are broadly underfunded (Fluharty & Scaggs, 2007; McClure et al., 2021; Orphan & McClure, 2019). Uniquely tied to their local region, rural institutions struggle to maintain consistent funding for both traditional collegiate and community-level activities, and at the rural community college level has meant institutions experience gaps in funding for both types of activities (Fluharty & Scaggs, 2007; Thornton & Friedel, 2016). In one examination of a rural anchor institution, Orphan and McClure (2019) found that the institution invested in many different forms of community capitals (cultural, social, political, financial, built, and natural capital) which was mutually beneficial to both the institution and the region. For example, rural colleges tend to be the region's larger employer, and Orphan and McClure (2019) found that this contributed to the overall financial stability of its region. Many rural counties have less than 65% of adults aged 25–65 who are employed, which is designated by the United States Department of Agriculture's Economic Research Service as a low employment county, and 17% of rural public colleges are located in such a county (McClure et al., 2021). However, without the employment opportunities provided by rural higher education, the number of counties designated as "low employment" counties would double (McClure et al., 2021). Rural higher education then serves as a nexus of mutual need and support for the institution and the local region.

Rural institutions continue to struggle with recruiting and sustaining employees. The challenge to attract and recruit K–12 educators in rural areas has been long documented (Biddle & Azano, 2016), but less attention has been paid to this similar challenge in rural higher education. One difficulty in rural higher education recruitment is that rural areas tend to be described as having less to offer, instead of offering different amenities such as access to outdoor spaces, lower cost of living, and so forth (Murray, 2007). Recruitment and retention have been examined at the rural community college level, where institutions experience challenges in identifying a pool of faculty members, particularly in specialized academic fields (Cejda, 2010). In the challenge to recruit faculty members at rural community colleges, retaining faculty members may also be challenging due to lower salaries compared to non-rural institutions (Cejda, 2010) and to the requirement to teach higher course loads compared to non-rural community college faculty (Murray, 2007). Employment in rural higher education offers many benefits. From the attraction to access to natural spaces and outdoor recreation, to directly witnessing student learning outcomes and influencing change within and outside of the institution (Eddy, 2007). Although the workload may be higher or challenging in unique ways, there are substantive benefits to seeking a career in rural higher education. Opportunities for professional development for individuals working in rural institutions can be found through organizations such as the National Association for College Admission Counseling's Rural and Small Town Special Interest Group, the American Educational Research Association's Rural Special Interest Group, and the National Rural Education Association.

FUTURE CONSIDERATIONS AND DIRECTIONS

This chapter highlights many important facets of rural institutions. Rural colleges are integral to improving access to higher education, are key components of regional community and economic development, and are hubs for cultural and civic engagement. Therefore, it is crucially important for researchers, policymakers, and practitioners to work not only to disrupt the inaccurate narratives held about rurality overall, but also about rural institutions, the students who attend them, and the regions they serve. Not only are these deficit narratives harmful to rural spaces, but they erase the lived experiences of those that live there. One meaningful way to change such narratives is to equally center and focus on rural colleges in practice, policy, and research.

Practitioners

At the individual level, it is important for all to remember that place is inherently tied to rurality. Those employed at rural higher education institutions can work to disrupt the deficit narratives around rurality, both internally and externally. Practitioners can foster inclusive spaces on campuses that center rurality and normalize rural ways of life. This can be reflected in student and community programming efforts. Further, providing information, awareness, and encouragement about employment in rural areas can help students explore greater career options and help reinvigorate interest in rural life.

Policymakers

Historically, most policies, educational and economic alike, are urban-centric. Policymakers must be more inclusive and intentional about rural higher education. For example, policymakers should work to address funding inequities faced by rural colleges and universities and incentivize individuals to pursue employment in rural higher education. Most importantly, publicly available data is needed on rural higher education institutions, rural-serving institutions, and rural students. Access to such data will aid in the production of empirical research on rurality and give greater insight into the experiences of rural colleges and universities.

Researchers

Broadly, research on rurality is underexamined empirically. With consideration to rural public higher education, there is much more to be gleaned about these unique institutions and the students who attend them. Research is desperately needed on student persistence and graduation rates at different rural institutional types. Further, as demonstrated in this chapter, there is much to be learned about the intersectionality of rural institutions and different rural institutional types. Given that rural students and rural institutions face unique financial challenges, research should explore how state and federal policies affect rural higher education. Lastly, these recommendations are consistent with recommendations from other researchers (McClure et al., 2021; Orphan & McClure, 2019; Thornton & Friedel, 2016).

As mentioned at the beginning of this chapter, it is imperative to remember that institutions that serve rural areas are different from institutions located in rural areas; however, both are crucially important to higher education in rural places. The authors suggest reviewing the Alliance for Research on Regional Colleges report on Rural-Serving Institutions (Koricich et al., 2022) to learn more about these institutions and get a deeper explanation of rural-servingness.

REFLECTION QUESTIONS

1. What are the key facets of a rural college or university?
2. What are your experiences with rural colleges?
3. How do the intersecting missions of rural colleges of different classifications or designations influence the communities they serve?
4. What policies and practices should be changed (or implemented) to better empower rural institutions?
5. How do you see rural institutions in action in your practice, leadership, and research? How can we be more inclusive of these institutions?

REFERENCES

Biddle, C., & Azano, A. P. (2016). Constructing and reconstructing the "Rural School Problem": A century of rural education research. *Review of Research in Education*, *40*(1), 298–325. https://doi.org/10.3102/0091732X16667700

Cejda, B. D. (2010). Faculty issues in rural community colleges. *New Directions for Community Colleges*, *2010*(152), 33–40. https://doi.org/https://doi.org/10.1002/cc.425

Crisp, G., Doran, E., & Salis Reyes, N. A. (2018). Predicting graduation rates at 4-year broad access institutions using a Bayesian modeling approach. *Research in Higher Education*, *59*(2), 133–155.

Eddy, P. L. (2007). Faculty development in rural community colleges. *New Directions for Community Colleges*, *2007*(137), 65–76. https://doi.org/https://doi.org/10.1002/cc.271

Fluharty, C., & Scaggs, B. (2007). The rural differential: bridging the resource gap. *New Directions for Community Colleges*, *2007*(137), 19–25. https://doi.org/10.1002/cc

Hillman, N., & Weichman, T. (2016). *Education deserts: The continued significance of" place" in the twenty-first century*. American Council on Education Center for Policy Research and Strategy. https://doi.org/10.1007/s11162-017-9459-x

Irvin, M. J., Byun, S., Meece, J. L., Farmer, T. W., & Hutchins, B. C. (2011). Educational barriers of rural youth: Relation of individual and contextual difference variables. *Journal of Career Assessment*, *20*(1), 71–87. https://doi.org/10.1177/1069072711420105

Koricich, A., Chen, X., & Hughes, R. P. (2018). Understanding the effects of rurality and socioeconomic status on college attendance and institutional choice in the United States. *The Review of Higher Education*, *41*(2), 281–305. https://doi.org/10.1353/rhe.2018.0004

Koricich, A., & Fryar, A. H. (2021). The critical role of broad-access institutions in serving rural communities: Good as gold. In G. Crisp, K. R. McClure, & C. M. Orphan (Eds.), *Unlocking opportunity through broadly accessible institutions* (pp. 51–64). Routledge.

Koricich, A., Sansone, V. A., Fryar, A. H., Orphan, C. M., & McClure, K. R. (2022). *Introducing our nation's rural-serving postsecondary institutions: Moving toward greater visibility and appreciation.* Alliance for Research on Regional Colleges. https://www.regionalcolleges.org/project/ruralserving

Koricich, A., Tandberg, D., Bishop, B., & Weeden, D. (2020). Doing the same (or more) with less: The challenges regional public universities face in serving rural populations. *New Directions for Higher Education*, *2020*(190), 59–70. https://doi.org/10.1002/he.20367

McClure, K. R., Orphan, C. M., Fryar, A. H., & Koricich, A. (2021). *Strengthening rural anchor institutions: Federal policy solutions for rural public colleges and the communities they serve.* Report Prepared by the Alliance for Research on Regional Colleges.

McDonough, P. M., Gildersleeve, R. E., & Jarsky, M. K. (2010). The golden cage of rural college access: How higher education can respond to the rural life. In K. A. Schafft & A. Y. Jackson (Eds.), *Rural education for the twenty-first century: Identity, place, and community in a globalizing world*. Pennsylvania State University Press.

Means, D. R., Clayton, A. B., Conzelmann, J. G., Baynes, P., & Umbach, P. D. (2016). Bounded aspirations: Rural, African American high school students and college access. *The Review of Higher Education 39*(4), 543–569. https://doi.org/10.1353/rhe.2016.0035

Murray, J. P. (2007). Recruiting and retaining rural community college faculty. *New Directions for Community Colleges*, *2007*(137), 57–64. https://doi.org/10.1002/cc.270

Orphan, C. M., & McClure, K. R. (2019). An anchor for the region: Examining a regional comprehensive university's efforts to serve its rural, Appalachian community. *Journal of Research in Rural Education*, *35*(9), 1–19.

Rosenboom, V., & Blagg, K. (2018). Disconnected from higher education. *Urban Institute* (January). https://www.urban.org/research/publication/disconnected-higher-education

Thelin, J. R. (2019). *A history of American higher education*. JHU Press.

Thornton, Z. M., & Friedel, J. N. (2016). Performance-based funding: State policy influences on small rural community colleges. *Community College Journal of Research and Practice*, *40*(3), 188–203. https://doi.org/10.1080/10668926.2015.1112321

Tieken, M. C. (2016). College talk and the rural economy: Shaping the educational aspirations of rural, first-generation students. *Peabody Journal of Education*, *91*(2), 203–223. https://doi.org/10.1080/0161956X.2016.1151741

U.S. Department of Education. (n.d.a). *White House Initiative on advancing educational equity excellence and economic opportunity through Historically Black Colleges and Universities*. Retrieved January 5, 2023, from https://sites.ed.gov/whhbcu/one-hundred-and-five-historically-black-colleges-and-universities/

U.S. Department of Education. (n.d.b). *White House Initiative on advancing educational equity excellence and economic opportunity for Native Americans and strengthening Tribal Colleges and Universities*. Retrieved January 5, 2023, from https://sites.ed.gov/whiaiane/tribes-tcus/tribal-colleges-and-universities/

CHAPTER 6

URBAN-SERVING INSTITUTIONS

Serving Students, Serving Cities

Yolanda M. Barnes and Tiffany J. Davis
University of Houston

The urban-serving institution (USI) is an institution of American higher education that uniquely centers its urban residency within how it creates knowledge, disseminates knowledge, and serves the local community. Representing 68% of colleges and universities in the United States and serving over 20 million students (Association of Public & Land-Grant Universities, n.d.), USIs were founded to serve as a resource for not only the residents within the region seeking a postsecondary credential but to also serve as a conduit to help improve the economic and social health of the city in which the institution is located (Davis & Walker, 2019; Friedman et al., 2014). With a history of exclusion in U.S. institutions of higher education, USIs for several decades have operated with a mission to extend access to populations that have historically experienced barriers to higher education, specifically, low-income, racial/ethnic minority, and first-generation students (Zerquera, 2016).

HISTORY

The USI emerged during the mid-20th century in response to increased population growth in urban settings. During the post-World War II era,

Institutional Diversity in American Postsecondary Education, pp. 71–80
Copyright © 2024 by Information Age Publishing
www.infoagepub.com
All rights of reproduction in any form reserved.

urban communities experienced an influx of diverse populations of individuals in search of housing and employment opportunities (Boustan et al., 2013; Cohen & Brawer, 2003). With growing urbanization, USIs materialized in "areas that were accessible to the influx of diverse communities moving to urban regions and to working class GI's moving into the newly developed suburbs within metropolitan areas" (Zerquera, 2016, p. 139). Often associated with the community college movement, USIs are considered as the third wave of U.S. higher education (Cohen & Brawer, 2003), following the land grant movement in the second wave, and the establishment of colonial colleges during the first wave (Thelin, 2019).

To understand the USI campus is to understand the context of where it is located. Most people in the United States live in or near urban areas, giving USIs access to diverse populations of students and community members to engage. Approximately 17.4% of people who live below the poverty line reside in the largest urban areas in the United States (Benzow & Fikri, 2020) and confront ongoing challenges in addition to poverty such as affordable housing shortages, economic segregation, and educational barriers. Given the high stratification of historically underserved populations within urban centers, USIs open their doors to many students who face barriers that can hinder their ability to experience academic success (Silva et al., 2015). USIs work within these communities to advance innovation, provide access, and address regional concerns through the production of knowledge—all avenues that reinforce their mission to serve urban students (Zerquera & Doran, 2017).

Operating with a multifaceted mission, in more recent years, USIs have been dubbed anchor institutions. In a 2001 study, the Aspen Institute introduced *anchor institution* into the higher education lexicon, defining it as an "urban institution with significant infrastructure in a specific community that is therefore unlikely to move" (Fulbright et al., 2001). Anchor institutions often serve as a pivotal hub for the distribution of knowledge to students, the local workforce, and community (Ehlenz, 2018; Harris & Holley, 2016). As curators of region-specific knowledge, anchor institutions uniquely address problems within the surrounding city to help promote economic and cultural growth (Barlow, 1998; van ser Wusten, 1998). Anchor institutions or USIs play a critical role in urban areas by helping to employ large workforces, encourage participation in civic engagement, influence policy, and improve local businesses in the region (Martin et al., 2010).

ORGANIZATION STRUCTURE AND CULTURE

The USI is tasked to reflect on its effectiveness by ensuring the organization's structure and culture are well-positioned to meet the growing needs of its diverse student populations. Accordingly, USIs must reimagine student services and campus policies as it relates to class scheduling, extended advising hours, and childcare (Riposa, 2003). It is not uncommon for USIs to schedule most of their academic classes in the afternoon and evenings to accommodate the needs of working students. Rather than a traditional 8-to-5 workday for most offices, most USIs extend hours and schedule student-facing services during times that make it possible for students to visit their academic advisor or financial aid officer before or after their work, which is often located off campus. For students who are parents, childcare centers on campus allow students to better focus while in class and promote a healthier work-life balance. USIs serve a wide-ranging population of students and meeting their needs means considering their life off campus and on. With this focus in mind, USIs can ensure their students have a rich academic experience, while also crafting programming efforts that accommodate their lives. This finds USIs creating an academic culture that must be both rigorous and accessible to students that are often balancing childcare responsibilities and full-time employment (Riposa, 2003).

For many enrolled at USIs, their student identity is one of multiple hats they must balance on any given day, and they need a campus culture that recognizes the various life responsibilities that guide their decision-making. One-way USIs can find balance while acknowledging the real experiences of their students is to create opportunities enabling students to develop marketable skills for future employment the moment they first set foot on campus. USIs can embed career readiness activities throughout campus services to ensure students are developing the necessary skills to be competitive in the workforce post-college. Due to external constraints, USI students do not always have the flexibility to leave their full-time employment for say a semester-long internship experience in a field in which they wish to work. Because of barriers such as time constraints and work responsibilities, USIs work to offer practical trainings or integrate workforce competencies into the academic setting.

Whereas it is easy to focus the conversation regarding USIs on public, commuter, open access, teaching-centered institutions (as we foreground throughout this chapter), it is important to recognize the diversity within the USI institutional type. USIs include private and public institutions, 2- and 4-year colleges, equity-oriented institutions such Historically Black Colleges and Universities (HBCUs) and Hispanic Serving Institutions (HSIs), as well as liberal arts colleges, research-intensive universities, and religiously affiliated institutions. Further, there are USIs that have residential and international populations and boast national/international reputations and prestige. In *Student Affairs in Urban-Serving Institutions: Voices from Senior Leaders* (Ortiz, 2019), chapter authors examine the challenges and contributions of student affairs leaders that assist in presenting a nuanced perspective of the diversity and complexity of the USI structure, students, and missions; we encourage you to consult this important text for extending your understanding of this institutional type. It is the diversity within the USI community that necessitates professional spaces where academic leaders can network and strategize. The Coalition of Urban and Metropolitan Universities (CUMU) and the Coalition of Urban Serving Universities (USU) are two professional organizations that provide these opportunities (Davis & Walker, 2019).

STUDENT SUCCESS AND POPULATIONS

Given the student populations USIs serve, these institutions are often flattened and compared with other institutions with missions to improve and expand their capacity to serve marginalized communities, such as mission-based Hispanic Serving Institutions (HSI), Historically Black Colleges and Universities (HBCU), and Asian American and Native American Pacific Islander-Serving Institutions (AANAPISI). What makes USIs stand out is their unique mission to not only advance educational equity for marginalized communities, but to situate the city or region for which the institution resides within their approach to teaching, research, and service (Barlow, 1998).

USIs reflect the demographics of the community in which they reside. The traditional image of a college student is someone that resides on campus, is young, works part-time, is single, and childless. This image is a stark difference to the demographic of students that are significantly more likely to enroll at a USI—Students of Color, non-traditionally aged, work full-time, are parents or primary caregivers, identifies as a first-generation or returning student, is lower-income, and/or needs significant academic remediation (Attewell & Monaghan, 2016; Civitas, 2017; Riposa, 2003; Zerquera, 2016). Given the diversity of students USIs serve, assessing the campus environment to best capture the shifting needs of students can facilitate the development of postsecondary experiences that bolster retention, while ultimately serving the local community (Riposa, 2003).

A shared characteristic among many USI students, which should come as no surprise, is being placed based, meaning they need to earn their postsecondary credential closer to home (Riposa, 2003). USI students balance multiple responsibilities both inside and outside of the classroom. With strong commitments in their community due to family or employment obligations, USI students find it necessary to earn a postsecondary credential, sometimes literally, in their backyards. This allows for more flexibility in managing competing life responsibilities and increases their likelihood of college completion given the location of the USI is meeting the students where they are located geographically.

It is not uncommon for USIs to enroll a considerable number of first-generation students who have high potential but are often characterized as academically unprepared for the postsecondary experience. Like other institutional types, first-generation students at USI's are more likely to withdraw after their first year or struggle to stay on track to graduate within 6 years (Pascarella et al., 2004). University leadership often must strike a balance between creating a learning environment with academic rigor that meets the needs of a student population with various backgrounds in college preparation. One way that USIs can address this demographic is by partnering with national resource centers designed to meet first-generation college students' needs, such as The NASPA Center for First-Generation Student Success.

Many academically underprepared incoming students may be required to enroll in developmental education courses, for which they must pay and pass, before starting classes that count towards their degree. With the intent to fully prepare students for credit-bearing coursework, developmental education courses often delay USI students' timeline to graduation. Historically, it took about 4 years to complete a bachelor's degree. With competing demands, financial strains, and an ongoing pandemic, on average it is taking students 6 or more years to complete their college degree (NCES, n.d.). For USI students who have off-campus employment to support their households or caregiver responsibilities, making time for homework and other academic responsibilities prolongs their degree completion timeline.

Due to a higher percentage of their students being lower income, USI students are more susceptible to housing instability and food insecurity (Broton & Goldrick-Rab, 2018; Silva et al., 2017). On the housing front, most postsecondary institutions do not provide residential facilities for undergraduate students (Snyder & Dillow, 2012). And with the rising cost of higher education, three in five college students experience housing insecurity (Graham, 2020). Housing insecurity for urban students can involve moving several times a year or relying on other families and friends for safe housing due to financial challenges (Broton & Goldrick-Rab, 2018). A 2021 study revealed 52% of respondents at 2-year colleges and 43% at 4-year institutions were housing insecure (The Hope Center, 2021). Another study showed that 14% of all students who completed a survey on basic needs insecurity reported experiencing homelessness, specifically in the immediate 12 months prior to the survey (The Hope Center, 2021). Taken together, it is socially imperative that USIs consider their role in helping to address the totality of their students' needs beyond academic preparedness.

Another challenge USI students may confront is food insecurity. Food insecurity looks different for every student, but it can often be described as skipping meals or not eating for several days due to lack of resources (Silva et al., 2017). The inability to access nutritious foods can produce low academic performance for USI students. When faced with hunger, students experience feelings of anxiety, stress, and fatigue, all factors that make it more challenging to concentrate on academics and leads to lower GPAs (Maroto et al., 2015).

As previously stated, USIs reflect the demographics of the community in which they reside. Therefore, if the surrounding community has high rates of housing instability, difficulties with accessing healthy food, and academic under-preparedness, it can be assumed many of the students who enroll at the USI experience a similar predicament. For some USI students living with these intersecting identities, there is a stronger possibility that one might experience disengagement from the academic experience due to the chronic stress they must manage when faced with critical competing priorities, such as simply trying to live. While this is not the case for all USI students, it is significant for enough members of this demographic to warrant consideration.

PROFESSIONAL CONTEXT

For professionals that work at USI's, there is an unspoken pressure to do more with fewer resources. Such pressures are often associated with the USI quest to emulate the policies, practices, and positions of their research-intensive land-grant counterparts (Zerquera & Doran, 2017) while under-resourced and serving a very different student population. The faculty and staff of USI's work to create learning environments that meet students where they commonly are as caregivers, full-time employees, academically unprepared, and lower income. Faculty and staff at USIs are considered quite creative given competing demands they experience as employees of institutions of higher education needing to meet their core function of research, teaching, and service, while considering various needs of a diverse student population. Faculty and staff recognize their students have varied lives outside of campus and work to create opportunities that emphasize practical life skills and career connections.

Because USIs are so diverse, faculty and staff may feel that they are serving multiple missions while trying to meet the needs of every type of student population on their campus. This moving target of a mission can often lead to burnout. With extended office hours and many evening classes, faculty and staff can experience feelings of being overworked and chronically stressed. Serving such a high-need population of students makes it more challenging to meet every need, which can leave faculty and staff feeling as if their efforts are not moving the needle toward student success.

Not only do faculty and staff experience the pressure to create a culture that is welcoming, accessible, and promotes transformative growth and development, but they are also called to engage in prestige chasing, which is a common characteristic of USIs in recent years. The external and internal pressure to do more through the achievement of excellence is often tied to their quest to seek academic prestige. When USIs take steps to become a more academically competitive institution that attracts sentiments of prestige, the founding mission of the institution is challenged—a form of *mission creep* (Davis & Walker, 2019).

And with this challenge, faculty and staff are asked to lean in and help the university achieve greater heights to be viewed as a premier institution of learning. Faculty feel the pressure to produce more research and spend less time in the classroom teaching, which has an impact on the academic experience for students. Strong research activities portray value and faculty are expected to increase grant funds and the profile of the institution via academic publications and conference presentations. Additionally, faculty are encouraged to adjust their academic offerings by moving away from developmental and career readiness courses to classes that are viewed as more academically rigorous to help with the recruitment of higher academic achieving students (Zerquera, 2018). Not only do faculty feel the pressure to produce academically, but they also must juggle their teaching and service responsibilities at an excellent level, which makes it challenging to find a healthy work-life balance.

Administrators are asked to be creative with limited resources and reallocate funds that would allow for greater investments to increase their prestigious profile (Zerquera, 2018). While building residence halls can be viewed as an act of building prestige, they are also a way for USIs to address students' basic needs and/or lack of access to affordable housing, often characterized by urban and metropolitan areas. USIs, then, must consider how to facilitate a student live-in experience that is as unique as their student populations, rather than reproducing a more traditional living-learning academic community. The pressure to allocate funding to new efforts can cause stress for administrators, especially at resource constrained USIs, where campus leaders are balancing the needs of the students in their backyard while also striving toward institutional prestige and isomorphism.

FUTURE CONSIDERATIONS AND DIRECTIONS

Historically founded with the mission to expand access to communities most in need over the last several decades, USIs have scaled and expanded their mission to address challenges brought on by the inherent undertaking of serving diverse communities. Similarly, USIs continue to sustain despite declining federal and state financial support. This combination is why the most common modern challenge USIs experience is striving to achieve more with fewer resources (Zerquera & Doran, 2017). In recent years, USIs have experienced great tension with the very identity that made them quite unique—urban. It is not uncommon for USI's to remarket themselves as being more of a metropolitan campus rather than urban (Serverino, 1996). The desire to put distance between the institutional identity and the urban area for which it resides is to avoid common negative associations when describing an urban community—poverty, crime, and academic unprepared (Severino, 1996). This rebranding is also an attempt to help USIs capture the prestige of institutions that more easily fit into the Carnegie system of classifications.

Since USIs do not fit into traditional academic classifications, the language we have, use, and continue to develop, as well as the funding structures we center in higher education, fail to fully capture their nuance. The resulting culmination positions USI leaders to make difficult decisions, usually in the form of *mission creep* change, which negatively impact the population of students they were intended to serve (Davis & Walker, 2019; Zerquera & Doran, 2017). While it is easy to critique these shifts as counter to their historical positioning, these changes have material consequences to admission standards and the population of students USIs recruit therein. Ultimately, USI leaders must consider new avenues beyond admissions criteria and overall mission creep to address and manage their core purpose and historic populations or else the nuance of their positioning may be forever lost.

DISCUSSION QUESTIONS

1. In the race for institutional prestige, how can urban serving institutions strike a healthy balance for remaining an accessible university for diverse communities, without excluding students they were founded to serve?

2. USI institutions sometimes have dual or even multiple classifications and designations, how might new USI leaders remain true to their USI designation while honoring the other affiliations they may hold?

3. Social identity demographics of urban areas have dramatically shifted in the 21st century. What role should USI institutions hold in continuing to facilitate access for students typically relegated to the margins of higher education?

4. As first-generation students, students with basic needs insecurities, and students from racially minoritized backgrounds grow to become the largest share of students enrolling in higher education, how might USIs lead the charge in their retention and persistence?

REFERENCES

Association of Public & Land-Grant Universities. (n.d.). *Coalition of urban serving universities.* https://www.aplu.org/members/commissions/urban-serving-universities/

Attewell, P. & Monaghan, D. (2016). How many credits should an undergraduate take? *Research in Higher Education, 57*(6), 682–713.

Barlow, M. (1998). Developing and sustaining an urban mission. In H. van der Wusten (Ed.), *The urban university and its identity* (pp. 149–166). Springer.

Benzow, A., & Fikri, K. (2020). *The expanded geography of high-poverty neighborhoods.* The Economic Innovation Group.

Boustan, L. P., Bunten, D. M., & Hearey, O. (2013). *Urbanization in the United States, 1800–2000* (No. w19041). National Bureau of Economic Research.

Broton, K. M., & Goldrick-Rab, S. (2018). Going without: An exploration of food and housing insecurity among undergraduates. *Educational Researcher, 47*(2), 121–133.

Civitas Learning. (2017). *Community insights: Emerging benchmarks and student success trends from across the Civitas.* Inside Higher Education. https://www.insidehighered.com/sites/default/server_files/media/Civitas_Community_Insights_Spring2018_VF.pdf

Cohen, A. M., & Brawer, F. B. (2003). *The American community college.* John Wiley & Sons.

Davis, T. J., & Walker, R. (2019). Understanding the urban-serving institution. In A. M. Ortiz (Ed.), *Student affairs in urban-serving institutions: Voices from senior leaders* (pp. 19–37). Routledge.

Snyder, T. D., & Dillow, S. A. (2012). *Digest of Education Statistics, 2011. NCES 2012-001.* National Center for Education Statistics.

Ehlenz, M. M. (2018). Defining university anchor institution strategies: Comparing theory to practice. *Planning Theory & Practice, 19*(1), 74–92.

Friedman, D., Perry, D., & Menendez, C. (2014). *The foundational role of universities as anchor institutions in urban development: A report of national data and survey findings.* Retrieved from http://usucoalition.org/images/APLU_USU_Foundational_FNLlo.pdf

Fulbright-Anderson, K., Auspos, P., & Anderson, A. (2001). *Community involvement in partnerships with educational institutions, medical centers, and utility companies.* Coalition of Urban Serving Universities. http://usucoalition.org/images/APLU_USU_Foundational_FNLlo.pdf

Graham, C. (2020, September 30). *COVID-19 worsens housing insecurity for college students*. Best Colleges. https://www.bestcolleges.com/blog/covid-19-housing-insecurity-college-students/

Harris, M., & Holley, K. (2016). Universities as anchor institutions: Economic and social potential for urban development. In L. W. Perna (Ed.), *Higher education: Handbook of theory and research* (pp. 393–439). Springer.

Martin, S. A. (2010). *Urban universities: Anchors generating prosperity for America's cities*. Coalition of Urban Serving Institution. http://strategicplan.iupui.edu/media/b4910ced-7475-4268-b06d-3e011164719e/cYDdhw/StrategicPlanContent/PDF/Urban%20Universities%20-%20Anchors%20Generatng%20Prosperity%20for%20America's%20Cities.pdf

Maroto, M. E., Snelling, A., & Linck, H. (2015). Food insecurity among community college students: Prevalence and association with grade point average. *Community College Journal of Research and Practice, 39*(6), 515–526.

Ortiz, A. M. (2019). *Student affairs in urban-serving institutions: Voices from senior leaders* (1st ed.). Routledge.

Pascarella, E. T., Pierson, C. T., Wolniak, G. C., & Terenzini, P. T. (2004). First-generation college students: Additional evidence on college experiences and outcomes. *The Journal of Higher Education, 75*(3), 249–284.

Riposa, G. (2003). Urban universities: Meeting the needs of students. *The ANNALS of the American Academy of Political and Social Science, 585*(1), 51–65.

Severino, C. (1996). The idea of an urban university: A history and rhetoric of ambivalence and ambiguity. *Urban Education, 31*(3), 291–313.

Silva, M. R., Kleinert, W. L., Sheppard, A. V., Cantrell, K. A., Freeman-Coppadge, D. J., Tsoy, E., & Pearrow, M. (2017). The relationship between food security, housing stability, and school performance among college students in an urban university. *Journal of College Student Retention: Research, Theory & Practice, 19*(3), 284–299.

Thelin, J. R. (2019). An embarrassment of riches: Admission and ambition in American higher education. *Society, 56*(4), 329–334.

The Hope Center. (2021). *Basic needs insecurity during the ongoing pandemic*. https://hope4college.com/wp-content/uploads/2021/03/RCReport2021.pdf

Wusten, H. V. D. (1998). A warehouse of precious goods. In H. van der Wusten (Ed.), *The urban university and its identity* (pp. 1–13). Springer.

Zerquera, D. D. (2016). Urban-serving research universities: Institutions for the public good. *Higher Learning Research Communications, 6*(2), 9.

Zerquera, D. D., & Doran, E. E. (2017). Charting ahead: Navigating threats and challenges to the urban-serving research university mission. *Metropolitan Universities, 28*(2), 46–62.

Zerquera, D. (2018). Prestige-seeking across urban-serving research universities. *International Journal of Leadership and Change, 6*(1), 5.

SECTION II

EQUITY-ORIENTED INSTITUTIONS

Tiffany J. Davis
University of Houston

The second section of this text amplifies the contributions of institutions that are often commonly and collectively referred to as minority-serving Institutions (MSIs). We, instead, title them equity-oriented institutions (Blake, 2017) to acknowledge the colleges and universities that address barriers of postsecondary access and opportunity for students. Some of these institutions (namely historically Black colleges and universities [HBCUs] and tribal colleges and universities [TCUs]) were founded to serve particular demographics of racially minoritized students and have always had open door policies for all, while others are institutional designations that evolved from shifting enrollment patterns and intersecting social class considerations. As Blake (2017) advocated:

> A shift in language from minority-serving institution to equity-oriented institution will signal the growing urgency with which all postsecondary institutions must approach educating a society that is becoming more diverse and serve as a badge of honor in these changing times. Whereas "minority" is a word that connotes lesser-than status, equity is a disposition and commitment that embodies all members of a campus community and does not misleadingly imply that only students in the demographic minority are being educated. (para. 9)

Institutional Diversity in American Postsecondary Education, pp. 81–83
Copyright © 2024 by Information Age Publishing
www.infoagepub.com
All rights of reproduction in any form reserved.

82 SECTION II: EQUITY ORIENTED INSTITUTIONS

As a group, the servingness of these equity-oriented institutions can offer opportunities for belonging and social mobility for Students of Color, low-income students, first-generation students, and students with disabilities particularly in ways that disrupt generational patterns of societal, economic, and cultural marginalization and oppression. Each of the chapters in this section, presented in chronological order of their appearance within the higher education marketplace, provide context and complicates differences in the ways in which U.S. higher education provides access and opportunity to diverse populations of students.

In Chapter 7, Johnson and Tisdale offer the distinctive and significant role that Historically Black Colleges and Universities (HBCUs) contribute to higher education and their students. They center the role of student empowerment through cultural transmission and practices such as "other-mothering." HBCUs have a rich, storied legacy and this is illuminated through individual quotes from HBCU student alumni, which is a unique contribution of this chapter and within this text.

In Chapter 8, Carales and Doran trace the history of community colleges to contextualize the structure and culture of these institutions, the unique student diversity that exist and its influence on success outcomes, and their responsiveness to changing social, economic, and workforce needs. Carales and Doran's work amplifies the purpose of community colleges in the larger college completion agenda by increasing access to postsecondary education, yet they assert the evolving and expansive "goal should be to educate a new generation of critical thinkers who are able to make informed decisions about their future and who are civic-minded, globally conscious contributors to society."

In Chapter 9, Sands, Chavis, Brannon Yazza, and Davis, Jr. offer a complete composite of Tribal Colleges and Universities (TCUs) and Native American Serving Non-Tribal Institutions (NASNTI). Their work juxtaposes the harmful history that frames Indigenous education in America alongside the contemporary and significant role that TCUs and other Native Serving Institutions play in centering Indigenous scholars and rebuilding tribal ways of knowing. The story of TCUs and NASNTIs continues to evolve and shift to better support the next generation of Indigenous students.

In Chapter 10, Aguilar-Smith explores the growth of Hispanic Serving Institutions (HSI) which are designated to support Latina/o/x students. She describes "the complexities of HSIs which represent an increasingly vibrant and crucial part of the U.S. higher education landscape." Notably in this chapter, Aguilar-Smith contends with issues of servingness, mission drift/creep, faculty diversity, and institutional funding as these contemporary and emerging issues all have direct impact on HSIs leaders' capacity to serve their campus communities and support *Latina/o/x/e* uplift.

In Chapter 11, Nguyen, Toso-Lafaele Gogue, Cruz Espinoza, Duncan, Venturanza, and Dinh contribute a significant piece about Asian American and Native American Pacific Islander-Serving Institutions (AANAPISI). While one of the more recent federally designated minority-serving institutions, Hguyen et al. remind us that "although AANAPISIs encompass a small proportion of all postsecondary institutions in the country, they play an increasingly large role in serving AANHPI students" as they enroll nearly 40% of all Asian American, Native Hawaiian, and Pacific Islander (AANHPI) students in American higher education.

In Chapter 12, Yocum and Hughey engage in placemaking for Disability Serving Institutions despite this not being a federally or state recognized institutional type. They highlight the nuanced ways in which institutions offer access and support to move beyond the compliance notions of the American with Disabilities Act. These universities are distinctive in their service to ability in undergraduate education.

Taken together, these chapters suggest how equity-oriented institutions not only serve a critical role in increasing the number of college graduates, but also—and importantly—represent levers for change to lower barriers and promote access to, and success within, postsecondary education for marginalized populations. The authors offer a significant contribution to the discussion for how institutional agents at equity-oriented institutions successfully support, retain, and graduate students in culturally responsive and affirming ways, despite the large resource gap that exists across these institutions in the ways in which they are funded and sustained. Understanding the power and possibilities of these institutions as sites for student success is critical as we prepare educated citizens for the increasingly diverse communities and industry workplaces that they will serve.

REFERENCE

Blake, D. (2017, January 17). The case for rebranding minority-serving institutions. *Diverse Education*. https://www.diverseeducation.com/students/article/15099800/the-case-for-rebranding-minority-serving-institutions

CHAPTER 7

LITERACY AND LIBERATION

Historically Black Colleges and Universities and Culturally Relevant Praxis

Jennifer M. Johnson and Stephanie J. Tisdale
Temple University

Historically Black Colleges and Universities (HBCUs) represent a unique and diverse set of mission-specific institutions of higher education. Established prior to 1865, these 2- and 4-year campuses were founded with the explicit purpose of supporting and expanding educational opportunities for Black students. Mobley (2017) described HBCUs as one of the few spaces where, "Black culture is placed at the forefront, appreciated, and sustained" (p. 1036). As of 2020, there were 101 HBCUs located in 19 states, the District of Columbia, and the U.S. Virgin Islands, enrolling approximately 279,000 students (National Center for Education Statistics [NCES], 2022). Although these institutions continue to diversify in terms of the enrollment of students from diverse racial/ethnic backgrounds, Black students comprise about 76% of enrollment at HBCUs (NCES, 2022).

Within a sociopolitical context where the lives of Black people and the livelihood of Black educators is under attack, access to spaces like HBCUs can be particularly liberating. For generations, the institutional agents of HBCUs (i.e., administrators, advisors, student affairs professionals, and faculty), have been responsible for directing and engaging students in

Institutional Diversity in American Postsecondary Education, pp. 85–95
Copyright © 2024 by Information Age Publishing
www.infoagepub.com
All rights of reproduction in any form reserved.

a variety of educational programs designed to enhance their academic and professional development in culturally affirming ways. Graduates of HBCUs have highlighted the impact of relationships with institutional agents and the ways institutionalized practices inspired students to both actualize and expand their aspirations, while deepening their knowledge and appreciation of Black history and culture (Baker et al., 2018; Johnson & Winfield, 2022; Williams et al., 2022).

In this chapter, we describe the historical origins of Black colleges, the organizational culture and professional context of HBCUs, and discuss the ways these institutions continue to serve as spaces for professional and psychological liberation through culturally relevant praxis. To further crystalize these connections, we center the voices of HBCU students by including quotes from participants in a national study on HBCU student outcomes (Johnson, 2019). This project, the National HBCU Alumni Study, was a qualitative exploration of the college choice processes and early career outcomes of 117 HBCU alumni from 33 different HBCUs between the years 2000-2019. We conclude with future considerations for HBCUs and how they can continue to contribute to educational equity and access for all students on their campuses.

HISTORY

When you walk on campus, the buildings are named after people who impacted you, as compared to, "I just spent $5 million to get that building named after me." It's different. The buildings are named for people who were part of history, or they made a difference. They fought for me, or they did something for me.

—Pearl, Howard University

HBCUs emerged out of a meaning-making tradition existing in the hearts and minds of people of African descent (Carr, 2001). The relationship between literacy and liberation was a part of a larger intellectual pursuit for a community whose members were either enslaved or free, and disenfranchised by law. Prior to the formal founding of HBCUs, people of African descent developed and funded institutions—churches, schools, mutual aid societies, and publications—to address the needs within their own community (Anderson, 1988). In many of these institutional spaces, teaching and learning was paramount and education was incorporated into an overarching need for communal self-determination.

The first HBCUs were founded before the Civil War. The Institute for Colored Youth (Cheyney University of Philadelphia) was founded in 1837. Lincoln University was chartered as Ashmun Institute in 1854, becoming the first institution founded with the expressed purpose of granting degrees to people of African descent (Redd, 1998). Both institutions were established in collaboration with white philanthropists and evolved as an extension of existing educational efforts in the African American community. Although several HBCUs were similarly established with support from white philanthropists, Black educators were actively involved in the development of intellectual and cultural structures on HBCU campuses. Lucy Craft Laney, Mary McCleod Bethune, Booker T. Washington, and Lucy Diggs Slowe are just a few names of individuals who cultivated these educational spaces (Beauboeuf-Lafontant, 2018; Bethune et al., 1999; Slowe, 1933; Smith, 2009).

With the establishment of Wilberforce University in Ohio (1856), Bowie State University in Maryland (1865), and Howard University in Washington, DC (1867), HBCUs presented opportunities for intellectual advancement and socioeconomic elevation at a critical time in U.S. history marred by segregation and Jim Crow politics (Wilder, 2014). These expanded educational opportunities also contributed to the emergence of the Black Middle Class (Pattillo, 2007). These professionals leveraged their social and economic capital to continue the investment in the growth and development of Black education spaces. As additional HBCUs were established, Black educators had the opportunity to serve as faculty, staff, and administrative leaders on these campuses, further influencing the direction of the curriculum across academic programs and co-curricular opportunities across campus. Consequently, historically Black institutions emerged as spaces where social and economic capital was cultivated and exchanged (Brown & Davis, 2001).

ORGANIZATIONAL STRUCTURE AND CULTURE

I think that it was beautiful. It was positive. It was inclusive. It was just so encouraging to see. The majority of our staff, the people that you saw every day, the people that are teaching you, from the professors to the adjuncts, to those in the administration, to the Dean, everyone looked like us. Everyone.

—Tori, Cheyney University of Pennsylvania

HBCUs have distinct organizational structures and campus cultures that are grounded in Black cultural traditions. Although each Black college has its own unique characteristics, they are part of a larger network categorized by mission, history, student population, and educational outcomes (Simms, 2014). Presidents of public land-grant HBCUs describe an institutional commitment to providing underserved populations with access to higher education to develop Black leaders who can create positive change in Black communities (Esters & Strayhorn, 2013). At private HBCUs, institutional advancement leaders are responsible for more than just fundraising; they see themselves as "soul builders" who maintain the legacy of their institutions by building relationships with stakeholders and cultivating alumni giving (Leathers & Okpala, 2020). Collectively, HBCUs encourage students and graduates to contribute to the larger society through their scholarship, service, and philanthropic activities.

Thurgood Marshall, Martin Luther King, Jr., Stacey Abrams, and Kamala Harris are a few historical and contemporary political leaders educated at HBCUs. Others, such as mathematician Katherine Johnson, actor Chadwick Boseman, and philanthropist Oprah Winfrey, have talked about how their HBCU education inspired them to continue to advocate for, and uplift community interests and issues. Former HBCU students can be found in every major sector/industry, shaping policies, programs, and professional opportunities in a variety of ways. HBCU alumni give back as mentors, recruit students for internships or career opportunities, and contribute financially (Johnson & Winfield, 2022). For some, knowledge of these individuals and their commitment to service was a key motivating factor for choosing to attend an HBCU over other college options (Albritton, 2012). This campus culture has also inspired HBCU graduates to intentionally seek employment at HBCUs as staff and faculty.

Community-based partnerships are also embedded in the HBCU historical framework. With institutional missions that explicitly identify a commitment to racial uplift and collective advancement, HBCUs perpetuate the kinds of town-gown relationships that foster interaction and support between students, staff, and community members. Cheyney University of Pennsylvania emerged out of a community-based approach to teaching and learning, grounded in the efforts of the African American literary societies, schools, churches, and organizations that preceded it (Favors, 2019). Other HBCUs founded in the South mirror a similar origin story, with a deliberate focus on communal self-determination. Of HBCUs that still remain, close to 50% are in predominantly Black communities and the increase of the median income for Black households nationwide is correlated to their proximity to an HBCU (Perry, 2017). Aside from this, HBCUs impact their local and regional economies; for every HBCU campus-based job, 1.3 jobs are created as a result of HBCU-based spending (Humphreys, 2017). Thus, Historically Black Colleges and Universities partner both formally and informally with their surrounding communities.

> *The most diverse group of Black people I personally have ever been around ... it was a lot more diverse than I expected.*

> —King, Coppin State University

When asked, Black students often describe HBCUs as diverse educational environments. While most HBCUs remain predominantly Black in terms of undergraduate enrollment, by no means are they monolithic institutions. Students from all economic backgrounds seek admission to the diverse academic programs at HBCUs. Some HBCUs are more selective, drawing academically talented students from across the globe, while others follow an open admission policy, attracting and supporting students with modest pre-college academic records (Johnson, 2019). Regardless of pre-college economic and academic background, the educational experiences and degrees earned by HBCU students position them for economic and social mobility.

These trends, then should spark interest in gaining a better understanding of *how* institutional leaders, student affairs professionals, and faculty at HBCUs are able to successfully support the students on their campuses. As HBCUs continue to grow and expand, there has been interest in understanding the impact increased racial diversity may have on campus culture and traditions. In this regard, there are mixed opinions. Scholars who investigated this notion in the early 2000s found that some felt the "HBCU concept" may be antiquated or even divisive in a "post-racial" society (Palmer et al., 2018). However, contemporary issues reveal that safe educational spaces for racially minoritized students to thrive are just as necessary now as it was 150 years ago (Walker, 2018). Anti-Black racism, police brutality, the #BlackLivesMatterMovement, and overall racial hostility directed towards Black people and Black communities in present times mirror the issues experienced by past generations. As a result, HBCU leaders report receiving more undergraduate applications and positive enrollment patterns, although Black students continue to enroll at predominantly white colleges and universities. Accordingly, institutional leaders must continuously monitor these trends, and plan for any necessary infrastructure changes (e.g., housing availability, technological upgrades, staff support) to properly support the students admitted to their campuses. Furthermore, members of the HBCU campus community viewed a diversified campus as beneficial, attracting student affairs professionals who had "a different perspective" and who were "bringing in a lot of [different] practices" (Palmer et al., 2018, p. 8). This infusion of administrative talent was viewed as vital for the continued growth of HBCU operations.

PROFESSIONAL CONTEXT

My advisors were like mothers. They were very in tune to everything I was doing ... I think they went above and beyond building relationships with the students. [As a result] I knew there were adults [on campus] who weren't going to allow me to fall through the cracks. They weren't going to allow me to not give them my best, and they would call me out on that. It was good because I felt accountable, and I felt that they truly were looking out for me.

—Alfonso, University of Arkansas—Pine Bluff

On campus, some HBCU staff and faulty engage in practices of "other-mothering" by cultivating healthy student interactions that mirror familial and caring patterns of relationships (Flowers et al., 2015; Hirt et al., 2008). When institutional agents demonstrate an ethic of care and concern about the well-being and personhood of a student, students can feel a deeper connection to that community member, and by extension, the HBCU. This illustrates an important mindset that may be critical to a long and sustained career as a higher education professional at an HBCU. Walker (2018) explored the important connection between an othermothering approach to student support and improved mental health outcomes among Black men at HBCUs. He argued, for example, "Counselors and residence life staff can utilize HBCUs' emphasis on culture to convince men to speak with someone they trust about their struggles" (p. 10). Extending training to staff and faculty would allow for the identification and monitoring of students in need of counseling.

They fed me, gave me resources, challenged me, told me what I was not doing well, and gave me second chances. They absolutely loved me.

—June, Grambling State University

The expectation for othermothering or intrusive advising practices is a tremendous responsibility shouldered by individuals working within the HBCU setting. It is also important to recognize the ways that faculty and staff balance these responsibilities while maintaining other expectations for career success. For instance, faculty at research focused HBCUs must find ways to engage in authentic professional relationships outside of the classroom with students, while also balancing increasing pressures to engage in the types of research and scholarship that can secure external grants and resources for the institution (Williams & Johnson, 2019).

Student affairs professionals may be particularly over-extended as they too work to engage in these holistic othermothering practices with students, while also managing other staff members and campus programs (DeCrescenzo, 2021). Increased demands on institutional agents at HBCUs is also a reflection of the COVID-19 pandemic, as executive leaders are grappling with a "mass exodus" of talent from the field of higher education. Thus, HBCUs must actively engage in networks of collaboration between faculty and student affairs to continue to promote student success while navigating limited resources (Commodore et al., 2018; Coupet & Barnum, 2010).

It is well documented that HBCUs are historically under-resourced—due to a lack of state funding as well as inadequate tuition income and smaller endowments. From an equity standpoint, however, it is unfair to continue to expect the institutional agents at HBCUs to "do more with less." These individuals need to be compensated financially, recognized for their work (e.g., compensation, award ceremonies), and ultimately given more support (increased staffing in high-volume areas).

There are several professional organizations and spaces for those who work in student and academic affairs roles in higher education, and some that are specific to working within the context of HBCUs. Within these spaces, individuals can learn more about how to build their skills as a higher education professional while cultivating networks with others in the field. For example, in 2022, NASPA—Student Affairs Administrators in Higher Education hosted a "HBCUs Educate Webinar Series" with a stated purpose to "to provide professional development intentionally designed for HBCU professionals and practitioners seeking to work at these institutions." The series featured topics such as starting a career in the field of higher education/student affairs, programming for first-generation college students, and strategies for socio-emotional wellness, led by panelists who "work, research, and collaborate with HBCUs." As another example, the Frederick D. Patterson Research Institute of the Thurgood Marshall College Fund conducts and disseminates research that "informs policymakers, educators, philanthropists and the general public on how to best improve educational opportunities and outcomes for African Americans and other underrepresented minorities across the pre-school-through-college-graduation pipeline". The Howard University HBCU Center for Research, Leadership, and Policy, is focused on "illuminating the collective success of HBCUs through institutional collaboration, research-informed advocacy, capacity-building programs, and leadership development." Additionally, ACPA—College Student Educators International, has featured several workshops and programs focused on the practices at Minority Serving Institutions. These and other similarly structured communities are critical for addressing some of the concerns raised about the over-extension of professionals at HBCUs and raise the visibility of the important work done at these institutions.

STUDENT SUCCESS AND POPULATIONS

Being exposed to this Black history when your entire life has been filled with learning about Edgar Allen Poe and Helen Keller, you know, and then to realize like Langston Hughes and Thurgood Marshall and just all these people that have had such a major impact on pretty much everything that happens around us is very important for understanding and development of sense of self and sense of who African Americans are.

—Felecia, Southern University and A&M College

Finally, a deeper exploration of in-class experiences, specifically curricular practices of faculty, can provide greater insights into how decisions related to the curriculum content can have a positive impact on students and perhaps better prepare them to appreciate diverse perspectives, worldviews, and peoples. Faculty are instrumental in structuring opportunities for self-exploration among students within an academic context. As a part of the general curriculum, some HBCUs require students to take a course or series of courses in Black history or the African American experience. These courses are often initiated during students' first or second term on campus. The intentional inclusion of courses focused on race and culture illustrates an institutional commitment to creating spaces where identity can be explored, even within a seemingly homogenous environment like an HBCU.

Predominantly white institutions often require the completion of a "race and diversity" course as a part of the general education curriculum. Where the intent of these course offerings may be the same, the impact and effectiveness of these courses is often shaped by the tone set by the faculty and the willingness among students to engage in potentially controversial and difficult dialogue. Within the structured setting of the college classroom, students can capitalize on opportunities to delve into an array of topics, including how race intersects with other salient aspects of identity. Some examples include thoughtful inclusion of the writings and teachings of critically conscious authors, analytical reviews of media images or movies, or visits to museums or artistic festivals (Rush, 2022). These activities can facilitate the exposure to new ideas and perspectives that influenced this understanding of identity. Student affairs professionals should be intentional in building from these curricular experiences through co-curricular programming designed to extend and deepen opportunities to engage in critical conversation outside of the classroom.

FUTURE CONSIDERATIONS DIRECTIONS

Some Black people do well in predominantly White institutions, but I needed to go to Florida A&M University. I feel like if I would have finished at the white school that I would have finished and that was it. I would have never tried to pursue getting my Master's [and now] I'm a semester away from finishing my Ph.D.

—Na'im, Florida A&M University

In the wake of renewed attention to the racial inequities facing Black communities in the United States, Historically Black Colleges and Universities are experiencing a surge in interest and enrollment among students and families. Although this analysis centered on race, it is important to acknowledge that within predominantly Black environments, racial identity is as important as other notions of identity, inclusive of gender, socioeconomic status, religion, or sexual orientation. As students navigate the college environment, they are seeking out opportunities to cultivate a sense of belonging and building meaningful connections with others through engagement with spaces that reflect these other salient aspects of identity. All institutions of higher education should work to ensure the diversity of student organizations, clubs, and services reflect the diversity of the campus community and these spaces need to continue to grow and evolve over time. As HBCUs continue to grow and the student population continues to diversify, HBCUs must continue to explore strategies to support the growth and development of their students from diverse backgrounds at the intersection of social identities.

REFLECTION QUESTIONS

1. Prior to engaging with this chapter, what types of experiences have you had within the context of Historically Black Colleges of Universities? How might you expand your understanding of this setting to better prepare yourself for success as a professional within these institutions?

2. To what extent did your student affairs and higher education graduate preparation program discuss HBCUs? How might you advocate for the inclusion of HBCU scholarship in the curriculum and practicum experiences?

3. What are some "best practices" of HBCUs that could be directly adopted by your university to promote student success?

REFERENCES

Albritton, T. J. (2012). Educating our own: The historical legacy of HBCUs and their relevance for educating a new generation of leaders. *The Urban Review, 44*, 311–331. https://doi.org/10.1007/s11256-012-0202-9

Anderson, J. D. (1988). *The education of blacks in the south, 1860–1935.* The University of North Carolina Press.

Baker, D. J., Arroyo, A. T., Braxton, J. M., Gasman, M., & Francis, C. H. (2021). Expanding the student persistence puzzle to minority serving institutions: The residential historically Black college and university context. *Journal of College Student Retention: Research, Theory & Practice, 22*(4), 676–698. https://doi.org/10.1177/1521025118784030

Beauboeuf-Lafontant, T. (2018). The new Howard woman: Dean Lucy Diggs Slowe and the education of a modern Black femininity. *Meridians, 7*(1), 25–48. https://doi.org/10.1215/15366936-6955065

Bethune, M. M. L., McCluskey, A. T., & Smith, E. M. (1999). *Mary McLeod Bethune: Building a better world: Essays and selected documents.* Indiana University Press.

Brown, M. C., & Davis, J. E. (2001). The Historically Black College as Social Contract, Social Capital, and Social Equalizer. *Peabody Journal of Education, 76*(1), 31–49.

Carr, G. (2011). What Black studies is not: Moving from crisis to liberation in Africana intellectual work. *Socialism and Democracy, 25*(1), 178–191.

Commodore, F., Gasman, M., Conrad, C., & Nguyen, T. (2018). Coming together: A case study of collaboration between student affairs and faculty at Norfolk State University. *Frontiers in Education, 3*(39), 1–10. https://doi.org/10.3389/feduc.2018.00039

Coupet, J., & Barnum, D. (2010). HBCU efficiency and endowments: An exploratory analysis. *International Journal of Educational Advancement, 10*(3), 186–197.

DeCrescenzo, D. L. (2021). *Understanding mid-level student affairs professionals' experiences through belonging* [Dissertation, Temple University]. Proquest Dissertations and Theses Global. http://dx.doi.org/10.34944/dspace/7212

Esters, L. L., & Strayhorn, T. L. (2013). Demystifying the contributions of public land-grant historically black colleges and universities: Voices of HBCU presidents. *Negro Educational Review, 64*(1), 119–135.

Favors, J. M. (2019). *Shelter in a time of storm: How black colleges fostered generations of leadership and activism.* The University of North Carolina Press.

Flowers, A. M., Scott, J. A., Riley, J. R., & Palmer, R. T. (2015). Beyond the call of duty: Building on othermothering for improving outcomes at historically Black colleges and universities. *Journal of African American Males in Education, 6*, 59–73.

Hirt, J. B., Amelink, C. T., McFeeters, B. B., & Strayhorn, T. L. (2008). A system of othermothering: Student affairs administrators' perceptions of relationships with students at Historically Black Colleges. *NASPA Journal, 45*(2), 210–236. https://doi.org/10.2202/1949-6605.1948

Humphreys, J. (2017). *HBCUs make America strong: The positive economic impact of historically Black colleges and universities.* UNCF Frederick D. Patterson Research Institute.

Johnson, J. M. (2019). Pride or prejudice? Motivations for choosing Black colleges. *Journal of Student Affairs Research and Practice, 56*(4), 409–422. https://doi.org/10.1080/19496591.2019.161493

Johnson, J. M., & Winfield, J. (2022). Institutionalizing success: Systems and practices of HBCUs that promote student development and degree attainment. *Journal of Higher Education.* Advanced Publication. https://doi.org/10.1080/0221546.2022.2082759

Leathers, E., & Okpala, C. O. (2020). An exploration of the perceptions of institutional advancement leaders on their role in the survival of private HBCUs: A qualitative study. *Journal of Research Initiatives, 5*(2), 1–9.

Mobley Jr., S. D. (2017). Seeking sanctuary: (Re)claiming the power of historically Black college and universities as places of Black refuge. *International Journal of Qualitative Studies in Education, 30*(10), 1036–1041. https://doi.org/10.1080/09518398.2017.1312593

National Center for Education Statistics. (2021). *Integrated postsecondary education data system.* U.S. Department of Education, Institute of Education Sciences.

Palmer, R. T., Arroyo, A. T., & Maramba, D. C. (2018). Exploring the perceptions of HBCU student affairs practitioners toward the racial diversification of Black colleges. *Journal of Diversity in Higher Education, 11*(1), 1–15. https://dx.doi.org/10.1037/dhe0000024

Pattillo, M. (2007). *Back on the block: The politics of race and class in the city.* University of Chicago Press.

Perry, A. (2017). *Black colleges can revive American cities.* Brookings Institute.

Redd, K. E. (1998). Historically Black colleges and universities: Making a comeback. *New directions for higher education, 1998*(102), 33–43.

Rush, A. (2022). A new look: HBCU museums as dynamic educational spaces. In A. Bagasara, A McLetchie, & J. Wesley (Eds.), *Contributions of Historically Black Colleges and Universities in the 21st Century* (pp. 179–200). IGI Global. https://doi.org/10.4018/978-1-6684-3814-5.ch009

Simms, K. (2014). Educational outcomes at Historically Black Colleges and Universities: Eclectic or cohesive? *SAGE Open, 4*(2), 1–9. https://doi.org/10.1177/2158244014530131

Slowe, L. D. (1933). Higher education of Negro women. *The Journal of Negro Education, 2*(3), 352–358. https://www.jstor.org/stable/2292205

Smith, J. L. (2009). Lucy Craft Laney (1855–1933) and Martha Berry (1866–1942): Lighting fires of knowledge. In A. S. Chirhart & B. Wood (Eds.), *Georgia women: Their lives and times* (pp. 318–418). University of Georgia Press.

Walker, L. J. (2018). How othermothering and support systems can improve mental health outcomes among African American males at HBCUs. *Spectrum: A Journal on Black Men, 7*(1), 1–16.

Wilder, C. S. (2014). *Ebony and ivy: Race, slavery, and the troubled history of America's universities.* Bloomsbury.

Williams, K. L., Mobley, S. D., Campbell, E., & Jowers, R. (2022). Meeting at the margins: Culturally affirming practices at HBCUs for underserved populations. *Higher Education, 84*(5), 1067–1087. https://doi.org/10.1007/s10734-022-00816-w

Williams, M. S., & Johnson, J. M. (2019). Predicting the quality of Black women collegians' relationships with faculty at a public historically Black university. *Journal of Diversity in Higher Education, 12*(2), 115. https://doi.org/10.1037/dhe0000077

CHAPTER 8

AMERICA'S MOST ADAPTABLE INSTITUTIONS
Community Colleges

Vincent D. Carales
University of Houston

Erin E. Doran
Iowa State University

Considered a uniquely American invention, historians and scholars point to the founding of Joliet Junior College as the genesis of what is known today as community colleges. In 1901, University of Chicago President William Rainey Harper and Joliet High School principal J. Stanley Brown coordinated efforts to establish Joliet Junior College (Baber et al., 2019). Other junior colleges began appearing in the early 1900s as extensions of high schools for the sole purpose of preparing students to transfer to four-year institutions (Meier, 2018; Thelin, 2019). This chapter begins with a historical overview and evolving mission, function, and purpose of community colleges over time. We continue with a description of the organization and culture of community colleges and then highlight the unique student diversity that exists within them. Next, we highlight the professional context by describing the role of faculty and student services in community colleges. Finally, we discuss the role of community colleges in addressing college completion and future considerations for community colleges.

Institutional Diversity in American Postsecondary Education, pp. 97–107
Copyright © 2024 by Information Age Publishing
www.infoagepub.com
All rights of reproduction in any form reserved.

HISTORY

At the turn of the 20th century, various social, political, and economic forces were contributing factors to the growth and development of community colleges, including the second industrial revolution and the expanding K–12 education system (Meier, 2018). In 1930, over 440 junior colleges existed in all but five states (Cohen et al., 2014). By this time, vocational and technical education dominated the curriculum, particularly at large urban community colleges (Meier, 2018). In the two decades that followed, community colleges were at the forefront of providing access to higher education for veterans returning home from World War II (Meier, 2018). Concomitantly, the landmark Truman Commission Report of 1947 argued that all adults, regardless of race, gender, religion, or economic status, could benefit from exposure to a community college education. Lastly, the Higher Education Act (HEA) of 1965 provided financial aid opportunities to low-income students who could not previously afford college. That year, enrollment was slightly over one million, and 50 years later, in 2015, it would peak to over seven million (Malcom-Piqueux, 2018). As of fall 2022, 6.1 million students attend 1,026 community colleges (American Association of Community Colleges [AACC], 2024).

Part of the growth of community colleges was due to the federal government's steadfast commitment to increasing access to higher education since the Truman Commission Report and the signing of the HEA. Community colleges have traditionally provided access to student populations who were historically excluded from higher education (Thelin, 2019) and serve as catalysts in providing equitable outcomes to diverse learners. As such, the present purpose of community colleges, according to Baber et al. (2019), is to provide an "accessible space to chase opportunity and shape future success—transfer credit for the refocused adolescent or returning adult, English as second language courses for the new immigrant, retraining for the displaced worker, and workshop series for the small business owner" (p. 203). Community colleges grew, changed, and adapted to eventually becoming institutions "for the people, by the people" (Baber et al., 2019, p. 203). As community colleges welcomed a new generation of college students into postsecondary education, the expansion and multiplicity of their mission and educational functions began to take shape.

In explaining their evolving mission, Boggs and McPhail (2016) argued that five generations of community colleges have existed. The first generation focused on transitioning high school graduates to college (1900–1930). The next generation concentrated on providing the first two years of college coursework (1930–1950). Then the following generation expanded access for vets and low-income groups (1950–1970) while the fourth generation centered around offering comprehensive community-based programs

(1970–1985). Complementing the latter period was a 1988 report sponsored by the American Association of Community and Junior Colleges (now called American Association of Community Colleges [AACC]) which set forth an agenda to strengthen the role of community-building and develop recommendations for the future of community, technical, and junior colleges (Commission on the Future of Community Colleges, 1988). The current generation of community colleges (1985–present day) has focused on responding to the needs of the ever-changing student population and ensuring their success (Boggs & McPhail, 2016). Regardless of how community colleges have functioned over time, their purpose for democratizing and increasing access to postsecondary education would forever change the landscape of American higher education.

ORGANIZATION STRUCTURE AND CULTURE

The mission of community colleges has always been to provide access to education beyond high school (Meier, 2018; Thelin, 2019). However, the function and purposes of these institutions have evolved and become more complex as they responded to social, economic, and educational developments over the last century. In addition to transfer to four-year institutions, community colleges offer comprehensive and localized curriculum including workforce training and development; career and technical education (CTE); developmental education; adult, basic, and community education; and dual enrollment programs (Cohen et al., 2014; Meier, 2018).

There are multiple layers to the community college mission that inform the structure of a college's administration and culture. It should be noted that most community colleges are administered by a locally run district or governing board and may be a single campus or part of a multi-campus system (Cohen et al., 2014). As previously noted, the community college fulfills a variety of curricular programs for both credit and non-credit-bearing students. There is no single structure or organization for community colleges (Cohen et al., 2014), so here we discuss the ways that a community college may divide its administration along curricular lines—specifically between its liberal arts programs and its career and technical education programs. The liberal arts programs, which normally offer Associates of Arts (AA) and Associates of Sciences (AS) degrees, are the programs that prepare students to transfer to a four-year institution (Cohen et al., 2014). The career and technical education programs house degrees and certificate programs that prepare students for jobs in a wide variety of occupations including health-related professions (e.g., nursing, sonography) and fields like plumbing and heating, ventilation, and air conditioning (HVAC) maintenance. While community colleges may not have distinct colleges in the same way that four-year institutions do, the liberal arts and CTE programs may constitute the two biggest divisions within a college with departments falling underneath these units to create a programmatic structure for the college (e.g., arts and humanities, sciences).

Community colleges provide a critical bridge between high school and four-year institutions for many students. Dual enrollment programs have provided high school students with another opportunity to gain college-level credit before their high school graduation, and in many states, these programs are free to students and their families (Pierce, 2017). These include Early College High School programs that provide supportive structures to enhance college readiness for historically marginalized populations (Calhoun et al., 2019). In the context of student enrollment declines, these types of programs represent not only significant community outreach activities for community colleges but also important sources of revenue. Strong partnerships with four-year institutions also enable community colleges to provide effective advising to their students and adequate preparation for transfer. Strengthening these partnerships involves providing clear articulation agreements with four-year universities and offering services and programs that promote seamless student transfer.

Other units in a community college may include adult, basic, and community education; administrative services and/or business affairs; enrollment management; and institutional effectiveness. The adult, basic, and community education programs may offer an array of services from adult literacy, GED, and English as a Second Language (ESL) courses to community enrichment events such as lectures and film screenings that are free and open to the public. These events may be tailored to the histories of the local community or tied to broader celebrations, like Black History Month and Women's History Month. Most community colleges also offer developmental education, consisting of classes and skills workshops for students who have been labeled academically underprepared by a placement test in reading, writing, or math as mandated by a college's respective state (Cohen et al., 2014). The administrative services and/or business affairs units oversee the human resources and financial aspects of the institution. Enrollment managers direct strategic initiatives to recruit and retain students at the college from admission through graduation. Next, institutional effectiveness offices at community colleges manage the data of the institution in order to spur continuous improvement, data-driven decision making, accreditation efforts, and mandatory state and federal reporting efforts.

Finally, community colleges have both academic affairs and student affairs, like their four-year counterparts, though the latter is often called student services. As Ozaki and Hornak (2014) pointed out, student services work in community colleges is often more intertwined with academics than at four-year institutions. The number of student services offered at any community college can vary widely, but student services may include residence life, tutoring, career services, student activities, honors programs, community service initiatives, orientation, and athletics (Cohen et al., 2014). While a four-year institution may have offices and personnel who can focus their work on specific aspects of student services/affairs (e.g., advising, career counseling, orientation), in community colleges student services employees may be cross trained to work in more than one area in part because they work with fewer staff members (Ozaki & Hornak, 2014). In all, the structure of the community college enables administrators to serve a diverse student body.

STUDENT SUCCESS AND POPULATIONS

The ability to meet the needs of the diverse students and communities they serve is a source of pride for these two-year institutions. Given their open-access mission, community colleges are more likely than four-year institutions to enroll students who identify as women, Students of Color, low-income, part-time, first-generation, and/or students who have been declared academically underprepared by the K–12 system. As Malcom-Piqueux (2018) noted, community colleges historically served as an entry point into postsecondary education for those deemed "unworthy of admission into flagship state university systems" (p. 25). However, lower tuition costs, location, class size, and flexible course scheduling—characteristics that demonstrate a commitment to access and affordability—are aligned to what community college students value and why they prefer to attend them. Students enroll at community colleges due to their varying levels of academic preparation and educational goals, which contribute to the persistent gaps that remain across transfer and degree completion (Malcom-Piqueux, 2018). As a result, community colleges are faced with the challenge of addressing the inequitable educational outcomes that exist across the racial and economically disadvantaged populations they serve (Baber et al., 2019; Malcom-Piqueux, 2018).

Community colleges have seen an explosion of diverse student populations over the last several decades. For example, in 1976, African American, Latina/o/x, Asian and Pacific Islanders, and Native American students comprised 19.6% of students enrolled in community college (Malcom-Piqueux, 2018). Forty years later, students from those racially minoritized groups made up 49% of the community college student population (Malcom-Piqueux, 2018). Recent AACC data from its 1,044 member institutions tells a similar story. For example, in fall 2022, community college students enrolled for credit were 43% White, 28% Latina/o/x, 12% Black, and 6%

Asian American. The remaining groups include Native Americans (1%), students of two or more races (4%), and other groups including international students (6%) representing a total of 6.1 million students (AACC, 2024). Of this group, 66% (4.0 million) attend part-time, approximately one-third of students are first-generation, and 43% are 22 or older with an average age of 27 (AACC, 2024). In addition, approximately 7% (80,000) of all international students in the United States attended community colleges in the 2019–2020 academic year (Baer & Martel, 2020). Lastly, nearly half (48%) of community college students receive some type of federal financial aid, including 36% who receive federal grants (AACC, 2024). The current compositional diversity that exists undoubtedly presents a challenge and an opportunity for community colleges to accelerate equitable outcomes for historically disadvantaged populations (Baber et al., 2019; Goldrick-Rab, 2010; Malcom-Piqueux, 2018). As noted above, nearly half of community college students are from racially and ethnically minoritized student groups. Further, states like California (56.7% Asian and Latino) and Texas (54.3% Latino and African American) have reached a majority-minority student population in community colleges, and Florida is on pace to reach this status with 47.9% of students (Malcom-Piqueux, 2018). It is also important to note that community college students are uniquely different from traditional college students in that they have varying attendance patterns, educational goals, and levels of academic preparation. As a result, community colleges have the responsibility of serving students who have a diverse set of needs.

PROFESSIONAL CONTEXT

Faculty and advisors play an important role in navigating students through community college, regardless of their academic goals. The literature is clear that validating interactions with faculty positively contributes to student success (e.g., Alcantar & Hernandez, 2020; Barnett, 2011). Under most regional accreditation standards, community college faculty are qualified to teach with a master's degree and at least 18 graduate-level credits in their respective teaching field (Twombly & Townsend, 2008). Faculty in adult and basic education or in career and technical education may have differing standards for the required education and ongoing professional development needed, such as relevant professional experience (Bartlett, 2002). There are also student services jobs that may include teaching student success courses. It has been noted that community colleges are increasingly relying on adjunct instructors, or those who teach on a part-time, non-tenure eligible basis (Thirolf & Woods, 2018). The American

Association of University Professors (2018) found that approximately 65% of associate's level (two-year college) faculty members were part-time.

As previously noted, student services contribute to the work of community college campuse—though the day-to-day work of professionals in this area may look different from student affairs professionals in other types of institutions. Royer and colleagues (2021) argued that many graduate students in student affairs graduate programs do not receive adequate (or any) explicit training focused on community colleges. This gap in their training means that graduates from these programs may not fully understand how these institutions operate, how they are different from four-year institutions, nor any comprehension of the needs of community college students. Organizations that provide important professional development for community college-focused leaders and practitioners include the American Association of Community Colleges, the Council for the Study of Community Colleges, and the National Institute for Staff and Organizational Development.

FUTURE CONSIDERATIONS AND DIRECTIONS

Community colleges have shifted from providing access to ensuring student success since former President Obama's college completion initiatives were launched in the summer of 2009. Labeled as the American Graduation Initiative (AGI), President Obama challenged the country to increase its college-educated population and specifically called upon community colleges to take the lead in helping America once again become a world leader in education. This call once again put the spotlight on community colleges to meet national educational attainment goals that were followed by several other college completion campaigns (Lester, 2014). AACC even created its own 21st Century Initiative and subsequent Commission on the Future of Community Colleges report to reimagine the mission and focus of these institutions (AACC, 2012).

Given that community college students are diverse in their goals, intentions, or motivations for attending, it is important to reconsider how their success is measured. Traditional measures of transfer and degree completion are flawed because they do not tell the full story of their educational pathways (Carales, 2020). Goldrick-Rab (2010) argued students' transitions to college from high school and their experiences in developmental or credit-bearing courses may impact their success and should be considered when evaluating their outcomes. Furthermore, policymakers note that extending the amount of time used to calculate completion or transfer rates influences these outcomes and provides a better evaluation of success for community college students. For example, graduation rates for full-time students are more than doubled (11.3% to 26.7%, respectively) by extending the measure from two to three years. Moreover, 38.2% of community college students completed a college credential at either a community college or four-year college within six years (Juszkiewicz, 2016). From an equity standpoint, serving community college students should be more than just providing access, facilitating transfer to four-year institutions, or preparation for entry-level jobs. The goal should be to educate a new generation of critical thinkers who are able to make informed decisions about their future and who are civic-minded, globally conscious contributors to society.

We described the evolution of community colleges–from early extensions of high schools to an important sector of postsecondary education. Their mission and purpose evolved as they became responsive to state, business, labor market, and local community interests. We highlighted how their functions expanded to address these developments while remaining accessible to and serving diverse student populations. Arguably the most democratic higher education institutions in the country, the strength of community colleges lies in their ability to adapt to current challenges and contexts. While a myriad of issues are worthy of discussion, we have chosen to focus on two that are currently receiving the most attention.

Free Community College

With the election of Joe Biden in 2020, the issue of free community college has been revitalized and was proposed as part of (but ultimately struck from) President Biden's massive infrastructure package. Given the place of community colleges as drivers of workforce development and employment training (D'Amico, 2016), free community college programs may provide more students with access to job training and retraining programs as less expensive pathways to a baccalaureate degree. Despite the failure to pass free community college at the federal level in 2021, more than half of states in the U.S. offer some form of tuition-free college to students (Douglas-Gabriel, 2022), which include promise programs that can provide financial aid to students in various forms (e.g., first-dollar vs. last-dollar aid, place-based aid; see Perna & Leigh [2017] for a detailed discussion of promise programs).

Community College Baccalaureate

Community colleges have traditionally offered associate degrees as their highest degree awarded. However, more community colleges are now offering baccalaureate degrees, particularly in technology fields (McKinney et al., 2013). These programs are notable for providing access to bachelor's programs, particularly in education deserts. However, research has shown that community college baccalaureate programs may have unintended consequences like tuition hikes and the elimination of associate's and certificate programs at the expense of building baccalaureate programs (Martinez, 2020).

DISCUSSION QUESTIONS

1. How can community colleges maintain their status as open-access institutions and balance their multiple missions, including transfer to four-year institutions and workforce development, while also contributing to the nation's college completion agenda?
2. What function should community colleges focus on to ensure equitable outcomes for the next generation of students?
3. What are the potential challenges for community colleges as they consider offering baccalaureate degrees?
4. How might graduate programs in higher education and student affairs prepare their graduates to work in community colleges?

REFERENCES

Alcantar, C. M., & Hernandez, E. (2020). "Here the professors are your guide, tus guías": Latina/o student validating experiences with faculty at a Hispanic-serving community college. *Journal of Hispanic Higher Education, 19*(1), 3–18. https://doi.org/10.1177/1538192718766234

American Association of Community Colleges. (2012). *Reclaiming the American Dream: Community colleges and the nation's future*. Washington, DC. https://files.eric.ed.gov/fulltext/ED535906.pdf

American Association of Community Colleges. (2024). *Community college fast facts*. Retrieved on April 15, 2024, from https://www.aacc.nche.edu/research-trends/fast-facts/

American Association of University Professors. (2018, October 11). *Data snapshot: Contingent faculty in US higher ed*. Retrieved September 14, 2021, from https://www.aaup.org/news/data-snapshot-contingent-faculty-us-higher-ed#.YUDo2lNKjyV

Baber, L. D., Zamani-Gallaher, E. M., Stevenson, T. N., & Porter, J. (2019). From access to equity: Community colleges and the social justice imperative. In M. B. Paulsen & L.Perna (Eds.), *Higher education: Handbook of theory and research* (pp. 203–240). Springer.

Baer, J., & Martel, M. (2020, November). *Fall 2020 international student enrollment snapshot*. Institute for International Education. https://www.iie.org/wp-content/uploads/2022/12/Fall-2020-Snapshot-Report-Full-Report.pdf

Barnett, E. A. (2011). Validation experiences and persistence among community college students. *The Review of Higher Education, 34*(2), 193–230. https://doi.org/10.1353/rhe.2010.0019

Bartlett, J. E. (2002). *Preparing, licensing, and certifying postsecondary career and technical educators*. Paper prepared for the National Career and Technical Education Institute. Retrieved September 14, 2021, from https://files.eric.ed.gov/fulltext/ED461770.pdf

Boggs, G. R., & McPhail, C. J. (2016). *Practical leadership in community colleges: Navigating today's challenges*. John Wiley & Sons.

Calhoun, Y., Rangel, V. S., & Coulson, H. L. (2019). Educational resilience at risk? The challenges of attending an early college high school. *The Urban Review, 51*(2), 301–325.

Carales, V. D. (2020). Examining educational attainment outcomes: A focus on Latina/o community college students. *Community College Review, 48*(2), 195–219.

Cohen, A. M., Brawer, F. B., & Kisker, C. B. (2014). *The American community college* (6th ed.). Jossey-Bass.

Commission on the Future of Community Colleges. (1988). *Building communities: A vision for a new century*. American Association of Community Colleges and Junior Colleges. Retrieved on September 11, 2021, from https://files.eric.ed.gov/fulltext/ED293578.pdf

D'Amico, M. (2016). Community college workforce development in the student success era. In M. B. Paulsen (Ed.), *Higher education: Handbook of theory and research, 31* (pp. 217–273). https://doi.org/10.1007/978-3-319-26829-3_5

Douglas-Gabriel, D. (2022, March 5). Tuition-free college movement gains momentum, despite Biden's stalled plans. *The Washington Post*. https://www.washingtonpost.com/education/2022/03/05/tuition-free-college-states/

Goldrick-Rab, S. (2010). Challenges and opportunities for improving community college student success. *Review of Educational Research, 80*(3), 437–469.

Juszkiewicz, J. (2016, March). *Trends in community college enrollment and completion data, 2016*, American Association of Community Colleges.

Lester, J. (2014). The completion agenda: The unintended consequences for equity in community colleges. In M. B. Paulsen (Ed.), *Higher education: Handbook of theory and research* (Vol. 29, pp. 423–466). Springer.

Malcom-Piqueux, L. E. (2018). Student diversity in community colleges: Examining trends and understanding the equity challenge. In J. S. Levin, & S. T. Kater (Eds.), *Understanding community colleges* (pp. 37–58). Routledge.

Martinez, E. (2020). Trading inequities: Hispanic-serving community colleges and baccalaureate degree programs. *New Directions for Community Colleges, 190*, 59–68.https://doi.org/10.1002/cc.20387

McKinney, L., Scicchitano, M., & Johns, T. (2013). A national survey of community college baccalaureate institutions. *Community College Journal of Research and Practice, 37*(1), 54–63. https://doi.org.10.1080/10668926.2021.711140

Meier, K. (2018). The historical origins of the comprehensive college mission, 1901–1965. In J. S. Levin & S. T. Kater (Eds.), *Understanding community colleges* (pp. 1–19). Routledge.

Ozaki, C. C., & Hornak, A. M. (2014). Excellence within student affairs: Understanding the practice of integrating academic and student affairs. *New Directions for Community Colleges, 166*, 79–84. https://doi.org/10.1002/cc.20104

Perna, L. W., & Leigh, E. W. (2017). Understanding the promise: A typology of state and local college promise programs. *Educational Researcher, 47*(3), 155–180. https://doi.org/10.3102/0013189X17742653

Pierce, D. (2017). The rise of dual enrollment. *Community College Journal, 87*(5), 16–24.

Royer, D. W., Latz, A. O., Ozaki, C. C., Hornak, A. M., & Qi, W. (2021). Making community college student affairs visible in master's-level student affairs preparation: A longitudinal curricular audit. *Community College Journal of Research and Practice, 45*(7), 525–539. https://doi.org/10.1080/10668926.20 20.1771627

Thirolf, K. Q., & Woods, R. S. (2018). Contingent faculty at community colleges: The overlooked and under-engaged faculty majority. *New Directions for Institutional Research, 176*, 55–66. https://doi.org/10.1002/ir.20244

Thelin, J. R. (2019). *A history of American higher education* (3rd ed.). JHU Press.

Twombly, S., & Townsend, B. K. (2008). Community college faculty what we know and need to know. *Community College Review, 36*(1), 5–24.

CHAPTER 9

PATHWAYS OF SUPPORT FOR INDIGENOUS STUDENTS

Understanding the Role of Tribal College and Universities and Other Native Serving Institutions

Tara Leigh Sands
University of Rochester

Terry Chavis
University of North Carolina at Greensboro

April Brannon Yazza
University of New Mexico

Roger Davis, Jr.
University of Mississippi

Education for Indigenous students in the United States has historical trauma and failed domestic policies (Boyer, 1995). Historically, formal education occurred at Boarding Schools whose philosophy was harmful in preserving Indigenous culture and language (Deloria & Wildcat, 2001). While this historical trauma is now at the collective forefront, it is important to acknowledge the harmful history of American education and its

Institutional Diversity in American Postsecondary Education, pp. 109–118
Copyright © 2024 by Information Age Publishing
www.infoagepub.com
All rights of reproduction in any form reserved.

impacts on Indigenous students (Crazy Bull & White Hat, 2019). This chapter explores the history of United States education and its impact on Indigenous communities and the growth and support of Indigenous-based learning.

Within today's higher education system, there are two types of institutions serving Indigenous Students: Native American Serving Non-Tribal Institutions (NASNTI) and Tribal Colleges and Universities (TCU). Native American Serving Non-Tribal Institutions have an Indigenous enrollment of greater than 10% and are not considered a Tribal College or University (U.S. Department of Education, 2022). These institutions are not organized by tribes but instead serve a population of American Indian and Alaskan Native students (U.S. Department of Education, 2022). There are approximately 100 Native American Serving Non-Tribal Institutions.

TCUs originated from the pressing need for educational opportunities and resources to be provided specifically for Native students. Which mirrored the call to action for other Minority-Serving Institutions (MSIs), such as Historically Black Colleges and Universities (HBCUs). TCUs are unique and not governed by the U.S. Department of Education (DOE). TCUs are recognized and receive funding through the Bureau of Indian Education (BIE) within the Department of the Interior (DOI). Starting in 1968 with the first institution to receive the TCU designation, Navajo Community College (renamed Diné College in 1997), the U.S. now has 36 TCUs with more than 75 campuses within 15 states (American Indian Higher Education Consortium, 2021). TCUs receive their designation based on a multitude of criteria established by the BIE and the Tribally Controlled College or University Assistance Act of 1978 (TCCUA). More specifically, the TCCUA authorizes *"Federal assistance to institutions of higher education that are formally controlled or have been formally sanctioned or chartered by the governing body of an Indian Tribe or Tribes."* (Grants to Tribal Colleges and Universities and Diné College, 2016). Tribal Colleges and Universities serve 30,000 students with a 78% Indigenous Enrollment (U.S. Department of Education, 2022), are located primarily in the Midwest and Southwest and can often be the only higher education institute in the poorest rural areas of the United States (Ambler, 2006).

HISTORY

The evolution of education in the United States and its impacts on tribal sovereignty and knowledge is grounded in colonization and policies. Colonization devastated Indigenous educational practices, both formal and informal, since first contact from a lack of desire to understand the vast natural world knowledge of Indigenous Peoples in the Americas (Deloria & Wildcat, 2001). Instead, formal education was used by European settlers as a weapon in tribal identity, culture, and family relationships (Crazy Bull & White Hat, 2019). Indigenous peoples were removed and sent to Europe or boarding schools, while missionaries were sent to teach Christianity to Indigenous people. Used by the federal government, these practices were designed to remove the *Indian* and force assimilation into the colonial culture while changing the ways Indigenous peoples lived, identity, relations, and well-being (Crazy Bull & White Hat, 2019). This allowed settlers to claim Indigenous land through removal (Crazy Bull & White Hat, 2019).

During the 1800s and until 1969, boarding schools were established as a means of assimilation through Christianity and the promotion of traditional gender roles of the European settlers (Wilder, 2013). Boarding schools removed numerous Indigenous people from their traditional homelands and culture and language were lost (Crazy Bull & White Hat, 2019). In 1871, the United States government passed the Appropriations Act of Indian Education, which required day schools on reservations, but in 1873 was deemed ineffective as children were still speaking their native language at home (Bowker, 2007). This led to the forced assimilation and removal to boarding schools away from Indigenous home communities (Bowker, 2007). During this period, there was a high level of disease, death, and abuse (Evans-Campbell et al., 2012). In the 1970s, there was a rise in activism and complaints regarding boarding schools, which led to the passage of the Indian Self-Determination and Education Assistance Act in 1975 (Bowker, 2007). This allowed tribes to manage education and with the passage of the Indian Child Welfare Act, Indigenous families were able to refuse placement in boarding schools (Bowker, 2007). From the 1800s until the present, hundreds of thousands of Indigenous people attended Indian boarding schools (Crazy Bull & White Hat, 2019). This period of U.S. Education is still felt in Indigenous families today (Deloria & Wildcat, 2001).

In the era of tribal self-determination and self-governance, the 1960s, there was a passage of civil rights legislation and federal law that allowed Indigenous people to create and implement educational practices that reflected Indigenous methodologies on their own lands and reservations of federally recognized tribes (Crazy Bull & White Hat, 2019). The first Tribal College established in 1968 is Diné College, formerly Navajo Community College, and is tribally controlled and teaches indigenous languages and cultures. Following the founding of Diné College, other TCUs began to appear. Native Studies programs also begin to appear that allow traditional knowledge education (Crazy Bull & White Hat, 2019).

ORGANIZATION STRUCTURE AND CULTURE

To inform one's understanding of Native culture, it is important to know that not every Native tribe is federally recognized by the Bureau of Indian Affairs (BIA) and DOI. According to the National Conference of State Legislatures (NCSL), there are 574 federally recognized tribes and 200+ tribes that are not federally recognized (NCSL, 2020). Tribes not federally recognized do not have the complete sovereignty to govern an institution as a tribal nation. Institutions of higher education (IHEs) that are not recognized as TCUs, but serve a large population of Native American students relative to other IHEs, are called Native American-Serving Nontribal Institutions (NASNTI). NASNTIs are designated and funded by the DOE. They must meet a different set of criteria, with the forefront being that at least 10% of undergraduate students enrolled identify as Native American (U.S. Department of Education, 2014).

Though there are two different title designations and two different government departments that primarily fund them, these institutions have been the pillar of Native education for three reasons: (1) to facilitate nation-building through self-determination (Boyer, 2015); (2) to increase the completion rates of Native Americans and Alaskan Natives (NA/AN) (Marroquín, 2019); and (3) to reject the colonial, Eurocentric, and religious ideals and practices that forced the assimilation of Indigenous students. These institutions provide more space, resources, and cultural support for Native students than non-Native institutions. The culture of these institutions challenges the western ideals and Eurocentric practices that center Whiteness under the guise of a neoliberal environment (i.e., color-blindness, surface-level use of intersectionality, etc.).

Additionally, non-Native institutions provide little space for Native students to refute acculturation and assimilation as the pressures to respect and participate in campus traditions. These intuitions lag behind TCUs and NASNTIs in understanding the cultural inputs that Native students show up to campus with and carry within them as they navigate the environment.

As Amiotte and Allen (1989) stated, "One of the key reasons for the tribal colleges' success has been the belief and practice that students can remain Indian, can practice tribal traditions and retain tribal values and also be successful students" (as cited in Pavel & Colby, 1992, p. 2). A study completed by Marroquín (2019) aimed to understand the effects of support from intersecting communities of a Native student and their cultural integrity (maintenance of cultural traditions and cultural identity). This study found that Native students who attended a TCU had significantly higher perceptions of cultural reciprocity and cultural resiliency than Native students who attend predominantly White institutions (PWIs). These perceptions were influenced by several institutional systems and environments, including Native students' comfortability with speaking their tribal language, culturally relevant outcomes, and support from faculty, staff, social, and institutional/financial.

TCUs and NASNTIs have proven to be the most reliable campuses to provide spaces of belonging and cultural support to Native American students. It is well known in educational statistical data reports that Native American students have one of the lowest enrollments per capita than any other ethnicity. According to the Postsecondary National Policy Institute (PNPI; 2021), 24% of 18–24-year-old Native American students were enrolled in college, compared to 41% of the overall U.S. population. Since only 21% of Native American children under the age of 18 lived in a household with a parent holding at least a bachelor's degree in 2017, the added challenges of the hidden curriculum and biases in favor of continuing generation students poses a problem for NA/AN students' broader academic success. This is compared to 52% of White households in the U.S. (PNPI, 2021). This large number of prospective first-generation students impacts the enrollment projects for Indigenous institutions.

In the 2017–2018 academic year, 86% of all students at TCUs and NASNTIs identified as Native American (PNPI, 2021). More excitingly, this is an 8% increase from the 2016–2017 academic year. However, Native enrollment across the country has declined over the past five years. Undergraduate enrollment of Native students decreased by 9.5% from 2016–2017 ($N = 128,6000$) to 2019–2020 ($N = 116,400$). Moving in tandem, post-baccalaureate enrollment for Native students decreased by 2.2% from 2016–2017 ($N = 13,700$) to 2019–2020 ($N = 13,400$) (PNPI, 2021). As we find ourselves on the other side of the COVID-19 pandemic, we will begin to see how the enrollment of Native students suffered along with other ethnically marginalized communities. This impact adds to the looming enrollment cliff projected in 2026–2027 and 2027–2028 academic years due to the 2008 U.S. economic recession.

STUDENT SUCCESS AND POPULATIONS

True to Indigenous student(s') resiliency, the College Board (Howell et al., 2021) reports that despite the odds, post-early COVID retention rates have increased 1.5% for NA/AN and 4.8% for Native Hawaiian/Pacific Islanders at four-year public and private institutions from 2018 to 2019 cohorts (Howell et al., 2021). With this academic momentum, institutional data continue to focus largely on academic performance and graduation rates as a measure of NA/AN student success. But due to NA/AN realities outside of academics e.g., their identities, family duties, and community responsibilities), NA/

AN student success is far more complex. It is important to understand the student identity and varying cultural knowledge that stems from spiritual healing, tribal medicine, family relations, language, and geographical location (i.e., on or off-reservation or homeland). These pillars play a factor in that student's overall confidence in navigating the classroom and campus environments. In addition to academic performance, campuses can better represent NA/AN student success by recognizing the Indigenous genius students bring with them to campus, which ultimately can inform institutional curriculum and student support practices. Similar to considering the histories of Native American education (e.g., boarding school assimilation), this approach encapsulates a deeper narrative of the student experience regarding navigating and surviving a westernized environment.

Ultimately, educators of Indigenous students who acknowledge and nurture the foundational knowledge of Indigenous students would encourage greater engagement in and out of the classroom. For example, land-based learning is a meaningful approach in which land is utilized in connecting modern concepts with the natural world of the students. NA/AN students can not only survive in westernized environments, but also thrive in their academic environments without jeopardizing their Indigenous identity.

Additionally, identifying where an Indigenous student's mental, physical, social, and spiritual well-being stands, could ultimately expose access and equity issues that prevent academic success for that student (e.g., food insecurity, financial burden, lack of ceremonial practice spaces, physical and mental disabilities, etc). *Bini'ba' hozho*, translated in the Diné language for mental well-being, takes into consideration a student's "mind and thinking processes ... and developmental changes" (Secatero, 2021). A common experience of Native students begins in history and social studies courses, where students often experience emotional responses after enduring lessons that gloss over the Native perspective, perpetuate stereotypes, and sometimes speak of indigenous people in the past tense language (Chandler, 2010). Due to the ongoing mental challenges NA/AN students endure, Indigenous communities have emphasized "personal adjustment" (Pottinger, 1989, p. 342) as being important to their students' success which can be achieved through intentional support and Indigenous-based curriculum and practices.

PROFESSIONAL CONTEXT

Native American-Serving Nontribal Institutions (NASNTIs) and Tribal Colleges and Universities (TCUs) have the unique opportunity to intentionally adapt the unique opportunity to intentionally adapt the on-campus experiences for both Indigenous students and practitioners. Indigenous identities represented at all levels within an organization can influence and often challenge standardized approaches. Fort Lewis College (FLC), a NASTNI, located in Durango, Colorado mirrors this approach and represents a tribal melting pot. FLC is well known for being one of two public universities in the country that grants a Native American tuition waiver (NATW) to qualified students from federally recognized tribes. In the case of FLC, this is due to the college's history of beginning as a federal boarding school in 1891. FLC currently has 189 tribes represented in their student population (Fort Lewis College, n.d.).

Unique to the first-year student experience, many NA/AN identifying students attend Native American Orientation. This orientation is hosted by the Native American Center (NAC) which focus on introducing the student and families to the NATW, the closest Indian Health Service enrollment process, and local tribal leadership, and encourages the use of their free book, computer, and calculator loan programs. On an institutional level, in efforts to nurture spiritual healing and medicinal practices, FLC's student housing facilities contain a smudging policy in which the burning of traditional herbs is allowed within their living spaces. Lastly, FLC's Registered Student Organization (RSO) Wanbli Ota is one of many RSOs to host a large community pow wow every year where a young student can vie to represent FLC as a Hozhoni Ambassador. Each experience is unique yet essential to the belongingness of an Indigenous student's identity.

When considering the FLC Indigenous practitioner experience, it is important to consider the added layer of the prominent institutional culture of race and white privilege across various institutional types (Chandler, 2010). Similar to the student experience, the Indigenous practitioner navigates the institutional political environment in their workplace daily. Professional practices such as listing their alumni status, tribal affiliation, and pronouns can be found on their business cards, printed FLC name tags, and or email signatures. This overall visibility attracts the attention of Indigenous students and fellow Indigenous colleagues/relatives. Often sharing the same clan, last names, or tribal relations, Indigenous staff are uniquely positioned to develop strong relational bonds quickly, even in the professional setting. Lastly, Indigenous alumni can often find themselves empathizing with the students' hardships and homesickness as they too were once in the shoes of their students at the same institution.

FUTURE CONSIDERATIONS AND DIRECTIONS

Tribal college and university (TCUs) graduation rates for first-time, full-time students are frequently criticized (Stull et al., 2015). These institutions, however, perform a wide range of other tasks, like many other land-grant institutions. These institutions support local economies, academic fields, and the achievement of students in a variety of ways (Stull et al., 2015). Nation building and Indigenous knowledge systems, affordability for low-income students, economic development and job training, a diverse faculty and staff, and research on American Indian issues from an AIAN viewpoint are just a few examples of TCUs' services and advantages.

As mentioned earlier in this chapter, the first institution, currently known as Diné College, was founded on the Navajo reservation in 1968, marking the beginning of the tribal college movement (American Indian Consortium, 2021). Native American knowledge and history need to be preserved, honored, and advanced with the establishment of these institutions; local academic and extracurricular talent had to be supported, and there had to be a substitute for the traditional American universities that were failing to properly educate and support American Indian students. These types of institutions are particularly effective educational settings that blend individualized care with cultural relevance to motivate American Indians, particularly those who reside on reservations, to overcome obstacles to higher education (Guardia & Evans, 2008). Tribal colleges have a significant impact on advancing self-awareness, social competence, cognitive growth, acculturation, and identity development of their enrolled students by addressing barriers, exposure to Native culture, assistance, preparation for further education, and a sense of empowerment (Merisotis & McCarthy, 2005).

On the other hand, many of the issues affecting American Indian communities today, such as language shift and loss and the low number of students graduating from colleges and universities, can be understood theoretically through the lens of TribalCrit (Brayboy, 2005; Writer, 2008). TribalCrit, also known as tribal critical race theory, can be utilized to more thoroughly address the problems faced by Indigenous people in the United States. This theoretical framework was developed by Brayboy (2005) and covers the complex relationship between American Indians and the federal government of the United States by looking at historically and geographically located epistemologies and ontologies founded in Indigenous communities.

Indigenous education is shifting for the better. Focusing on Tribal needs and understanding the historical context is important for Indigenous education while focusing on rebuilding Indigenous ways of knowing. TCUs and NASNTIs are important to student success and persistence. There is a need to continue to study and learn from Indigenous education scholars. The research on Indigenous students and their experiences is growing and discusses critical needs and support. Indigenous practitioners, scholars, and advocates are needed to continue to build on knowledge. More advocacy and support are needed to assist in the continuing development and growth of TCU and NASNTIs. They have the opportunity to support development, persistence, and tribal ways of knowing while focusing on the next generation of Indigenous students.

DISCUSSION QUESTIONS

- How does the past education experience of Indigenous People impact Indigenous students today?
- What are the differences between TCUs and NASNTIs? How do they serve Indigenous students?
- How can the decolonial approaches to higher education utilized by TCUs and NASNTIs be integrated into our campuses?
- How can institutions work alongside surrounding tribal communities to establish a sense of place and belonging for Native students?
- What challenges are TCU and NASNTIs facing in future years?

REFERENCES

Ambler, M. (2006). While globalizing their movement, tribal colleges import ideas. *Tribal College Journal of American Indian Higher Education, 16*(4).

American Indian Higher Education Consortium (2021). Tribal Colleges & Universities: Advancing Native Students—Advancing Native Nations Advancing Our Nation. http://aihec.org/what-we do/docs/FY22/AIHEC_ LegislativePrioritiesBrochure_FY2022.Feb.pdf

Amiotte, L., & Allen, T. (1988). *The 4 Year Community College: Tribal College.* Some Lessons in Success for Indian Students in College.

Bowker, K. M. (2007). *The boarding school legacy: Ten contemporary Lakota women tell their stories.* Montana State University. Retrieved September 21, 2022, https:// scholarworks.montana.edu/xmlui/bitstream/handle/1/958/BowkerK1207. pdf?sequence=1

Boyer, P. (2015). *Capturing education: Envisioning and building the first tribal colleges.* Salish Kootenai College Press.

Brayboy, B. M. J. (2005). Toward a tribal critical race theory in education. *The Urban Review, 37*(5), 425–446.

Chandler, P. (2010). Critical race theory and social studies: Centering the Native American Experience. *The Journal of Social Studies Research, 34*(1), 29–58.

Crazy Bull, C., and White Hat, E. R. (2019). Cangleska Wakan: The ecology of the sacred circle and the role of tribal colleges and universities. *International Review of Education, 65,* 117–141.

Deloria, V., Jr., & Wildcat, D. (2001). *Power and place: Indian education in America.* Fulcrum Resources.

Evans-Campbell, T., Walters, K. L., Pearson, C. R., & Campbell, C. D. (2012, September). Indian boarding school experience, substance use, and mental health among urban Two-Spirit American Indian/Alaskan Natives. *The American Journal of Drug and Alcohol Abuse, 38*(5), 421–427.

Fort Lewis College. (n.d.). *Native American Tuition Waiver (NATW)*. https://www.fortlewis.edu/tuition-aid/scholarships/native-american-tuition-waiver

Grants to Tribal Colleges and Universities and Diné College 2016, 81 Fed. Reg. 38585 (2016, June 14)

Guardia, J. R., & Evans, N. (2008). Student development in tribal colleges and universities. *NASPA Journal, 45*(2), 237–264.

Howell, J., Hurwitz, M., Ma., J., Pender, M., Perfetto, G., Wyatt, J., & Young, L. (2021). *College Enrollment and Retention in the Era of Covid*. The College Board.

Marroquín, C. (2019). *Tribal colleges and universities: A testament of resilience and nation building*. https://www.academia.edu/38975594/Tribal_Colleges_and_Universities_A_Testament_o f_Resilience_and_Nation_Building

Merisotis, J. P., & McCarthy, K. (2005). Retention and student success at minority-serving institutions. *New Directions for Institutional Research, 2005*(125), 45–58.

National Conference of State Legislatures. (2020). *Federal and State Recognized Tribes*. https://www.ncsl.org/legislators-staff/legislators/quad-caucus/list-of-federal-and-state-recognized-tribes.aspx

Pavel, D. M., & Colby, A. Y. (1992). *American Indians in Higher Education: The Community College Experience*. ERIC Digest.

Postsecondary National Policy Institute. (2021, November 19). *Native American Students in Higher Education*. https://pnpi.org/native-american-students/#:~:text=Undergraduate%20enrollment%20among%20Native%20Americans,private%20institutions%20of%20higher%20education

Secatero, S. (2021). Ataa'dadiin Ba' Hane'. The Corn Pollen Model Curriculum. Unpublished document. (PDF) UNM COEHS Copy Center.

Stull, G., Spyridakis, D., Gasman, M., Samayoa, A., & Booker, Y. (2015). *Redefining success: How tribal colleges and universities build nations, strengthen sovereignty, and persevere through challenges*. https://www.researchgate.net/publication/304049818_Redefining_Success_How_Tribal_Colleges_and_Universities_Build_Nations_Strengthen_Sovereignty_and_Persevere_Through_Challenges

U.S. Department of Education. Office of Postsecondary Education. (2014). *Native American-Serving Nontribal Institutions Program*. https://www2.ed.gov/programs/nasnti/eligibility.html

U.S. Department of Education. (2022). White House initiative on advancing educational equity, excellence, and economic opportunity for Native Americans and strengthening Tribal Colleges and Universities. https://sites.ed.gov/whiaiane/tribes-tcus/tribal-colleges-and-universities/

Wilder, C. S. (2013). *Ebony and ivy: Race, slavery, and the troubled history of America's universities*. Bloomsbury Press.

Writer, J. H. (2008). Unmasking, exposing and confronting: Critical race theory, tribal critical race theory, and multicultural education. *International Journal of Multicultural Education, 10*(2).

CHAPTER 10

HISPANIC-SERVING INSTITUTIONS

Levers of Latina/o/x/e Uplift

Stephanie Aguilar-Smith
University of North Texas

Over time, the Latina/o/x community in the United States (U.S.) has boomed, now representing just shy of 20% of the total U.S. population (U.S. Census Bureau, 2020). Notably, this growth has cascaded throughout the U.S. educational system, resulting in a growing number of Hispanic-Serving Institutions (HSIs). HSIs refer to historically underfunded public and private U.S. colleges and universities enrolling a minimum of 25% full-time equivalent (FTE) Latina/o/x and 50% Pell-eligible undergraduate students (Higher Education Opportunity Act, 2008). As a result of continued underinvestment, definitionally, these institutions also operate with low core expenses (Higher Education Opportunity Act, 2008). To date, 569 postsecondary institutions, or more than 1 in every 6 U.S. colleges and universities, classify as an HSI, and collectively, these institutions educate slightly over two-thirds of all Latina/o/x undergraduates in the United States (*Excelencia* in Education [*Excelencia*], 2021).

This chapter will explore the complexities of HSIs which represent an increasingly vibrant and crucial part of the U.S. higher education landscape. HSIs are serving as the primary point of access to higher education for most Latina/o/x undergraduates and countless other students with

---

Institutional Diversity in American Postsecondary Education, pp. 119–129
Copyright © 2024 by Information Age Publishing
www.infoagepub.com
All rights of reproduction in any form reserved.

120   S. AGUILAR-SMITH

minoritized/marginalized identities. Despite the substantial uptick in research on HSIs in recent years, HSIs' growing numbers and ongoing institutional diversification leave much to be further understood in terms of what it means to be Hispanic-serving and how these colleges and universities can fully embrace this federal designation and, more importantly, their campus communities.

HISTORY

Despite the pivotal role HSIs play in the higher education of Latina/o/x and other marginalized students, the formal legal and political recognition of HSIs only occurred about 30 years ago with the 1992 reauthorization of the Higher Education Act of 1965 (HEA). Specifically, after decades of lobbying efforts by groups like the Hispanic Higher Education Coalition and later the Hispanic Association of Colleges and Universities (HACU), Congress finally recognized HSIs under the HEA's Strengthening Institutions Program (Valdez, 2015). Beyond creating this official designation and providing these institutions access to federal grant funding, the codification of this statute (i.e., Higher Education Amendments of 1992 [U.S. Government Publishing Office, 1992])) also acknowledged a new type of Minority-Serving Institution (MSI)—one predicated on enrollment. Following this precedent, Congress later recognized other enrollment-contingent MSIs, including Asian American and Native American Pacific Islander-Serving Institutions (AANAPISIs; see Chapter 11) and Predominantly Black Institutions.

Unlike any other federally recognized MSI at that time (i.e., Historically Black Colleges and Universities [HBCUs; see Chapter 7] and Tribal Colleges and Universities [TCUs; see Chapter 9]), most HSIs were not created with the deliberate mission to serve the Latina/o/x community. Instead, gaining this federal designation because of their Latina/o/x enrollment, HSIs organically surfaced in areas with established or emerging Latina/o/x and working-class/poor populations (Laden, 2004). In short, the creation of the HSI designation introduced a novel type of MSI—one contingent on student enrollment and, thus, responsive to demographic shifts. Notably, ongoing enrollment trends show that Latina/o/x students increasingly attend HSIs. In 1994–1995, HSIs enrolled roughly 345,000 FTE Latina/o/x undergraduates, whereas today, they matriculate just under 1.5 million such students—an impressive 333% increase over this period (Santiago et al., 2020).

While retaining these distinct qualities, HSIs generally mirror other MSIs in terms of their financial circumstances. Like other MSIs, many HSIs operate with pronounced budgetary constraints due to systematic underfunding. That is, despite serving as a central access point to higher education for Latina/o/x and other minoritized students, HSIs historically have and presently still receive less federal and state funding than non-HSIs. Specifically, between 1999–2010, Ortega et al. (2015) found that public 4-year non-HSIs averaged $9,913 per student compared to $8,636 per student for 4-year public HSIs. More recently, HACU (2021) reported that HSIs receive approximately 68 cents for every federal dollar allocated to non-HSIs. Exacerbating matters further, HSIs often also have limited alternative revenue streams, endowment holdings, and resources for institutional advancement, rendering many HSIs in a constant, exigent state of financial precarity.

ORGANIZATIONAL IDENTITY AND CULTURE

In the time since Congress formally recognized HSIs, these institutions have not only grown exponentially in number but have also institutionally diversified. Consequently, as shown in Table 1, HSIs now represent an increasingly heterogeneous mix of 2-year and 4-year public and private institutions across the United States, Puerto Rico, and the District of Columbia. Specifically, the most recent estimates indicate that more than half of all HSIs (56%) are 4-year colleges and universities (*Excelencia*, 2021). Despite the growing number of 4-year HSIs, public community colleges make up 41% of the HSI population, thus still representing the single most prevalent type of HSI (*Excelencia*, 2021).

Considering enrollment, most HSIs are small to medium-sized institutions. Specifically, 64% of all HSIs matriculate 5,000 or fewer FTE undergraduate students, and 17% enroll fewer than 500 FTE students (*Excelencia*, 2021). Evidencing this trend, in their descriptive analysis of 140 U.S. mainland HSIs offering both undergraduate and graduate degrees/certificates, Garcia and Guzman-Alvarez (2019) found that most HSIs ($n = 51$) had a total enrollment of between 1,000–4,999 students, followed by HSIs ($n = 30$) with enrollments between by 5,000–9,999. However, while most HSIs are relatively small, some are remarkably large. For example, as of 2019–2020, the largest reported HSI enrolled more than 49,000 FTE undergraduates (*Excelencia*, 2021). Furthermore, within the last decade, more 4-year universities have become HSIs, and with this shift, HSIs' average enrollment size has incrementally grown. Illustratively, as of 2019–2020, nearly a fifth of HSIs enrolled between 5,000–10,000 students, and another fifth enrolled 10,000 or more students (*Excelencia*, 2021).

In terms of HSIs' geographic spread, most remain regionally concentrated in the West and Southwest United States and Puerto Rico. Yet, with Latina/o/xs' ongoing growth and settlement in new geographic areas, even states without long-standing Latina/o/x enclaves will soon have HSIs. Case

122 S. AGUILAR-SMITH

in point, Santiago et al. (2020) reported that, as of 2018–2019, states such as Arkansas, Idaho, and Wisconsin each had at least one HSI. Moreover, based on recent estimates, only a mere 10 states have neither an HSI nor an Emerging HSI (eHSI) as of 2019–2020. As a point of clarity, eHSIs refer to postsecondary institutions on the cusp of reaching the 25% Latinx FTE enrollment rate required for designation as an HSI (Santiago & Andrade, 2010).

Table 10.1

Hispanic-Serving Institutions' Growth and Evolution Over Time

	HSIs		Emerging HSIs		HSIs With Graduate Programs	
	2019–2020	1994–1995	2019–2020	1994–1995	2019–2020	1994–1995
Sector						
Public, 4-year	150	30	93	—	96	—
Public, 2-year	235	91	102	—		
Private, 4-year	169	56	156	—	141	—
	15	12	11	—		
Total	569	189	362	146	237	48
FTE Enrollment						
Total	3,244,469	448,151	1,692,212	—	416,960	—
Total Latina/o/x	1,490,244	344,406	339,523	114,561	120,199	23,308
Location						
# of States & Territories	30	14	38	15	19	10

Note. All institutions included are non-profits. Public 4-years include HSIs that offer graduate degrees/certificates. FTE enrollment for HSIs and Emerging HSIs refers to the FTE undergraduate enrollment, but for HSIs with graduate programs, these numbers reflect FTE graduate student enrollment. Total enrollment represents students across all racial/ethnic groups. These numbers reflect HSIs' legal definition, not the official number of institutions that have applied for HSI designation. Data are from *Excelencia*.

Because of HSIs' immense and increasing institutional diversity, these colleges' and universities' structures, including their organizational identities and cultures, vary widely. Some institutions proudly lean into or embrace their identity as an HSI. For instance, based on their content analysis of the strategic plans of 19 HSIs in Texas, Flores and Leal (2020) described some institutions as *Latinx-serving*, as they explicitly acknowledged their campus's HSI designation and Latina/o/x population in an asset-based way. In contrast, other colleges and universities have limited awareness of their current or impending HSI status or seemingly "closet" this designation (Contreras et al., 2008). As a result, such institutions often do not intentionally evolve their organizational identity to fully embrace their HSI status. Nevertheless, although scholars and practitioners still heatedly debate the meaning and responsibilities of this designation, a growing body of research grapples with HSIs' complicated organizational identity and what this federal designation does, could, or should mean, particularly for how these institutions serve Latina/o/x students.

Notably, among such work, Garcia et al. (2019) conducted a systematic analysis of the HSI literature and, in turn, proposed a multidimensional conceptual framework of servingness. Specifically, within this framework, they identified multiple *indicators for serving* and *structures for serving*. In short, the former includes measurable academic outcomes, such as students' GPAs and 6-year graduation rates, as well as non-academic outcomes, like their academic self-efficacy, social agency, and leadership identity. Meanwhile, structures for serving encompass a range of observable, although less clearly measured, organizational elements, including an institution's mission statements, diversity plans, incentive structures, curricula, and decision-making practices.

STUDENT SUCCESS AND POPULATIONS

By definition, at least a quarter of an HSI's undergraduates identify as Latina/o/x, and half are eligible for federal financial aid (Higher Education Opportunity Act, 2008). However, recent reports indicate that, on average, just under half (46%) of all students at HSIs identify as Latina/o/x (*Excelencia*, 2021). HSIs are also a critical access point to higher education for Students of Color beyond the Latina/o/x community. For instance, a recent report indicated that HSIs enrolled an estimated 285,000 Black/ African American students, 311,000 Asian/Pacific Islander students, and 15,000 American Indian/Alaskan Native students in 2018–2019 (Santiago et al., 2020). Additionally, HSIs play a significant role in the postsecondary education of other chronically underserved student populations, including first-generation college goers, English language learners, immigrants, and transfer students (Cuellar, 2015).

STUDENT SUCCESS AND POPULATIONS

Within the HSI literature on student success, most studies focus on Latina/o/x students' academic outcomes (e.g., persistence rates, degree completion, and GPAs), particularly compared to their peers at non-HSIs. Barring a few exceptions, these studies' findings are mostly consistent: Latina/o/x students at HSIs perform roughly the same as their counterparts at other institutions (Garcia et al., 2019). Furthermore, within this scholarship, other studies examine students' nonacademic outcomes, such as academic self-concept, leadership development, and civic engagement. For example, based on longitudinal data on HSIs, eHSIs, and non-HSIs, Cuellar (2014) found that the academic self-concept of Latina/o/x students at HSIs increased more than their peers at non-HSIs. Moreover, studies have shown that HSIs provide a range of affirming, transformative curricular and co-curricular opportunities, some of which even help Latina/o/x students develop their racial/ethnic identity (e.g., Garcia et al., 2018). Altogether, evidence suggests that HSIs help foster Latina/o/x student success, at least in some key ways.

Meanwhile, research on students' experiences at HSIs generally centers on Latina/o/x students and explores their peer and faculty interactions. For instance, Contreras Aguirre et al. (2020) interviewed Latina undergraduates in STEM programs at two HSIs and found that peers and faculty provide academic support, a favorable learning climate, and guidance on how to excel in college and beyond. Furthermore, Alcantar and Hernandez (2020) illustrated how faculty, specifically at a Hispanic-serving community college, validated Latina/o/x students both in and out of class, in turn supporting these students' sense of belonging, persistence, and academic self-concept. Collectively, the research is consistent; as is the case throughout higher education, faculty help define students' academic lives and collegiate experiences at HSIs.

Additionally, within the literature on the student experience at HSIs, studies increasingly examine students' perception of campus racial climate. For example, through a case study of an HSI within the California State University system, Serrano (2020) explored Black and Latino male students' understanding of the institution's campus racial climate. He concluded that students did not feel uniformly welcomed at the university. Specifically, participants perceived most academic departments as hostile and unwelcoming, but viewed the Pan-African Department, the Latin American Studies Program, and two race-based student organizations as positive racial microclimates. Relatedly, based on focus groups and individual interviews with Black male students at a Hispanic-serving community college, Abrica et al. (2019) found that anti-Black racism, in the form of rejection and appropriation, shaped their experiences. In sum, as with most colleges and universities, HSIs likewise can have contentious campus racial climates. At the same time, however, the HSI literature is also replete with examples of ways that HSIs provide validating learning environments and actively work to foster Latina/o/x students' sense of belonging (e.g., Garcia, 2020).

PROFESSIONAL CONTEXT

Despite the vast institutional diversity among the HSI population, several studies still speak to these institutions' working conditions and experiences, namely for faculty. Within the HSI scholarship, studies explore (a) the racial/ethnic composition of the HSI professoriate and (b) faculty members' curricular decisions and pedagogical practices. In addition, other work highlights the experiences of faculty of Color at HSIs, including their involvement in both faculty and student mentoring programs.

Notably, although the higher education scholarship, writ large, documents the benefit of students seeing themselves reflected among their professors, existing research evidences the pronounced underrepresentation of Latina/o/x faculty at HSIs. For instance, Vargas et al. (2019) found that the average Title V awardee employed between 9–920 tenure-track faculty members and an average of 213. However, while the total student-to-faculty ratio at these institutions was 28:1, the average and median ratio of Latina/o/x students to Latina/o/x faculty was a staggering 146:1 and 93:1, respectively (Vargas et al., 2019). In comparison, the average student-to-faculty ratio for their White counterparts was 10:1 (Vargas et al., 2019). Because of the racial/ethnic makeup of the faculty at most HSIs, Vargas et al. (2019) further found that these institutions typically offer limited opportunities for Latina/o/x students to engage with Latina/o/x faculty especially compared to their peers of other racial/ethnic identities.

Contreras (2018) likewise documented the underrepresentation of Latina/o/x faculty at HSIs. Specifically, she found that although 42.5% of the student population at California community colleges (84% of which are HSIs) is Latina/o/x-identified, only 15% of tenure-eligible faculty at these colleges similarly identified. She discovered a similar discrepancy across the California State University system, of which 78% of institutions are HSIs.

Taken together, these studies troublingly signal that Latina/o/x faculty at HSIs likely shoulder a high service load, as Latina/o/x students may disproportionately rely on them for guidance and mentorship. To note, such intensive service loads may especially be the case for Latina/o/x faculty at private HSIs since the Latina/o/x faculty-to-student ratio at such institutions is nearly double that of their public counterparts (Vargas et al., 2019).

Asides from research about faculty at HSIs, some work, although exceedingly sparse, considers the experiences of student affairs professionals at HSIs. Instead, more often, the literature simply describes or assesses innovative or effective student affairs programming or possibilities at HSIs. As a notable exception, Garcia (2016) explored how student affairs professionals at an HSI experience and perceive diversity on campus. In brief, she found that their experiences with the institution's campus racial climate varied based on their specific workplace's microclimate. Specifically, those working within positive microclimates voiced encouraging comments about the campus's diversity efforts, whereas participants within negative microclimates shared stories of uncomfortable, invalidating coworker interactions. Ultimately, despite the limited published research in this specific area, the HSI literature broadly suggests that professionals at HSIs would be best equipped by having a well-developed understanding of Latinidad and the intersectional needs of Latina/o/x students. Additionally, a willingness to develop and implement curricular and co-curricular programming based on the racial and cultural ways of knowing Latina/o/x students is essential for those working at these institutions (Garcia, 2017). Toward developing such knowledge and skills, HSI professionals may lean on several organizations, including the Alliance for Hispanic Serving Institution Educators, *Excelencia* in Education, and HACU.

FUTURE CONSIDERATIONS AND DIRECTIONS

There are several significant contemporary and emerging issues currently at play at HSIs. First, given HSIs' existing and projected student demographics, the hiring, promotion, and retention of faculty of Color at these institutions is a pressing issue. As Vargas et al. (2019) explained, "should HSIs more systematically recruit and retain Latina/o/x faculty, they will be better suited to expend federal HSI resources on initiatives that serve to slow or ameliorate ethnoracial inequalities facilitated, in part, by systems of higher education" (p. 40).

Second, given HSIs' evolving institutional landscape, another prime issue revolves around mission drift/creep or striving at HSIs. For example, both Doran (2015) and Deturk and Briscoe (2020) investigated how the University of Texas at San Antonio negotiated its access-oriented mission while striving for Tier One status. However, the implications of such a culture of striving at HSIs, specifically how such aspirations come to bear on faculty, staff, students, and other campus members, need further attention.

Third, in the context of persistent declines in higher education spending, HSIs increasingly come to rely on alternative revenue streams. In particular, given the limits on tuition and fee increases, securing external funding, including competitive grants, will become more crucial. Amid this context, it is vital for HSI administrators, advocates, and researchers to critically examine HSIs' grant-seeking and grant management and how these institutional efforts translate into serving their campus communities, especially Latina/o/x students. Such work is particularly necessary considering recent research indicating that some HSIs pursue Title V funding—capacity-building, federal grants for HSIs—to finance broad-based, race-evasive institutional efforts, not initiatives designed to serve Latina/o/x students (Aguilar-Smith, 2021). Finally, to advance equity and justice at HSIs, it is imperative to continuously monitor this group's evolving institutional profile and consider what the shifting composition of this population means for public policies regarding HSIs.

DISCUSSION QUESTIONS

- Bearing in mind HSIs' ongoing growth and evolving institutional profile as well as existing HSI scholarship, consider the following:
- What does or should Hispanic-Serving or servingness mean in practice for administrators, faculty, and staff at HSIs? Specifically, how can institutional actors at HSIs, including student affairs practitioners and faculty, embody the campus's HSI designation and, indeed, serve Latina/o/x students?
- Considering HSIs' increasing institutional diversity, what issues are potentially present for educational equity and access, particularly for racially/ethnically minoritized or otherwise marginalized student groups?
- To what extent should HSIs' faculty and staff represent their students and neighboring communities, and how might HSIs realistically go about diversifying their faculty and staff?

REFERENCES

Abrica, E. J., García-Louis, C., & Gallaway, C. D. J. (2020). Antiblackness in the Hispanic-serving community college (HSCC) context: Black male collegiate experiences through the lens of settler colonial logics. *Race Ethnicity and Education*, *23*(1), 55–73. https://doi.org/10.1080/13613324.2019.1631781

Aguilar-Smith, S. (2021). Seeking to serve or $erve? Hispanic-serving institutions' race-evasive pursuit of racialized funding. *AERA Open*. https://doi.org/10.1177/23328584211057097

128 S. AGUILAR-SMITH

Alcantar, C. M., & Hernandez, E. (2020). "Here the professors are Your guide, tus guías": Latina/o student validating experiences with faculty at a Hispanic-serving community college. *Journal of Hispanic Higher Education*, *19*(1), 3–18. https://doi.org/10.1177/1538192718766234

Contreras, F. (2018). Latino faculty in Hispanic-serving institutions: Where is the diversity? *Association of Mexican American Educators Journal*, *11*, 223–250. https://doi.org/10.24974/ amae.11.3.368

Contreras, F. E., Malcom, L. E., & Bensimon, E. M. (2008). Hispanic-serving institutions: Closeted identity and the production of equitable outcomes for Latino/a students. In M. Gasman, B. Baez, & C. S. V. Turner (Eds.), *Understanding minority-serving institutions* (pp. 71–90). State University of New York.

Contreras Aguirre, H. C., Gonzalez, E., & Banda, R. M. (2020). Latina college students experiences in STEM at Hispanic-serving institutions: Framed within Latino critical race theory. *International Journal of Qualitative Studies in Education*, *33*(8), 810–823. https://doi.org/10.1080/09518398.2020.1751894

Cuellar, M. (2014). The impact of Hispanic-Serving Institutions (HSIs), emerging HSIs, and non-HSIs on Latina/o academic self-concept. *Review of Higher Education*, *37*, 499–530. https://doi.org/10.1353/rhe.2014.0032

Cuellar, M. (2015). Latina/o student characteristics and outcomes at four-year Hispanic-serving institutions (HSIs), emerging HSIs, and non-HSIs. In A. M. Núñez, S. Hurtado, & E. Calderón Galdeano (Eds.), *Hispanic-serving institutions: Advancing research and transformative practice* (pp. 101–120). Routledge.

Deturk, S., & Briscoe, F. (2020). From equity and enlightenment to entrepreneurialism: An HSIs pursuit of "tier-one" status in the neoliberal era. *Review of Higher Education*, *43*(4), 967–988. https://doi.org/10.1353/rhe.2020.0027

Doran, E. E. (2015). Negotiating access and tier one aspirations: The Historical evolution of a striving Hispanic-serving institution. *Journal of Hispanic Higher Education*, *14*(4), 343–354. https://doi.org/10.1177/1538192715570638

Excelencia in Education (2021). *Hispanic-serving institutions (HSIs): 2019-20*. https://www.edexcelencia.org/Hispanic-Serving-Institutions-HSIs-2019-2020

Flores, A., & Leal, D. R. (2020). Beyond enrollment and graduation: Examining strategic plans from Hispanic-serving institutions in Texas. *Journal of Latinos and Education*. Advanced online publication. https://doi.org/10.1080/153484 31.2020.1791121

Garcia, G. A. (2017). Decolonizing Hispanic-serving institutions: A framework for organizing. *Journal of Hispanic Higher Education*, *17*(2), 132–147. https://doi.org/10.1177/1538192717734289

Garcia, G. A. (2016). Exploring student affairs professionals' experiences with the campus racial climate at a Hispanic serving institution (HSI). *Journal of Diversity in Higher Education*, *9*(1), 20–33. https://doi.org/10.1037/a0039199

Garcia, G. A. (2020). (Ed.) *Hispanic serving institutions (HSIs) in practice: Defining servingness at HSIs*. Information Age Publishing.

Garcia, G. A., & Guzman-Alvarez, A. (2019). Descriptive analysis of graduate enrollment trends at Hispanic-serving institutions: 2005–2015. *Journal of Hispanic Higher Education*. https://doi.org/10.1177/1538192719835681

Garcia, G. A., Núñez, A.-M., & Sansone, V. A. (2019). Toward a multidimensional conceptual framework for understanding "servingness" in Hispanic-serving institutions: A synthesis of the research. *Review of Educational* Research, *89*(5), 745–784. https://doi.org/10.3102/0034654319864591

Garcia, G. A., Patrón, O. E., Ramirez, J. J., & Hudson, L. T. (2018). Identity salience for Latino male collegians at Hispanic serving institutions (HSIs), emerging HSIs, and non-HSIs. *Journal of Hispanic Higher Education*, *17*, 171–186. https://doi.org/10.1177/1538192716661907

Higher Education Opportunity Act, 20 U.S.C. §1101 et seq. (2008). https://www. govinfo.gov/content/pkg/PLAW-110publ315/pdf/PLAW-110publ315.pdf

Hispanic Association for Colleges and Universities (2021). *2021 Hispanic higher education and HSIs facts*. https://www.hacu.net/hacu/HSI_Fact_Sheet.asp

Laden, B. V. (2004). Hispanic-serving institutions: What are they? Where are they? *Community College Journal of Research and Practice*, *28*(3), 181–198. https://doi. org/10.1080/10668920490256381

Ortega, N., Frye, J., Nellum, C.J., Kamimura, A., & Vidal-Rodriguez, A. (2015). Examining the financial resilience of Hispanic-serving institutions. In A.M. Núñez, S. Hurtado, & E. Calderón Galdeano (Eds.), *Hispanic-serving institutions: Advancing research and transformative practice* (pp. 155–176). Routledge.

Santiago, D. A., & Andrade, S. J. (2010). Emerging Hispanic-serving institutions (HSIs): Serving Latino students. *Excelencia in Education*.

Santiago, D.A., Laurel, J, & Labandera, E. (2020). *25 years of Hispanic-serving institutions: A glance on progress*. Excelencia in Education. https://www.edexcelencia. org/research/publications/25-yrs-hsis-glance-progress

Serrano, U. (2020). 'Finding home': campus racial microclimates and academic homeplaces at a Hispanic-Serving Institution. *Race Ethnicity and Education*. https://doi.org/10.1080/13613324.2020.1718086

U.S. Census Bureau. (2020). *Hispanic heritage month 2020*. https://www. census.gov/newsroom/facts-for-features/2020/hispanic-heritage-month. html#:~:text=60.6%20million&text=Hispanics%20constituted%20 18.5%25%20of%20the%20nation%E2%80%99s%20total%20population

U.S. Government Publishing Office. (1992). *Higher Education Amendments*. https:// www.govinfo.gov/app/details/COMPS-10659

Valdez, P. L. (2015). An overview of Hispanic-serving institutions' legislation: Legislation policy formation between 1979 and 1992. In J. P. Mendez, F. A. Bonner II, J. Méndez-Negrete, & R. T. Palmer (Eds.), *Hispanic-serving institutions in American higher education* (pp. 5–29). Stylus.

Vargas, N., Villa-Palomino, J., & Davis, E. (2019). Latina/o/x faculty representation and resource allocation at Hispanic Serving Institutions. *Race Ethnicity and Education*, *23*(1), 39–54. https://doi.org/10.1080/13613324.2019.1679749

CHAPTER 11

ASIAN AMERICAN AND NATIVE AMERICAN PACIFIC ISLANDER-SERVING INSTITUTIONS (AANAPISI) AS CRITICAL SITES FOR ASIAN AMERICAN, NATIVE HAWAIIAN, AND PACIFIC ISLANDER (AA&NHPI) STUDENTS IN HIGHER EDUCATION

Mike Hoa Nguyen
University of Denver

Demeturie Toso-Lafaele Gogue
University of California

Kristine Jan Cruz Espinoza
University of Nevada

Becket C. Duncan
University of Denver

Rikka J. Venturanza
University of California

Dong M. Dinh
University of Denver

Institutional Diversity in American Postsecondary Education, pp. 131–143
Copyright © 2024 by Information Age Publishing
www.infoagepub.com
All rights of reproduction in any form reserved.

131

132 M. H. NGUYEN ET AL.

Asian American and Native American Pacific Islander-Serving Institutions[1] (AANAPISI) are one of the federal government's most recent Minority-Serving Institution (MSI) designations. The AANAPISI designation was established by Congress in 2007 to support and expand the educational opportunity of Asian American, Native Hawaiian, and Pacific Islander (AANHPI) students. Colleges and universities that become AANAPISIs are critical sites in U.S. higher education that enrich AANHPI students' learning experiences through culturally relevant curriculum, co-curricular activities, resources and services, and research.

Although AANAPISIs encompass a small proportion of all postsecondary institutions in the country, they play an increasingly large role in serving AANHPI students. Today, AANAPISIs enroll nearly 40% of all AANHPI undergraduates, while comprising only 5% of all colleges and universities in the United States and Pacific Islands (Nguyen et al., 2020). Despite their outsized role in educating AANHPI students, little is known about this institutional type within the larger canon of scholarship on MSIs. Thus, the purpose of this chapter is to offer a detailed perspective into the work of AANAPISIs, and the role that these MSIs play in serving and advancing educational access and success for AANHPI college students.

HISTORY

The AANAPISI designation was established in 2007 when the College Cost Reduction and Access Act (CCRAA) was signed into law. However, the advocacy to create AANAPISIs can be documented well before Congress passed CCRAA. From conception to establishment, the origin story of AANAPISIs includes the organizing efforts of students, faculty, and administrators; the advocacy of community-based and AANHPI organizations; and leadership of AANHPI federal policymakers, among others. According to Park and Teranishi (2008), some of the earliest discussions for an AANHPI serving institution were held in the 1980s by then U.S. Congressmembers Norman Mineta and Robert Matsui who noted the exclusion of AANHPIs in the reauthorization of the Higher Education Act. However, it was not until 2000 when the Congressional Asian Pacific American Caucus (CAPAC) hosted a forum to discuss the educational experiences of AANHPIs that a greater legislative movement to create the AANAPISI designation began (Park & Teranishi, 2008). This forum was subsequently followed by a 2001 summit on Southeast Asian and Pacific Islander issues in higher education, led by the Southeast Asia Resource Action Center (SEARAC) and CAPAC, where further public conversations regarding AANAPISIs were held. Then, on January 19, 2001, the White House Initiative on Asian Americans and Pacific Islanders (WHIAAPI) issued a policy report with recommendations for the creation of a federal MSI designation for AANHPIs. In 2002, then U.S. Congressmember Robert Underwood introduced H.R. 4825 to create an AANHPI serving institution designation to be housed in the U.S. Department of Education, along with other MSIs. U.S. Congressmember Underwood then left the U.S. House of Representatives to run for Guam's gubernatorial office. Thus, the bill was later reintroduced as H.R. 333 by U.S. Congressmember David Wu in 2003, and then again as H.R. 2616 in 2005. Additionally, then U.S. Senators, Barbara Boxer and Daniel Akaka, introduced the Senate companion bill, S. 2160 in 2005.

However, the introduction of legislation to establish an AANAPISI designation was met with resistance from various stakeholders. Park and Chang (2009) detailed that even with Democratic control of Congress and of the House Committee on Education and Labor, these did not automatically lead to "the legislation's success as [Chairman] Miller and other Democrats were not convinced that having a special designation for AAPI [Asian American and Pacific Islander] serving institutions was necessary" (p. 112). Indeed, many of the Democratic members of Congress, even those representing Congressional districts with high concentrations of AANHPIs, assumed that AANAPISI funding would be used primarily at highly selective institutions rather than public regional comprehensive institutions and community colleges, where the majority of AANHPI students are enrolled (Teranishi, 2011).

These Democratic members of Congress assumed that AANHPI college students are "model minorities" who are academically high achieving and primarily attend elite institutions—a problematic and dangerously harmful stereotype with serious implications for AANHPI students (Poon et al., 2016; Yi et al., 2020). This proved to be a significant challenge toward the advancement of the legislation. Ironically, U.S. Congress member George Miller's district encompassed large concentrations of Asian Americans, mainly Southeast Asian Americans, who are heavily underserved in higher education. These concerns were eventually addressed, and the support of Chairman Miller was garnered. As a legislative strategy, the AANHPI serving institutions bill was incorporated into the larger College Cost Reduction and Access Act (CCRAA) of 2007. Thus, the AANAPISI designation was created in 2007, when Congress passed the CCRAA, which was subsequently signed into law by President George W. Bush (Park & Chang, 2009). After the AANAPISI designation was created, U.S. Congress member Mike Honda, as a senior member of the House Appropriations Committee, secured $2.5 million through the Fiscal-Year 2009 Omnibus Bill to provide additional funding to AANAPISIs.

Reflecting the demographic concentrations of AANHPI populations throughout the country, AANAPISIs today are heavily concentrated on the

134   M. H. NGUYEN ET AL.

West and East coasts, as well as in the Pacific Islands (Nguyen, 2019).[2] Additionally, a growing number of AANAPISIs are in the Midwest, specifically in Minnesota and Illinois, as well as in the Southern states like Georgia and Texas. Given their growing numbers, advocacy for AANAPISIs continues in Washington, D.C., and across college campuses to ensure that AANAPISIs can strengthen their ability to serve AANHPI students.

ORGANIZATIONAL STRUCTURE AND CULTURE

The AANAPISI designation is administered by the U.S. Department of Education and is operationalized as a competitive grant that provides federal funding for colleges and universities that meet federal eligibility requirements. Specifically, to become an AANAPISI, an institution's enrollment must be comprised of at least 10% AANHPI undergraduates and meet Section 312(b) of the Higher Education Act's eligibility criteria of Title III and Title V programs, which is commonly understood as maintaining a significant proportion of low-income students and a low average of educational and general expenditures, among other requirements (Nguyen et al., 2021). Since 2007, about 217 institutions have met eligibility requirements for AANAPISI status and are nearly evenly split between community colleges and universities. However, the number of eligible AANAPISIs changes every year due to dynamic enrollment patterns and shifting institutional expenditures. After meeting eligibility requirements, institutions can then apply for funding under the AANAPISI designation. From 2007 to 2022, 50 institutions have been awarded AANAPISI funds, totaling approximately $100 million in federal appropriations over the past 15 years. These funded AANAPISIs receive an average of $300,000 to $350,000 each year, over a five-year grant period, which is the least amount of funding for MSIs per capita (M. H. Nguyen et al., 2021; Nguyen et al., 2020).

If an institution is awarded AANAPISI funding, an AANAPISI program is typically established on campus to serve AANHPI students. Teranishi (2011) noted AANAPISI programs primarily serve AANHPI students, faculty, and staff through three primary areas: academic and student support services; leadership, mentorship, and community-based opportunities; and research and resource development. For example, De Anza College used their AANAPISI funding to sustain the Initiatives to Maximize Positive Academic Achievement and Cultural Thriving (IMPACT) AAPI program, a learning community to support Pacific Islander and Southeast Asian American students' academic and transfer success (Impact AAPI, n.d.). Alternatively, University of Massachusetts, Boston used its federal funds to enhance its current services to support Asian American students on campus through the Asian Americans Student Success Program, which bridged both the academic and co-curricular aspects of campus (Asian American Student Success Program, n.d.).

However, it is important to note that most AANAPISIs are historically white institutions (HWIs) that have, over time, increased enrollment of AANHPI students due to changing demographics in the United States. Unlike Historically Black Colleges and Universities (HBCUs) and Tribal Colleges and Universities (TCUs), AANAPISIs were not established with the explicit mission to serve AANHPI students. In other words, like Hispanic-Serving Institutions (HSIs; see Chapter 10), the overall structure and culture of AANAPISIs may not be designed with AANHPI students in mind. For example, research has examined how AANAPISIs communicate serving AANHPIs in campus artifacts at varying levels of equity, reflecting more of a "becoming" AANHPI-serving than "being" AANHPI-serving (Alcantar et al., 2020; Alcantar, Rincón, et al., 2020). On the other hand, research has demonstrated how AANAPISI funding, and the subsequent establishment of funds, can begin to shift the overall institution to better serve AANHPI students, beyond the individual AANAPISI program on campus (Alcantar et al., 2019).

Indeed, this tension exists on campus due to the unique way AANH-PIs are racialized and minoritized on campus. Through their existence and work, AANAPISIs draw attention to the racial positioning of AANH-PIs, thus positioning AANAPISI programs as a *racial project*, a project that does the racializing "work" of linking structure and representation (Omi & Winant, 2015). The existence of AANAPISI programs communicates a commitment to serving AANHPIs to aggressively oppose the common stereotypes of academic exceptionalism and overrepresentation, often at odds with institutional or societal pressures (Nguyen, 2019). Nonetheless, the organizational structure and culture of AANAPISIs vary across the country due to the racial diversity of the student body, governance styles, founding model, financial expenditures, and design of the institution's AANAPISI program.

STUDENT SUCCESS AND POPULATIONS

Over one million AANHPI students are enrolled at institutions of higher education across the country, and over half (51.7%) of all AANHPI community college students are enrolled at an AANAPISI, where one out of three (33.2%) AANHPI students attend a four-year AANAPISI (Nguyen et al., 2020). With respect to degree completion, nearly half (47.5%) of all associate degrees that were awarded to AANHPI college students were at AANAPISIs and nearly 30% of baccalaureate degrees conferred to AANHPIs were from eligible or funded AANAPISIs (Nguyen et al., 2020). These data points underline how AANAPISIs are positioned to more purposefully align resources to support AANHPI students' educational needs. Moreover, as white-centered structures continue to influence the experiences of AANHPI students at AANAPISIs, their programs must be intentional in creating and sustaining courses, practices, and services, among many others, geared towards serving AANHPI students.

Complicating the operations of AANAPISIs is the harmful, lingering, and racialized view of, particularly, Asian Americans as a high academically achieving model minority (Poon et al., 2016; Yi et al., 2020). This highly problematic stereotype leads to notions against, and resistance towards, providing programs, services, and resources for AANHPIs. Integral to countering this model minority myth is including AANHPIs in ongoing efforts towards equity. This can be achieved by highlighting and responding to the heterogeneity within the AANHPI umbrella, with regards to ethnic, class, citizenship and immigration status, and language differences, among others. By disaggregating data by ethnicity, researchers have argued how certain subgroups (e.g., Native Hawaiians and Pacific Islanders, Filipinos, Southeast Asian Americans) have experienced academic challenges otherwise made invisible when AANHPIs are looked at as a monolith (e.g., National Commission on Asian American and Pacific Islander Research in Education [CARE], 2013, 2014; Gogue et al., 2021a, 2021b; Poon et al., 2021; Museus & Chang, 2009; Teranishi, 2007; Teranishi et al., 2013). Indeed, many AANHPI students identify as first-generation and come from low-income backgrounds (CARE, 2014). Data from the U.S. Census Bureau reveals how a high proportion of AANHPIs also speak a language other than English at home (39.4% of Asian Americans and 29.2% of Pacific Islanders) as compared to the total U.S. population (9.8%), and language needs vary when disaggregated by ethnic subgroup (CARE, 2008). At the same time, characterization of Asian Americans as a model minority makes invisible the insidious history of how anti-Blackness and white supremacy birthed the myth. In the wake of advocacy for social justice by minoritized communities of Color in the 1960s, Asian Americans were racially positioned to discredit these protests and demands (Suzuki, 2002). The model minority myth is predicated on "disciplining and shaming other People of Color" which "deflects attention away from how the myth is integral to a project of maintaining White supremacy" (Poon et al., 2016, p. 489). AANAPISIs, as racial projects, have an opportunity to contribute towards the dismantling of these issues for AANHPI students (Park & Teranishi, 2008).

In addition to (re)framing how AANHPIs are viewed, AANAPISI programs have demonstrated their ability to yield positive academic (e.g., persistence, retention, transfer, transition from basic skills or developmental to college-level courses) and psychosocial outcomes (e.g., facilitating self-concept, fostering engagement on campus, increasing sense of belonging) for students (CARE, 2014; Museus et al., 2018; Nguyen et al., 2018), through the prioritization of targeting specific AANHPI subgroups and intentionally designing initiatives that are culturally relevant and responsive to these diverse populations (Nguyen, 2021). For example, some AANAPISI programs have collaborated with their Asian American Studies departments to encourage cross-campus efforts as well as promote more awareness of the types of course offerings available within the discipline (Nguyen, 2020, 2021). Partnering with racial-specific academic departments also affords institutions opportunities to build in culturally relevant curriculum across other disciplines and programs (Catallozzi et al., 2019). However, there is still room to grow. Critical to the work of AANAPISIs is a focus on serving the AANHPI students upon whose enrollment the AANAPISI designation relies on in the first place. AANAPISI designation and funding gives institutions an opportunity to bolster their capacity to better serve AANHPIs, especially if they maximize this opportunity to do so.

PROFESSIONAL CONTEXTS

Given that AANAPISIs are HWIs and/or predominately white institutions that have received federal funding to design programs and initiatives to serve AANHPIs on campus, the professional context at AANAPISIs can vary substantially. As previously discussed, most AANAPISIs established programs and initiatives on their campuses may or may not have overarching aims to serve AANHPI students. At the same time, there is often an initial hiring of new student affairs professionals and, in some cases, faculty to support these programs. In these capacities, new student affairs professionals serve in some of the most challenging roles, with an often-diverse set of responsibilities. For example, some student affairs professionals are tasked with running a cultural center that provides co-curricular programming for AANHPI students; others may be hired to support a particular effort being enhanced by an existing program, such as leadership development (Maramba & Fong, 2020).

To implement these programmatic initiatives, many AANAPISI program professionals are trained in Asian American Studies and/or Pacific Islander Studies or have some awareness of the AANHPI student populations and their needs. Given these contexts, many AANAPISI program professionals are often oriented towards social and racial justice, and intentionally develop initiatives on their campuses to address issues of diversity and equity (Gogue et al., 2021a, 2021b; Venturanza et al., 2021). Thus, the professional context generated from this culture often involves challenges to ensure that the work of AANAPISI program professionals reaches beyond the immediate federally funded program. AANAPISI programs often inhabit an institutional culture of resistance that have the potential to drastically transform institutional policies and practices toward more equitable and inclusive conditions (Mac et al., 2019). Towards this objective, AANAPISI program professionals are often called to serve as institutional change agents, or what Nguyen and colleagues (2021) have termed "institutional pathfinders" to sustain their efforts and promote the longevity of their programs.

Apart from using community-centered research-based pedagogy and practice to coordinate, direct, maintain, and strengthen their programs while being strategically resourceful, AANAPISI professionals are tasked to be visionaries in their roles. This requires innovation, creativity, and political acumen to design and establish curricula and services while galvanizing, cultivating, incentivizing, or mobilizing communities within and beyond their campus (Mac et al., 2019; Maramba & Fong, 2020; Nguyen, 2020). These formidable and boundless endeavors represent a significant portion of AANAPISIs' professional context. Of course, this work is not done alone. Instead, the work of AANAPISI programs is accomplished by a team of dedicated student affairs professionals and faculty to achieve long-term AANHPI student outcomes, with the goal of institutionalizing programs and initiatives to serve AANHPI across the institution (Nguyen, 2019). Moreover, professional organizations such as Asian Pacific Americans in Higher Education (APAHE) and APIA Scholars, hosts annual conferences, webinars, and convenings throughout the year to connect AANAPISI professionals and share strategies, practices, and policy recommendations to enhance the work at AANAPISIs.

Finding pathways amidst an increasingly complex institutional system is only part of the work at AANAPISIs. Consequently, the institutional culture of resistance inequitably increases the workload and overall responsibility of AANAPISI professionals (Gogue et al., 2021a, 2021b; Venturanza et al., 2021). Indeed, many professionals learn quickly to be strong advocates beyond their programs and the students they serve on campus. AANAPISI professionals must also practice the power of self-advocacy as the work becomes an extension of the professional, especially if they politically and racially identify as AANHPI. AANAPISI program's space, resources, and more specifically allies are also inherently provisional and may diminish as early as the next academic quarter or semester throughout the typical five-year cycle of the program. This often places AANAPISI professionals on a fast-track to interacting with the most influential stakeholders on campus and beyond, making their voice a critical force in all interactions. Nonetheless, AANAPISI program professionals remain committed to serving AANHPI students, especially in an era where widely accepted narratives that conflate Asian Americans, Native Hawaiians, and Pacific Islanders, as well as categorize Asian Americans, and in some instances, Native Hawaiians and Pacific Islanders, into high achieving monolithic stereotypes that and need little to no attention or resources in higher education institutions (Poon et al., 2016; Yi et al., 2020).

FUTURE CONSIDERATIONS AND DIRECTIONS

Since its establishment in 2007, AANAPISIs have undoubtedly shifted how colleges and universities serve AANHPI students. As this chapter has discussed, AANAPISIs have challenged misunderstandings of AANHPI students (Park & Teranishi, 2008), enhanced programs and services dedicated to the success of this population (Museus et al., 2018), and afforded faculty and staff opportunities to develop new research that illuminate the unique experiences of AANHPI communities in higher education (Nguyen, 2019). Although AANAPISIs have done tremendous work to transform the landscape of higher education, they continue to receive the least amount of federal funds compared to other MSIs (Nguyen et al., 2020). Consequently, the number of institutions eligible for the AANAPISI grant remains limited, given the finite resources available. As colleges and universities enroll more AANHPI students, the number of eligible AANAPISIs will also grow, warranting increased attention to ways to expand and increase funding for the current AANAPISI program. However, any funding increases for AANAPISIs should not come at the expense of other MSIs.

At the institutional level, student populations, especially AANHPI communities, possess a variety of intersectional identities, which means that higher education institutions must continue to reevaluate their approaches to supporting students. For AANAPISIs specifically, they must continue to develop innovative and culturally relevant programs and services that cater to the diverse students who identify within the larger AANHPI category (Nguyen et al., 2021). Moreover, AANAPISIs must also think about how this federal designation also impacts faculty, administrators, and staff and their understanding of and approach to serving AANHPI students on college campuses across the nation (Alcantar et al., 2019; Nguyen & Nguyen, 2019). As Alcantar et al. (2019) note, the AANAPISI program "provides opportunities for grant money, but is not necessarily accompanied by the substantive organizational culture change needed to make such institutions welcoming and attuned to the needs of racial/ethnic minority students" (p. 311). Thus, more research is needed to understand how AANAPISI programs move beyond simply being situated within a program or department on campus towards a commitment that is adopted and embraced by the entire campus. By investing more resources into this ever-growing program and continuously evaluating institutional efforts towards supporting this student population, AANAPISIs have the potential to advance educational equity and access for the next generation of AANHPI communities.

DISCUSSION QUESTIONS

- How do AANAPISIs serve AANHPI students? What mechanisms do they deploy to achieve positive student outcomes?
- What are some of the challenges at AANAPISIs? What are their benefits?
- Given the complex and different ways in which Asian American *and* Native Hawaiian and Pacific Islander students are racialized, how do AANAPISIs work to address these problematic issues?
- How are AANAPISIs similar and different from other MSIs?
- What structural challenges do AANAPISIs face within the broader postsecondary education landscape?

REFERENCES

Alcantar, C. M., Kim, V., Hafoka, I., & Teranishi, R. T. (2020). Space and place at Asian American and Pacific Islander–serving community colleges: The geography of campus student support for Asian American and Pacific Islander students. *Journal of Diversity in Higher Education*. Advance online publication. http://dx.doi.org/10.1037/dhe0000281.

Alcantar, C. M., Pazich, L. B., & Teranishi, R. T. (2019). Meaning-making about becoming a minority serving institution: A case study of Asian-American serving community colleges. *The Review of Higher Education, 42*(5), 309–335.

Alcantar, C. M., Rincón, B. E., & Espinoza, K. J. (2020). In a state of becoming: How institutions communicate Asian American and Pacific Islander-and Latinx-servingness through campus artifacts. *Association of Mexican American Educators Journal, 14*(3), 104–119.

Asian American Student Success Program. (n.d.). University of Massachusetts Boston. Retrieved March 30, 2022, from https://www.umb.edu/academics/vpass/aassp

Catallozzi, L. A., Tang, S. S., Gabbard, G., & Kiang, P. N. (2019). Modeling AANAPISI community college–university collaboration: A case study of Asian American studies-centered faculty and curriculum development. *New Directions for Higher Education, 2019*(186), 79–92.

Gogue, D. T.-L., Poon, O. A., Maramba, D. C., & Kanagala, V. (2021). Inclusions and exclusions: Racial categorizations and panethnicities in higher education. *International Journal of Qualitative Studies in Education*. https://doi.org/10.1080/09518398.2021.1982045

Gogue, D. T.-L., Venturanza, R. J., Cuenza-Uvas, A., & Nguyen, M. H. (2021). The role of Asian American and Native American Pacific Islander-serving institutions in reframing leadership education. *New Directions for Student Leadership, 2021*(171), 101–111. https://doi.org/10.1002/yd.20460.

Impact AAPI. (n.d.). De Anza College. Retrieved March 30, 2022, from https://www.deanza.edu/impact-aapi/

Mac, J., Sarreal, A. D., Wang, A. C., & Museus, S. D. (2019). Conditions that catalyze the emergence of Asian American and Native American Pacific Islander serving institutions. *New Direction for Higher Education, 2019*(186), 67–77. https://doi.org/10.1002/he.20324

Maramba, D. C., & Fong, T. P. (Eds.). (2020). *Transformative practices for minority student success: Accomplishments of Asian American and Native American Pacific Islander Serving Institutions*. Stylus.

Museus, S. D., & Chang, M. J. (2009). Rising to the challenge of conducting research on Asian Americans in higher education. *New Directions for Institutional Research, 142*, 95–105.

Museus, S. D., Wright-Mair, R., & Mac, J. (2018). *How Asian American and Native American Pacific Islander Serving Institutions (AANAPISIs) are creating the conditions for students to thrive*. University of Pennsylvania Center for Minority Serving Institutions.

National Commission on Asian American and Pacific Islander Research in Education [CARE]. (2008). *Facts, not fiction: Setting the record straight*.

National Commission on Asian American and Pacific Islander Research in Education [CARE]. (2013). *Partnership for Equity in Education through Research (PEER): Findings from the first year of research on AANAPISIs*.

National Commission on Asian American and Pacific Islander Research in Education [CARE]. (2014). *Measuring the impact of MSI-funded programs on student success: Findings from the evaluation of Asian American and Native American Pacific Islander-Serving Institutions*.

Nguyen, B. M. D., Nguyen, T. H., Gutierrez, R. A. E., Kurland, W. M., & Lee, N. W. (2021). Institutional pathfinders: Key lessons from program directors of AANAPISI grant-funded projects. *Journal of Diversity in Higher Education, 15*(5), 596–606. https://doi.org/10.1037/dhe0000313

Nguyen, M. H. (2019). *Building capacity at Asian American and Native American Pacific Islander Serving Institutions (AANAPISI): Cultivating leaders and civic engagement through federal policy* [Unpublished doctoral dissertation, University of California]. Los Angeles.

Nguyen, M. H. (2020). Asian American and Native American Pacific Islander Serving Institutions (AANAPISIs): Serving and advocating for the educational needs of Southeast Asian American Students. *Journal of Southeast Asian American Education and Advancement, 15*(2), Article 3. https://docs.lib.purdue.edu/jsaaea/vol15/iss2/3

Nguyen, M. H. (2021). Building capacity for student success at Asian American and Native American Pacific Islander-Serving Institutions (AANAPISI): Transforming the educational experiences of Asian American and Pacific Islander Students. *The Journal of Higher Education*. Advance online publication. https://doi.org/10.1080/00221546.2021.1996170

Nguyen, M. H., Espinoza, K. J., Gogue, D. T.-L., & Dinh, D. M. (2020). *Looking to the next decade: Strengthening Asian American and Native American Pacific Islander Serving Institutions through policy and practice*. National Council of Asian Pacific Americans. https://files.eric.ed.gov/fulltext/ED608022.pdf

Nguyen, M. H., Espinoza, K. J., Gogue, D. T.-L., & Dinh, D. M. (2021). AANAPISIs in context and practice: Strategies for serving Asian Pacific Islander Desi American Students. *About Campus, 26*(1), 5–9.

Nguyen, T. H., & Nguyen, B. M. D. (2019). AANAPISI program directors: Opportunities and challenges. In R. T. Palmer, D. Preston, & A. Assalone (Eds.), *Examining effective practices at minority-serving institutions* (pp. 161–177). Palgrave Macmillan.

Nguyen, T. H., Nguyen, B. M. D., Nguyen, M. H., Gasman, M., & Conrad, C. (2018). From marginalized to validated: An in-depth case study of an Asian American, Native American and Pacific Islander serving institution. *The Review of Higher Education, 41*(3), 327–363.

Omi, M., & Winant, H. (2015). *Racial formation in the United States* (3rd ed.). Routledge.

Park, J. J., & Chang, M. (2009). Asian American and Pacific Islander Serving Institutions: The motivations and challenges behind seeking a federal designation. *AAPI Nexus Journal: Policy, Practice, and Community, 7*, 107–128.

Park, J. J., & Teranishi, R. T. (2008). Asian American and Pacific Islander serving institutions: Historical perspectives and future prospects. In M. Gasman, B. Baez, & C. S. V. Turner (Eds.), *Understanding minority-serving institutions* (pp. 111–126). State University of New York Press.

Poon, O., Squire, D., Kodama, C., Byrd, A., Chan, J., Manzano, L., Furr, S., & Bishundat, D. (2016). A critical review of the model minority myth in selected literature on Asian Americans and Pacific Islanders in higher education. *Review of Educational Research, 86*(2), 469–502.

Suzuki, B. H. (2002). Revisiting the model minority stereotype: Implications for student affairs practice and higher education. *New Directions for Student Services, 2002*(97), 21–32.

Teranishi, R. T. (2007). Race, ethnicity, and higher education policy: The use of critical quantitative research. *New Directions for Institutional Research, 2007*(133), 47–59.

Teranishi, R. (2011). Asian American and Native American Pacific Islander-serving institutions: Areas of growth, innovation, and collaboration. *AAPI Nexus: Policy, Practice and Community, 9*(1–2), 151–155.

Teranishi, R. T., Lok, L., & Nguyen, B. M. D. (2013). *iCount: A Data Quality Movement for Asian Americans and Pacific Islanders in Higher Education*. National Commission on Asian American and Pacific Islander Research in Higher Education.

Venturanza, R. J., Lee, H. H., & Masulit, M. M. (2022). Asian American Native American and Pacific Islander Serving Institutions empowering students' civic engagement toward social justice agendas. *AAPI Nexus: Policy, Practice and Community, 19*(1–2). https://escholarship.org/uc/item/1j1324gz

Yi, V., Mac, J., Na, V. S., Venturanza, R. J., Museus, S. D., Buenavista, T. L., & Pendakur, S. L. (2020). Toward an anti-imperialistic critical race analysis of the model minority myth. *Review of Educational Research, 90*(4), 542–579.

ENDNOTES

1. More information about the federal AANAPISI designation can be found on the U.S. Department of Education's website: https://www2.ed.gov/programs/aanapi/index.html
2. The number of eligible AANAPISIs changes yearly with enrollment shifts. For the most updated list, please visit the U.S. Department of Education's eligibility matrix: https://www2.ed.gov/about/offices/list/ope/idues/eligibilityhtml. The number of funded AANAPISIs changes every five years given the new cycle of grants. For a list of awardees by years, please visit https://www2.ed.gov/programs/aanapi/awards.html

CHAPTER 12

SERVING STUDENTS WITH DISABILITIES

Institutions and Programs

Casey Yocum
Virginia Commonwealth University

Aaron W. Hughey
Western Kentucky University

There are around 26 million students enrolled in the 6,000 colleges and universities in the United States (Bareham, 2021). Approximately 11% of all postsecondary undergraduates report having some form of disability (Accredited Schools Online, 2022), and many institutions have programs tailored to students with special needs (Bryant, 2021; Ivywise, 2022). There is an important distinction between colleges and universities that have, as their primary mission, the provision of higher education to students with disabilities and institutions that have specialized programs and services for these populations. Yet, there are many campuses that fall into the latter category, but relatively few in the former group (National Center for College Students with Disabilities, 2022). Yet even as significant progress has been made in identifying and responding to the needs of college students with disabilities, discussions still take place among all level of administrators regarding what constitutes a disability and how accommodations can best be provided (ADA National Network, 2022). Cappex (2022) reinforced this notion:

Institutional Diversity in American Postsecondary Education, pp. 145–156
Copyright © 2024 by Information Age Publishing
www.infoagepub.com
All rights of reproduction in any form reserved.

145

> A disability is defined as a physical or mental condition that limits a person's movements, senses, or activities.... Whether it's a physical disability, a developmental one, or related to learning, there are programs at a number of great colleges ready to help students with everything from dyslexia to deafness, from ADHD to Autism Spectrum Disorder, from Down Syndrome to depression.

Finally, it is important to acknowledge at the onset of the chapter that words matter. As such, even the language college administrators use is important and should be taken into consideration when developing programs and services designed to meet the needs brought of students with disabilities (Boston University, 2022). Grant (2022) brings this issue into sharp focus and stated: "The disability community is split on language. Many people prefer person-first language—"person with a disability." Others prefer identity-first language—"disabled person." The best option is to use the language that the individual prefers. Do not assume all people prefer the same language.

The bottom line is that it is challenging to provide an organizational and administrative template for institutions that exist primarily to serve students with disabilities as there are very few common characteristics that these institutions possess. This chapter includes a discussion of the institutions and programs that could serve as role models for better serving students with disabilities.

HISTORY

Colleges and universities have evolved in the provision of services for students with disabilities in tandem with legislation that has steadily progressed to ensure they have the same access and opportunities afforded to other students (Sannes, 2008). Beginning in the early 1970s, these legislative milestones include Section 504 of the Rehabilitation Act of 1973, the Individuals with Disabilities Education Act of 1985, the Assistive Technology Act of 1988, and the Americans With Disabilities Act (ADA) of 1990 (Grant, 2022). The general philosophy and guiding principle behind the legislation is that students with disabilities should be afforded the same access to educational opportunities as their non-challenged counterparts. As Wilson (2022) noted, "By law, students with disabilities have the same rights as those without them in educational settings. Nearly all educational institutions in the U.S. must provide students with disabilities the same access to quality education as other students" (para. 4). The ADA, which was expanded in 2008 with passage of the ADA Amendments Act (ADAAA), is a major milestone with respect to its implications for institutional structure in that it "prohibits discrimination against individuals with disabilities in employment, education, transportation, public access, both physical and digital, as well as other facets of life" (University of Connecticut, 2022, para. 2). For more on the legislative history of students with disabilities, please review the "Milestones of the Disability Rights Movement Over the Years" presentation (University of Connecticut, 2022) at The Center for Students with Disabilities at the University of Connecticut's website.

ORGANIZATIONAL STRUCTURE AND CULTURE

The primary determinant of administrative structure at disability access institutions seems to be more related to the overall institutional type, control, and size (Cavallari, 2022). Interestingly, urban colleges and universities seem to be more suited to providing services to students with disabilities due to their access to more community-based resources (Johnson, 2019). A major consideration that institutions must take when deciding on an administrative structure most appropriate for students with disabilities is how best to facilitate the transition from high school to college. Whereas most of the services needed by students with disabilities are mandated at the elementary and secondary level, colleges and universities that want to meet the needs of these students must be more purposeful and resourceful (University of Rochester, 2022). And this can be a daunting responsibility, as noted by Accredited Schools Online (2022):

> The transition from high school to college is a big one. If you're a student with a disability, the additional stresses can be overwhelming. One of the largest changes that you will have to deal with is the substantial difference in scope between the special education services provided on the high school level and those at college. (para. 1)

As acknowledged previously, there are very few colleges and universities—relatively speaking—that have been established specifically to meet the needs of students with a particular disability (National Center for College Students with Disabilities, 2022). As such, providing an institutional administrative structure that could be used as a template or a model for so-called best practices is exceptionally difficult (StateUniversity.com, 2022). However, there are examples that college and university stakeholders can emulate when making decisions regarding administrative design. With respect to institutions that exist to serve the needs of students with learning and intellectual disabilities, there are a couple of colleges that administrators need to carefully study. First, there is Beacon College is Leesburg, Florida. According to Ivywise (2022):

Founded in 1989, Beacon is the first accredited college offering four-year degrees designed around the needs of students with diagnosed learning disabilities.... The group of parents who conceived of Beacon College did so knowing that given the right environment, support, and tools, all students can succeed. The College is committed to student success, offering academic and personal support services that help each student achieve his or her goals.

Moreover, Cappex (2022) highlights Landmark College in Putney, Vermont, which also serves students with learning disabilities:

Landmark College caters entirely to students who learn differently. Students receive individualized attention from instructors with classrooms offering a low 6:1 student-teacher ratio. Students are also provided with frequent visits with experiences advisors, executive function coaching, and education technology support. Landmark offers a Bridge Program as well as a number of summer programs, and is home to the Landmark College Institute for Research and Training.

There are also a few institutions that were established specifically to meet the needs of students with disabilities of a more physical nature. As administrators, it is important to recognize the distinction between students with "invisible" disabilities (ADHD, autism, psychiatric disabilities, diabetes, some vision and hearing deficiencies, and chronic pain) and those of a more "visible" nature (students using wheelchairs and other assistive or communication devices). These are critical considerations that have implications for administrative structure (Barnett, 2018, October 28). This difference is highlighted by Wilson (2022):

Getting around campus, using writing utensils and keyboards, and turning pages in a book, to name a few examples, can be challenging for individuals with physical disabilities, and universities typically have a range of human support services for students in this category. Sometimes referred to as "non-medical help," your school can make accommodations to help you carry out daily tasks on campus where you might need extra time or assistance. (para. 37)

Chief among the physical disabilities are students who have hearing impairments. There are institutions that have been established specifically to meet the needs of these students, including Gallaudet University, the only liberal arts college in the world exclusively devoted to deaf students, National Technical Institute for the Deaf (NTID), a private technical college for the deaf in Rochester, New York, and the Southwest Collegiate Institute for the Deaf, a community college for the deaf in Big Spring,

Serving Students With Disabilities   149

Texas. The complexities inherent to the administration of these institutions are underscored by Verywell Health (2021):

> While deaf or partially deaf students in the United States can attend any college in the country, many are drawn to schools that specifically serve deaf students. In addition to offering more resources and classrooms tailored to deaf and partially deaf learners, these schools provide a sense of identity, understanding, and pride for their students and alumni. Instructors may be deaf, partially deaf, or hearing, and communicate using American sign language (ASL), spoken language, finger spelling, printed and visual aids, and online resources. (para. 1)

Similarly, there are a few institutions that cater exclusively to students with visual disabilities. One such college is the Perkins School for the Blind. Many of the challenges facing administrators at these institutions are delineated by Leslie Thatcher, Director of College Success at the Perkins School (2022):

> As a student with a visual impairment, you may be wondering which campuses are most accessible? You may be wondering, more generally, where are the best colleges for students with visual impairments? Other disabilities? While we all like clear, immediate answers, there really is no short answer to these questions. The college process is complex, and many factors need to be taken into consideration.

Regardless of institutional type, culture seems to be more important than administrative structure when it comes to institutional factors that define colleges and universities are more responsive to the needs of students with disabilities. According to Shaewitz and Crandall (2020):

> Disability is part of the human condition. To ensure inclusion in higher education, campus leaders must consider how to fully embrace all students, faculty, and staff with and without disabilities. When developing a culture of inclusion, colleges and universities have specific responsibilities to students with disabilities to ensure they can learn and achieve their goals. (para. 2)

Specifically, institutions that establish and maintain cultural centers for their students with disabilities seem to represent best practice, according to Landin (2021):

> Higher education should provide the same efforts, support, and resources for students with disabilities as they do for other cultural student populations to help challenge ableism and validate the disability identity. A *Disability Cultural Center (DCC)* can serve university students with disabilities by providing a safe space for students to connect with other students.... A

Disability Cultural Center is needed at universities to enrich and cultivate a community of intersectionality and interconnectivity for students with disabilities, allies, and all other student populations.

A critical component in the culture of an institution that successfully meets the needs of students with disabilities is how the faculty see their inherent responsibility to accommodate students who may need enhanced support in the form of services and programs that effectively levels the playing field (Sniatecki et al., 2015). This is reinforced by Sullivan (2021):

As a faculty member, I believe we owe it to our students to hire more people with disabilities (PWD).... Over 22 percent of Americans have a disability, but only 4 percent of faculty members do, according to the National Center for College Students with Disabilities. We have no national statistics on staff. This means a wide swath of students may never interact with faculty and staff who may well be uniquely qualified to engage them. (para. 4)

STUDENT SUCCESS AND POPULATIONS

Historically, students with disabilities have had to overcome many inequities to succeed in higher education due to barriers colleges have put in place. However, with the rising rates of students with disabilities attending postsecondary education, it is essential to understand how to best support these students (Francis et al., 2019). At specialized disability-serving institutions, there seems to be a level of understanding of how best to help these students. Each college works to meet the specific needs of their students, leading to increased retention and graduation rates.

Though there is little research about the success of students with disabilities at 4-year colleges, this could be related to students with disabilities who are not required to disclose their disability status. Research shows that 12–13% of students do not inform their college of their disability status (NCES, 2022). When comparing the retention and graduation rates between traditional 4-year colleges for students who disclose their disability status and those who are at disability-serving institutions, there is a 20% increase in success when looking at 6-year graduation rates. The critical question to ask is what contributes to students with disabilities experiencing higher success rates on disability-serving campuses?

Comparing the student experience of students with disabilities at traditional 4-year colleges and specialized disability-serving institutions can provide some insight into student success. There were five common themes when working with students with disabilities at traditional 4-year colleges. Students stated feelings of discouragement, debasement, insecurity, isolation, and repeated cycles of disempowerment (Francis et al., 2019). In comparison, Daisy (2008) had a participant who discussed their experience at Gallaudet University:

> I would say my many visits to Gallaudet through my high school years and beginning of college was a major influence. Gallaudet is a very strong, pro-Deaf Culture campus, and my experiences there became an important stage for me because they allowed me to understand different perspectives, especially because I spent my middle school and high school years in a mainstreamed program. (p. 64)

Radder and Smith (2019) shared a student's academic journey with Landmark College. The student graduated with their associate's degree from Landmark, transferred to a 4-year institution to come back to Landmark College to complete their bachelor's instead, "People have brains that may operate in some ways a little bit different than other people, but it doesn't make them a deficient person it just makes them unique, and I think that uniqueness is important in a lot of ways ... it strengthens my learning to be around people that aren't exactly like me." The students' experiences at Landmark College and Galludet University highlighted here signal a sense of belonging and inclusion that was in opposition to what they experienced on traditional 4-year college campuses. Anecdotal data such as these point to the need for further research that explores the experiences of students with disability across institutional mission and type.

PROFESSIONAL CONTEXT

To work at a specialized disability-serving institution, understanding the student population and students' unique experiences before coming to higher education is essential. In addition, knowing the different pathways that lead them to this point is critical for them to continue success. As a faculty or staff member at a specialized disability-serving institution, this requires a unique set of skills or the ability to use a different language and understand a different culture on some campuses. Below are excerpts of two college presidents about their own experiences of how to support their student populations at their institutions. College President Hagerty (2017), shares his experience at Beacon College and with students with learning disabilities:

> A college culture that works for students who learn differently accepts the reality that we are part of a neurodiverse world.... So for institutions that accept students with special learning needs (and this is universal), the tone, expectations and priorities need to be set at the top ... we must prepare faculty and staff to embrace and accommodate the learning different resident

on campus; our academic support resources must be available in the right measures to address the needs of the mix of admitted students; adaptive technology should be accessible and convenient; and new and renovated learning spaces should be increasingly reflective of the best features of universal design.

Hagerty (2017) explained that his student support model mimics the K–12 experiences in higher education for supporting students with learning disabilities. This culture of support requires structured planning and support from the student, faculty, and staff to meet the student's needs. Previous College President, I. King Jordan, Gallaudet Universities' first deaf president, discussed what it is like to work on Gallaudet's campus:

> While Gallaudet, is a unique institution, the one thing people readily identify as special is the fact that we rely on visual communications. Most important, we sign. No matter where you are, in our classrooms, our meeting rooms, the offices where we work, public areas … visual communication access will always be present in the form of sign language or text messages. People who come to our campus and who do not know sign language are communicatively disabled.

This excerpt provides a glance at the experiences on Gallaudet's campus. When you work at Gallaudet university, you need to understand sign language and deaf culture. Jordan (2005) touched on this briefly, discussing how disability studies and deaf studies diverge on this point. Some deaf individuals view their deafness as not something that needs to be fixed and resent that idea. Though serving different groups of students with disabilities, there are common themes in both excerpts of college presidents. Both colleges discuss how they put students first. Everything they do and their campuses are designed around a culture of support and understanding to meet their student needs best.

A culture of support can also be found in professional organizations. Professional organizations can be instrumental for individuals working at specific disability-serving institutions. Due to the variety of specialized institutions and range of disabilities, there are countless organizations to provide individuals the ability to stay up to date on research in the field and connect with others on new technology or about best practices for meeting the needs of students with disabilities on traditional college campuses and at disability serving institutions. Notably, the Association on Higher Education and Disability (AHEAD; 2024) "is the leading professional membership association for individuals committed to equity for persons with disabilities in higher education." AHEAD publishes books and monographs, hosts an annual conference, is home to the Journal of Postsecondary Education and

Disability (JPED), and provides an online career center. Furthermore, both of the leading student affairs and higher education organizations offer spaces for connection and professional development—NASPA's Disability Knowledge Community and ACPA's Coalition for Disability.

FUTURE CONSIDERATIONS AND DIRECTIONS

The term "Universal Design" was mentioned briefly in the quote from Beacon College President Hagerty, yet it is an important idea to explore and adequately explain as we discuss the future needs of and considerations for students. Universal Design was a term coined in the Assistive Technology Act of 1998, defined as:

> A concept or philosophy for designing and delivering products and services that are usable by people with the widest possible range of functional capabilities, which include products and services that are directly usable (without requiring assistive technologies) and products and services that are made usable with assistive technologies. (p. 112)

Burgstahler (2008) discussed how universal design reinforces the characteristic that universal design is proactive and not reactive. Universally designed devices or environments have built-in features that anticipate the needs of a diverse group of users. This idea is critical when supporting students, both in and outside the classroom. Jordan (2005) discussed how all universities need to provide students with a complete experience beyond the classroom. Though there are not many disability-serving institutions currently, with the increase of students with disabilities entering higher education, there could be an increase in demand for disability-serving institutions or an increase in accountability at traditional 4-year colleges to meet the needs of students with disabilities better. This demand could move traditional 4-year colleges to adopt a universal design approach inside and outside the classroom.

Each disability-serving institution is unique by meeting the specific needs of its student population, providing them with an environment that leads to high rates of student success and retention. Though these colleges are unique in working with different groups of students with disabilities, they are brought together by the idea that they put students first not only in their mission and values but also in their actions. These specialized disability-serving institutions are creating spaces for students to feel a sense of belonging that is not currently replicated at traditional 4-year colleges.

DISCUSSION QUESTIONS

- Given the fiscal constraints colleges and universities are anticipated to have to negotiate over the coming decades, is the concept of a "disability-serving institution" going to continue to be a viable concept?
- What are some additional and/or emerging disabilities that may warrant the development of institutions designed to meet the needs of the affected students?
- What role should serving students with disabilities play in the institutional accreditation process?
- What special skills and competencies (pedagogical, administrative, etc.) are needed to effectively meet the needs of students with disabilities?

REFERENCES

Accredited Schools Online. (2022, May 25). *Higher education for students with disabilities.* https://www.accreditedschoolsonline.org/resources/best-accredited-colleges-schools-for-students-with-disabilities/

ADA National Network. (2022). *What are a public or private college-university's responsibilities to students with disabilities?* https://adata.org/faq/what-are-public-or-private-college-universitys-responsibilities-students-disabilities

Assistive Technology Act of 1998, Pub. L. No. 105-394. https://www.congress.gov/bill/105th-congress/senate-bill/2432

Association on Higher Education and Disability (AHEAD). (2024). About. Retrieved April 15, 2024 from, https://www.ahead.org/about-ahead/about-overview

Bareham, H. (2021, October 22). *College enrollment statistics.* Bankrate. https://www.bankrate.com/loans/student-loans/college-enrollment-statistics/

Barnett, C. (2018). Disabled at Vanderbilt: Visible vs. invisible disabilities. *The Vanderbilt Hustler.* https://vanderbilthustler.com/2018/10/28/disabled-at-vanderbilt-visible-vs-invisible-disabilities/

Boston University. (2022). *Accommodating students with disabilities: Guidelines for faculty and staff.* Disability and Access Services. https://www.bu.edu/disability/accommodations/procedures/faculty/

Bryant, J. (2021, May 25). *How many colleges are in the U.S.?* Best Colleges. https://www.bestcolleges.com/blog/how-many-colleges-in-us/

Burgstahler, S. E. (2008). Universal design in higher education. In S. E. Burgstahler & R. C. Cory (Eds.), *Universal design in higher education: From principles to practice* (pp. 3–20). Harvard Education Press.

Burgstahler, S. E., & Cory, R. C. (2010). *Universal design in higher education: From principles to practice.* Harvard Education Press.

Cappex. (2022). *2021 Best colleges & universities for students with disabilities*. https://www.cappex.com/articles/match-and-fit/2021-best-colleges-universities-students-with-disabilities

Cavallari, D. (2022, September 1). *What is the typical organizational structure of a university?* Practical Adult Insights. https://www.practicaladultinsights.com/what-is-the-typical-organizational-structure-of-a-university.htm

Daisy, B. (2008). Deaf people in a hearing world: A qualitative study of cultural identity issues. *Master's Theses and Capstones*. https://scholars.unh.edu/thesis/73

Francis, G. L., Duke, J. M., Fujita, M., & Sutton, J. C. (2019). "It's a Constant Fight:" Experiences of college students with disabilities. *Journal of Postsecondary Education and Disability, 32*(3), 247–262.

Grant, B. (2022, May 12). *College guide for students with disabilities*. Best Colleges. https://www.bestcolleges.com/resources/students-with-disabilities/

Hagerty, O. (2017). Scaffolding as a model for academic assistance. In W. Nesbitt (Ed.), *Teaching students with learning disabilities at Beacon College: Lessons from the inside* (New edition) (pp. 27–34). Peter Lang.

Ivywise. (2022). *Colleges with programs for students with special needs*. https://www.ivywise.com/ivywise-knowledgebase/resources/article/colleges-with-programs-for-students-with-special-needs/

Johnson, E. (2019, December 20). Education deserts. *Inside Higher Education*. https://www.insidehighered.com/news/2019/12/20/access-higher-education-tilts-heavily-toward-urban-areas

Jordan, I. K. (2005). The Gallaudet Experience: Deafness and Disability. *PMLA, 120*(2), 625–627. http://www.jstor.org/stable/25486197

Landin, Z. (2021, May 10). The importance of disability cultural centers in higher education. *The Advocacy Monitor*. https://advocacymonitor.com/the-importance-of-disability-cultural-centers-in-higher-education/

National Center for College Students with Disabilities. (2022). https://www.nccsdonline.org/

Radder, K., & Smith, J. (2019). *"I'm not afraid to talk about my experiences."* Bennington Banner. Retrieved September 27, 2022, from https://www.benningtonbanner.com/uncategorized/im-not-afraid-to-talk-about-my-experiences/article_ce40f6ea-b1c0-520e-a5ed-8e0c1ee3ca5f.html

Sannes, J. (2008). *History of disability services for students (DSS): 1971–2007*. UND Departmental Histories 73. https://commons.und.edu/departmental-histories/73/

Shaewitz, D., & Crandall, J. R. (2020, October 19). Higher education's challenge: Disability inclusion on campus. *Higher Education Today*. https://www.higheredtoday.org/2020/10/19/higher-educations-challenge-disability-inclusion-campus/

Sniatecki, J., Perry, H. B., & Snell, L. H. (2015). Faculty attitudes and knowledge regarding college students with disabilities. *Journal of Postsecondary Education and Disability. 28*(3), 259–275. https://files.eric.ed.gov/fulltext/EJ1083837.pdf

StateUniversity.com. (2022). *Colleges and organizational structure of universities*. https://education.stateuniversity.com/pages/1859/Colleges-Universities-Organizational-Structure.html

Sullivan, M. (2021, October 25). POV: Higher ed institutions would benefit from hiring more faculty and staff with disabilities. *Boston University Today*. https://www.bu.edu/articles/2021/higher-ed-institutions-hiring-more-faculty-staff-with-disabilities/

Thatcher, L. (2022). *College: Not a 'one size fits all.'* Perkins School for the Blind. https://www.perkins.org/resource/which-colleges-may-be-right-for-me-as-visually-impaired-student/

University of Connecticut. (2022). *Center for students with disabilities*. https://csd.uconn.edu/history/#

University of Rochester. (2022). *Differences between high school and college accommodations*. Office of Disability Resources. https://rochester.edu/college/disability/incoming/accomodation-differences.html

Verywell Health. (2021, January 5). *5 U.S. and international colleges for the deaf.* https://www.verywellhealth.com/deaf-education-colleges-for-the-deaf-1048366

Wilson, R. (2022, July 15). *Resources and support for college students with disabilities*. Student Training and Education in Public Service. https://www.publicservicedegrees.org/resources/college-students-with-disabilities/

SECTION III

SPECIAL MISSION COLLEGES AND UNIVERSITIES

SPECIAL MISSION INSTITUTIONS

The last section of this text "Special Mission Institutions" explores the narrower mission-specific institutions that offer professional or character education for their student populations. This section "Special Mission Colleges" explores these different formats and classifications of American higher education institutional types which straddle gender or professionally-based institutions. For example, the chapters in this section explore the contributions of historical institutional types such as military and maritime colleges which are the only directly federally-funded higher education institutions.

In Chapter 13, Negrete and Tanaka describe the distinctive environment of art and design colleges. They do not identify performing arts or music conservatories but instead focus on institutions that focus on visual arts. This chapter demystifies the culture of art institutions with a special attention on the ways in which they are a privileged history that needs to be decolonized.

Strayhorn, in Chapter 14, offers a historical development of men's colleges. He profiles the institutions of Hampden-Sydney College, Morehouse College, and Wabash College, which are all different styles of men's colleges. Strayhorn offers the distinction of each institution's character and signature curricula. He offers questions about the potential ways in which men's colleges can offer inclusive environments.

Institutional Diversity in American Postsecondary Education, pp. 157–159

Copyright © 2024 by Information Age Publishing

www.infoagepub.com

All rights of reproduction in any form reserved.

158 SECTION III: SPECIAL MISSION COLLEGES AND UNIVERSITIES

In Chapter 15, Kortegast describes the history and evolution of women's colleges. In her chapter, she notes, "Historically, access was primarily for White, Christian, and wealthier women." However, this chapter expands on the future possibilities that women's colleges have on the identity and gender development of their students.

Gregory and Bullington in Chapter 16, deconstruct the rich history of faith-based institutions in the United States, which are acknowledged as the initial founding institutions of American higher education. The authors cite that there are over 1,000 colleges and universities in the United States with religious affiliations. There is also a subsection about faith-based 2-year institutions as well. This chapter helps its readers understand the diversity of organizational differences influenced largely by their institutional proximity to their faith orientation.

Chapter 17 by Shank et al. offers one of the most complete descriptions of the different kinds of military institutions, including maritime colleges. The authors also even identify 2-year institutions, which are military colleges as well. This chapter does not focus on Reserve Officer Training Corps (ROTC). One of the major strengths of this chapter is the way it describes the rank-and-file organization of military colleges.

In Chapter 18, Davis offers an emphasis on the development of occupational and technical colleges or career and technical education (CTE) in the United States. This chapter does not center on community colleges, which is a separate chapter in this text, but acknowledges that these institutions tend to be 2-year colleges that offer professional associate-level degrees. Davis focuses on the role of apprenticeships and other cooperative education as a distinguishing feature of these institutions.

Additionally, other special mission institutions exist with very distinctive curriculums, such as Deep Springs College, which is a liberal arts institution operated on a student self-governance model and focused on manual labor. St. John's College is another historic liberal arts college that can be described as a "Great Books" institution where students draw their learning only from an undergraduate curriculum rooted in the classics and philosophy. Minerva University is a unique, highly selective liberal arts institution with a seminar-focused curriculum. Minerva has a very rigorous institutional curriculum where students rotate across different campuses each year around the world, including Europe and South America, to complete cooperative education experiences and a major capstone project similar to an undergraduate thesis. These three institutions highlight the vast differences across institutions and how curricula shape institutional character and student experiences.

Thus, this section has some limitations as the editors of this text were unable to find dedicated space for other special mission institutions, such as work colleges and music conservatories. These institutions offer distinctive

Section III: Special Mission Colleges and Universities   159

opportunities for professional education. Music conservatories such as the Eastman School of Music or Julliard offer unique performing arts environments which reinforce professional artist identity with very strong arts management and entrepreneurship programs. Work colleges such as Berea or Blackburn mandate all students participate in work-service experiences which are integrated into the college curriculum, rather than co-curricular experiences such as service learning. Students who attend these institutions receive significant scholarships and gain hands-on experience. Yet, the authors in this section have done an admirable job in complicating the wide array of special mission institutions within American higher education. These different styles of education and educational environments are truly congruent with what John Thelin described as "diversity of choice."

CHAPTER 13

ART AND DESIGN INSTITUTIONS

Nicholas E. Negrete
Otis College of Art and Design

Yoi Tanaka
College of Design in Pasadena

INTRODUCTION

Today, art and design colleges are demonstrating a focus on decolonizing their curricula, diversifying their student and faculty bodies, and creating more accessible opportunities for students from all backgrounds to pursue an art and design education. Decolonization of the art and design education is about decentering the Western canon of art and design and infusing other ways of knowing, including Indigenous perspectives, highlighting Black, Indigenous, and people of color (BIPOC) artists and designers, and other non-western approaches to art education. Much more work needs to be done in these areas to transform existing trends including more active recruitment of full-time faculty of color, increased retention and graduation among students of color, and enhanced faculty development to improve course curricula while also helping faculty create a sense of belonging within their classrooms.

This chapter will explore the history, curriculum, and professional contexts of art and design institutions. We center on diverse identities and

Institutional Diversity in American Postsecondary Education, pp. 161–175
Copyright © 2024 by Information Age Publishing
www.infoagepub.com
All rights of reproduction in any form reserved.

critique the ways in which they can be further developed, particularly to center student success. We conclude with future directions to consider future directions and ask these art and design institutions to reflect on their privileged past to make a more equitable future. We begin with a brief overview of their historical evolution.

HISTORY

Art and design colleges have a unique history within the context of higher education. We can reference art academies as early as the 1600s which took the form of more of an apprenticeship model, where a master artist (predominately European and male) would take on several apprentices and engage them while demonstrating their proficiency within their area of focus (Cole, 1983). It was not until the 19th century that art schools and small art programs within colleges would emerge within higher education (Efland, 1990). While this chapter is focused specifically on art and design institution, we will often use "art school" as shorthand, but it is an important note that "art school' is used as a term to refer to all those sites or departments within post-secondary art institutions where art is taught" (Houghton, 2016). Many art and design colleges started out as for-profit entities and served the privileged and those who had the cultural and social capital to engage and navigate within the art world. Not unlike other higher education institutions, art and design colleges primarily served those from elite and privileged backgrounds, and it was considered an area of expertise for whom only a small few had the resources to engage.

It was not until decades following World War I, that there was a burst in the teaching of visual arts in major colleges and universities, which led to a major shift in the development of professional art and design schools such as Pratt Institute, Rhode Island School of Design, Otis College of Art and Design, and many others (Efland, 1990). As professional art and design colleges emerged, a consortium was developed to connect these institutions across the United States and Canada, which is today known as the Association of Independent Colleges in Art and Design (AICAD). Prior to AICAD, many art and design schools were associated with the National Portfolio Day Association (NPDA) which was created in 1978 and had a primary focus to support portfolio day events in order to assist in the preparation and promotion of students enrolling in art and design institutions (National Portfolio Day Association [NPDA], 2021).

Over the course of many decades, there were significant curricular models from the apprenticeship approach, as noted above. Examples include technical skills and specific techniques, to more expressive forms of art making to conceptual approaches to art, and to what we now know as professionalism of art and design, where "the professional curriculum is tied tightly to a belief that education should be instrumental and be aligned to enabling students on leaving to earn a living and contribute to a nation's economy" (Houghton, 2016, p. 115). Many of today's art and design colleges have strong aspects of their curricula and co-curricula that place a focus on career preparation within the creative economy, with a focus in entrepreneurship and creating a career-oriented plan that provides students with some sense of economic promise within their professional craft. While the professionalism of art and design may seem more apparent today, especially due to the public expectation of a return on investment for an art education, there continues to be many historical aspects of the art and design curricula that are woven throughout today's art student's educational journey. This includes making art for art's sake, approaching art through a conceptual lens, and focusing on foundational skills such as life drawing, color theory, and form and space, to name a few.

In addition to the large four-year colleges and universities establishing art disciplines, there was a need and desire to have more established professional art schools that focused solely on a holistic approach to arts education, such as those within the AICAD consortium. These college's focused on a curriculum that supports studio practice as well as having a liberal arts and sciences curricula in order for students to be able to connect theory to creative practice and be able to understand historical and current societal issues that help them become informed, educated and forward thinking artists and designers. Many art and design colleges offer Bachelor of Fine Arts (BFA) and Master of Fine Arts (MFA) degrees, with some offering Bachelor of Science (BS) degrees such as ArtCenter in Pasadena, CA as well as BBA degrees in design management such as Parsons. Certificate programs have also become more prevalent across art and design colleges, allowing students to specialize in a specific area, or to help current artists and designers learn new technologies and techniques that bring more relevance. What is most unique among these types of institutions is that students can live and learn among an entire artist community, where all students and faculty have a shared purpose and passion. The art and design student community is one where everyone is laser focused on their craft, creativity is palpable, and student life includes "making" together, and experiencing co-curricular activities that support, enhance, and further affirm their artist identity.

Much has changed in the form of an evolving curriculum, which is marked by the initial apprenticeship approach, to a more holistic approach that includes a liberal arts education coupled with formal studio practice, in addition to more diverse faculty and expanded reach to students from all backgrounds. However, what remains the same is the level of privilege that exists within art education, more specifically, socioeconomic privilege where students and families from high income backgrounds have the resources to support pre-college programs, allowing their student to be in a strong position to attend art school. Additionally, most art and design colleges continue to be predominately white, along with a high enrollment of international students. There continues to be a lack of representation of domestic students of color, and this can be attributed to a variety of factors, from families not understanding the value of art education, to a limited and skewed view about what careers opportunities exist within art and design, as well as the ongoing myth of the "starving artist." All art schools continue to struggle with diversifying their student and faculty demographics, and depending on where one grows up, art education may not be accessible in their pre-K–12 educational experiences. In fact, white students are overrepresented in the arts, with Black and Latinx students being underrepresented (Elpus, 2014).

ORGANIZATION STRUCTURE AND CULTURE

Many art and design colleges are within the small college consortium, with the largest AICAD school having an enrollment of approximately 5,000 students, and the smaller schools sitting between 500 and 1,000 students. The small art and design school experience tends to be intimate in nature, with small class sizes, especially in studio classes. Given that the majority of courses are studio based, students make many one-on-one connections to faculty, and there is a focus on individual growth and development of the artists or designers' individual voice. Within these specialized small schools there are many of the same divisions and departments we see at larger schools, however it is not uncommon to see pairings of focus areas such as enrollment management and student affairs within one division. There may also be several one-to-two-person offices. While many of these schools are private colleges with a high price tag, their organizational structure is designed to maximize their financial capacity, requiring staff and faculty to wear several hats in order to effectively serve their student body. Resources are limited, both human and financial, and there is a huge emphasis on collaboration across several departments both within academic affairs as well as student affairs. The size and specialization of art and design schools have financial implications, often requiring donors to underwrite various operations, increasing tuition costs, and possibly create facilities fees in order to remain financially healthy (Langlois, 2020).

It is quite common to have a Student Life office oversee student organizations, in addition to orientation programs, and even commencement. Academic advising areas may have registration and financial aid collapsed within one department in order to serve students holistically and have cross trained staff members who can serve students in a "one stop" fashion. Depending on the college, you may experience a very flat structure with easy access to the President and Provost, while others may serve in a more traditional sense with a clear hierarchy. What is most common across most art and design colleges is the fact that departments will have combined services, and divisional areas are small enough where staff members will gain more exposure to other functional areas in such an intimate manner. For instance, an entry level or mid-level student affairs professional may likely be exposed to conversations on enrollment projections, retention and persistence, and have some knowledge of how other functional areas impact their specific department.

Within academic affairs, there are some art and design colleges that continue with the tradition of a "foundation year" program, where all first-year students have a similar curriculum they engage in prior to being able to declare a major. The philosophy behind this is to ensure all students have the basic foundational knowledge of art and design from color theory to life drawing, form and space, and other traditional art and design curricular components. Within this model, a student has only 3 years in their actual major, with much to learn over the course of their six semesters. Other art and design colleges have designed their curricular structure where students can go directly into their major and begin a specific focus right away, whether that is in graphic design, product design, fashion, digital media, game design, architecture, and so on. The difference between these two types of curricular models is essentially the academic philosophy the college is functioning under and how they imagine their students' achieving the learning outcomes outlined through their specific approach.

In terms of majors or programs offered at art and design institutions, there will be variations based on the size, location and specialty of the institution. According to AICAD enrollment figures, the most popular undergraduate programs offered at AICAD institutions are Graphic Design, Illustration, Fine Art/Studio Arts, Animation, and Photography and Film (AICAD, 2021). Some institutions will have larger programs divided into more specialized areas of emphasis or tracks. Program offerings are also dependent on the location of the institution, which plays into faculty availability to teach courses, internship and job opportunities. For example, Otis College of Art and Design in Los Angeles offers a unique Bachelor of Fine Arts program in Toy Design. This is possible because eight of the biggest toy companies in the world are headquartered or have offices within a short distance of Otis's campus (White, 2012). At the graduate level, you will find further specialization and most colleges will elect to have master's programs in the undergraduate degrees where they attract the most students. On occasion, the undergraduate Chair will also serve as the graduate Chair for their same discipline. At the graduate level, programs tend to be smaller than at the undergraduate level and often offer individual studio spaces with larger workspaces to build community amongst their students. In addition, many art and design colleges will use Extension departments to prepare students for degree programs, emphasizing portfolio development in the different disciplines that align with their programs offered in the Undergraduate and Graduate departments. Youth programs, certificate programs, travel-based programs, and executive, professional development programs are also areas where Extension will build programming to increase revenue and engage parents and alumni.

As previously mentioned in the history of these types of institutions, many of the not-for-profit art and design colleges are under the umbrella of the Association of Independent Colleges in Art and Design (AICAD), which was formed in 1991 and whose mission is "to help strengthen the member colleges individually and collectively, and to inform the public about these colleges and universities and the value of studying the arts and design (AICAD, 2022). This consortium of colleges works together to enhance the value of an art and design education, providing professional development opportunities such as annual conferences, diversity and equity symposiums, increasing visibility of art and design colleges and promoting a holistic educational experience with a specialized focus. All these colleges are fully accredited by their regional accreditors as well as some are accredited by the National Association of Schools of Art and Design (NASAD), further validating their commitment to a standard of excellence within art and design education. Every art and design school is different and has various foci on the specific art and design disciplines it offers, but their overall profile as small colleges produces a similar organizational structure with many small departments working collaboratively to serve the whole student. There is a shared goal of helping each student develop their creative voice, gain technical skills with career readiness in mind, to graduate successfully, and contribute to the creative economy, both locally and globally.

Art and design colleges will employ staff and faculty who identify as "creatives," someone who creates whether that be art, music, writing, animation or another practice. Within the ranks of the community, you will find a substantial number of staff members who are creatives maintaining their artistic practice outside of work and the majority of faculty consisting of professional practicing artists and designers teaching as adjunct faculty. This creates a culture on campus that is a bit atypical in higher education, with staff and faculty having a shared common interest in artistic creation and an appreciation of the arts. Many art and design institutions often permit staff and faculty to access shops, labs and making facilities on campus, as well as providing opportunities to take courses with tuition remission, which helps to attract creatives into various roles.

Having this artistic perspective represented in various positions across campus works to the advantage of the colleges, ensuring that there are some creative staff members working with creative students and representing their perspectives. They tend to approach problem solving creatively and are less afraid to experiment, innovate, and experiment. It also can present challenges for institutions who are employing staff in administrative roles who may not have the traditional higher education or administrative experience on their resume and require additional professional development and coaching. An interesting division sometimes exists, whereby an administrative staff person's background in art and design can give them further legitimacy when working with the academic side of the institution, and a lack of creative experience can make someone feel like they have no authority to give input in certain conversations.

Department Chairs are typically distinguished in their creative field, which also means that they typically wield a significant amount of power on campuses and a high degree of influence on policies and procedures. Within these departments, there is also a degree of influence based on whether they are meeting their enrollment goals and their stature in their field, the industry or the art world.

Fundraising ability and the attractiveness to donors is also a component of Chair favorability, as well as their tenure at the institution and how resource heavy their department is. Some institutions will rotate department chairs on a cycle and others will be at the helm until they decide to retire or part ways with the institution. On the academic side, there is also a dichotomy between the humanities, sciences and art history department(s) and the studio departments, as some academic leaders value the approximately 35% of the curriculum devoted to the humanities and sciences more than others (National Association of Colleges of Art and Design, 2022, p. 86). Art and design colleges share similar aspects of institutional culture with larger colleges, but there are some nuanced differences that make working and learning at an art and design school extremely unique and invigorating. More specifically, 65% of the overall curricula is generally focused on the studio aspect, with 35% being focused on liberal arts and sciences, making much more of an emphasis on the studio practice.

STUDENT SUCCESS AND POPULATIONS

Student access to art and design schools are limited by multiple factors including art and design skill development, as evidenced by the portfolio, the high cost of tuition of art and design colleges and their expensive, urban geographic locations. These accessibility factors drive student demographics at art and design colleges toward affluent U.S. and foreign students, predominantly from Asian countries, who can afford the preparation costs as well as the tuition and living costs of art and design education.

In order to apply to an art and design school, students must prepare a portfolio of creative work. At colleges where students will enter directly into their chosen major, this portfolio might be expected to be advanced in terms of skill, concept, and ability. Other institutions, those mostly with first-year foundation programs, have an open-ended portfolio requirement, only specifying the number of works that must be included, but otherwise leaving it open for the student to select the works to include. Both types of admission requirements hinder access for students that do not have the resources to build their skills to the level needed to develop a strong portfolio. For this reason, art and design schools are "highly biased toward those students from privileged socioeconomic and ethnic backgrounds" (Houghton, 2016, p. 116).

There are several reasons that students from privileged backgrounds are more able to gain access to art and design colleges. One aspect is the training that is required to develop a portfolio and the access to visual arts education in public secondary schools. National studies in art education, although limited, show that access to art courses varies significantly based on socioeconomic factors. Only 80% of schools with high poverty rates offered visual arts courses, which compared to 95% of schools with the lowest poverty concentration (Parsad & Spiegelman, 2012, p. 34). With this inequality in access, socioeconomically disadvantaged students are often left to build their skills and portfolio independently through free resources online or, if available in their area, arts non-profit groups that provide supplemental art education.

Additionally, it often takes successive courses in the visual arts to develop the advanced skills and practice needed to create a successful portfolio, so the limited number of courses offered in public schools are rarely sufficient. Only 40% of public schools offered five or more different courses in the visual arts, which leaves a significant skill gap for students who must rely on school courses to develop their portfolio for entry (Parsad & Spiegelman, 2012, p. 10). In addition, the number of public schools offering visual arts education continues to decline.

Similar to standardized test preparation, there are a number of organizations and consultants in the business of helping students to prepare portfolios for their college applications. Access to these types of services is often limited to the students whose families can afford the additional cost and live in places where they have access to these services: "millions of parents seek opportunities for their children to study the arts outside school, but millions more are not inclined to do so, cannot afford to, or lack convenient access to those opportunities" (Rabkin & Hedberg, 2011). The offerings of these businesses range from group courses and workshops to one-on-one tutoring and mentoring. They may include services on application preparation, writing an artist statement, photographing physical artwork, and recommending extracurricular activities and internships.

Creating a portfolio is not simply putting together a collection of approximately 10–20 images, but photographing the work, designing the slides (if required), editing, writing about each piece, and curating the organization of the work. Internationally, in countries such as China and Korea, portfolio preparation is a big business and often the graduates of American art and design schools are employed at companies that help students develop work that their alma maters would have liked to see. The average student attending a public high school without additional support and guidance is extremely disadvantaged in this process of putting together a portfolio. In addition, the portfolio is typically the most critical aspect of the application and can trump the academic record of the student in the admission review.

The portfolio plays such a critical role in the student gaining access to the institution, but also factors into the cost of education if they are accepted. High tuition costs at art and design schools are often a result of the expensive cities these schools are located in, their need for extensive specialized facilities, equipment, and small class sizes necessitated by the studio environment (Seltzer, 2019). One counterbalance to the high tuition costs for students are institutional scholarships. However, the portfolio still plays a strong determining factor for awarding these scholarships, which favors the privileged students who could afford portfolio preparation assistance. Some institutional scholarships will factor financial need and diversity as well as portfolio and GPA.

The demographics of student populations on art and design school campuses vary depending on the geographic location, size and cost to attend. Black or African American populations are underrepresented with the majority of AICAD institutions falling below 10% of their total fall 2020 population and the highest being University of the Arts, which has 21% of their full-time student population identifying as Black or African American (National Center for Education Statistics [NCES], 2021). Surprisingly, white students are underrepresented at many AICAD institutions located outside of the Midwest and Northeast compared to the national average and Asian students are overrepresented at the majority of institutions.

Hispanic students are mostly underrepresented as well, except for Otis College of Art and Design and Laguna College of Art and Design, which both reported 21% of full-time students identifying as Hispanic. High international student populations can be found at art and design institutions in major cities such as New York, Los Angeles or San Francisco. Based on IPEDS data for fall 2020, the full-time student population at the School of Visual Arts in New York City was 54% international students, compared to 1% at the Kansas City Art Institute in Missouri. The interest in pursuing higher education in the United States at art and design institutions has grown steadily pre-pandemic, with the greatest number of students originating from China. In 2020, there were reported 24,960 Chinese students studying in Fine or Applied Arts in the United States, followed by 5,877 Korean students (Institute of International Education, 2020). Due to the financial certification process that international students must go through to apply for a F-1 student visa, the majority of international students are of means to pay the high cost of art and design school tuition and the cost of living in some of the most expensive cities in the United States. They are also able to afford the costs of English language preparation courses and portfolio preparation assistance. Every art and design school wants all their students to succeed with robust student enrollment, retention and persistence goals. However, they must address the inequities that cause barriers for successful preparation and academic success.

PROFESSIONAL CONTEXT

Due to their small size, many art and design institutions have staff and faculty who serve multiple roles at their institutions and have positions that cover a wide range of responsibilities. Managerial level positions often require long hours to meet an overflowing to-do list with varied responsibilities stemming from student-centered work, diversity programs/ initiatives, enrollment challenges and being asked to serve on multiple committees, working groups and task forces. Most art and design institutions are not financially well resourced due to their tuition dependent status, in addition to the fiscal challenges of maintaining an abundance of space for studios, facilities, shops and labs, coupled with the necessity of studio classes needing to be capped at a small size. These fiscal challenges place a heavy burden on staff, who often manage a plethora of responsibilities, which only grew with the onslaught of challenges surrounding the COVID-19 pandemic. While committee and working group responsibilities lead to more collaboration, innovation, and addressing the student experience from multiple perspectives, these commitments add to the day-to-day responsibilities; hence, much of the staff's individual workload occurs after hours. Working with art and design students is often hands on, with staff and faculty making efforts to attend exhibitions, gallery openings, film screenings, fashion shows, open studios, pop-up shops and other events during the evenings and weekends to support students and faculty colleagues.

Amongst art and design college campuses, there are those that exist in the middle of large urban cities and those that have a more traditional

Art and Design Institutions 171

campus feel. The urban campuses of colleges like the School of Visual Arts in New York City or the School of the Art Institute of Chicago in Chicago exist within the city itself and have a less unified feel than colleges such as Otis College of Art and Design in Los Angeles or Pratt Institute in Brooklyn. While admissions offices can promote the "city as their campus" for prospective students, for staff it can be more difficult to collaborate and connect with other staff members when you feel siloed in separate buildings within a dense city environment. Interactions are more planned, and it can be more difficult to get to know staff members in other departments that you have little scheduled interaction with. Those art and design colleges with a traditional campus often feel like small villages where everyone knows each other and you regularly run into someone, oftentimes have impromptu meetings and ideas for collaboration.

Many of the art and design institutions are highly tuition dependent institutions, which relies on the contributions of many across campus to put forth effort to attract and enroll new students. No longer is enrollment and retention the sole work of Admissions and Enrollment Management. Collaboration across campus is required to successfully enroll each new class with the goal of retaining students and ensuring their persistence toward graduation. It takes the entire campus to ensure that enrollment goals are met each year, including recruitment workshops by faculty, personalized outreach to students from department chairs, events with the President and Provost, tours led by students, alumni panels from Career Services, on trend social media campaigns from Communications and Marketing, and CRM technology buildouts from IT. For staff outside of enrollment management, these added tasks can feel like an additional burden on an already overflowing list of priorities. However, the instability of many small, private art and design colleges, like the merger of Pacific Northwest College of Art and Willamette University or the planned closure of San Francisco Art Institute, requires everyone to get involved to protect their uncertain future.

One additional reason that many art and design institutions feel inadequately staffed is the difficulty in recruiting and retaining staff. Many art and design institutions look to hire staff with both creative and administrative experience, which can make it difficult to find the right fit for certain roles. The job description for an admissions counselor position at an art and design school will typically require an art background or BFA degree to ensure that the counselor has the experience to effectively evaluate an applicant's portfolio of creative work and offer constructive feedback to help them improve. A career services role will often require knowledge and experience working with creative industries and the ability to help know portfolio standards in a variety of positions and roles. An instructional designer will need to understand the unique challenges of both studio and liberal arts courses. This professional experience, coupled with creative experience, is both an asset to institutions and a hindrance in terms of recruitment. It also means that retaining staff can be challenging, especially when they have multiple modes of income generation they are pursuing or when they decide their creative path must take precedence. Many staff also leave to pursue further education, as MFA degrees are commonly required to advance to the next stage of their career. The small art school can be very flat organizationally, so the opportunity for upward mobility within one's professional career can also mean seeking those opportunities elsewhere.

The creative students that build their skills on these art and design campuses make incredible work, which is often on display in the hallways, galleries, runways, outdoor spaces and video screens across campus. Students are unique and vibrant, often finding growth in these supportive campus communities and the studios become their sanctuaries. Unlike other campuses where you may find more students studying at home or in the library or in the quad, art students are always on campus to use studio facilities, often late into the night. This makes for an inspiring, creative and supportive environment to work in. Seeing these students at work, and their creative output, are visual reminders that encourage staff to come to work each day and put in those long hours.

FUTURE CONSIDERATIONS AND DIRECTIONS

It is imperative that art and design schools begin to reflect on their deep history of privilege, limited scope in curricular and pedagogical practices, and the lack of diversity across faculty and student demographics to in order to truly commit to actions that prioritize access, equity, and inclusion across all dimensions of their institutions. This includes the following:

1. Examining and addressing rank and promotion policies for faculty to further identify areas of bias as faculty are reviewed and evaluated for their service and creative practice.
2. Improving efforts to create a more inclusive critique culture pertaining to student learning, where student work is evaluated in ways that do not reinforce western ideals and Eurocentric approaches to art, but rather allow room for other ways of knowing.
3. Examine and revise admissions practices that consider the varied access to art programs in pre-K–12 education and develop measures in the admissions evaluation process to account for the uneven experiences prospective students may have, particularly from historically marginalized communities.

Art and Design Institutions 173

4. Staff equity issues across the campus must be evaluated in terms of the depth and breadth of responsibilities as compared to their counterparts, with a focus on increasing more equity in workload and pay.
5. Address the financial need of a diverse student population and increase scholarship programs to offset the large tuition costs.
6. Partner with various industry leaders in the creative economy who support diversity, equity and inclusion efforts, and create career pipelines that will improve diverse representation in art and design.

In order for such institutions to move toward equity and true inclusion, they must acknowledge that historically "they privilege a finite set of methodologies, ontologies, and socialities, shaping and defining artistic production" (Langlois, 2020, p. 200) and expand beyond the western canon of art and design curricula to include more BIPOC artists and designers, Indigenous ways of knowing, and an active interrogation of the traditional European artist tradition. Additionally, faculty must be equipped to teach with inclusion at the forefront and be challenged to critically assess their curriculum to ensure it is representative of today's student demographics, as well as current sociocultural issues. "As student demographics continue to grow and shift, becoming more racially, culturally and ethnically diverse, art educators must begin to more thoughtfully consider how we may develop and maintain a comprehensive art education discourse in which inclusion is a primary objective" (Acuff, 2013, p. 219). Faculty development requires human and fiscal resources, and in this case, it would benefit art and design colleges to consider how they may allocate additional resources or reshuffle their budgetary areas in order to support curricular and pedagogical enhancements that are aligned with a commitment to diversity, equity, inclusion, and belonging.

Prospective art and design students must be given a fair opportunity to be able to develop and submit portfolios that demonstrate their promise. Admission departments must emphasize a holistic approach that considers the whole student, not just grades and portfolio scoring. Art and design colleges can benefit from investing in their local community, providing pre-college workshops and programs that are free and/or low-cost, which can in turn open opportunities and accessibility for those from underrepresented communities. Today's college students must be given more agency, allowing them to construct and center their lived experiences and move toward creative action within their own practice (Freedman, 2007).

Faculty at art and design colleges continue to be predominately white, lacking in racial and ethnic diversity. Specific and actionable steps must be thoroughly outlined if we are to diversify our hiring practices, interrogate our own biases, including our bias toward a specific academic framework. Colleges should inspire and encourage new ways and new directions for faculty to be empowered to revolutionize their curriculum in order to meet today's students' needs and experiences. This means being more interdisciplinary in their approaches and moving toward helping students articulate how they use and value art, and what statements they are making about their art socially and politically. In essence, we must leverage more cultural complexity in order to bring more marginalized voices to the center, creating a critical multicultural art education for students (Acuff, 2013).

Finally, if we are to commit to a more diverse and inclusive campus community, we must address financial access and affordability. Art and design colleges are notorious for being some of the most expensive colleges to attend, due to several key factors: (1) a commitment to keep the student to faculty ratio low in studios, (2) high cost of location and rentals of buildings, and (3) remaining competitive with their caliber of facilities that provide students with state-of-the-art equipment. Prospective students who are privileged enough to access the social and cultural capital it requires developing their own brand as an artist and designer are more prepared than those who come from communities where art education is not accessible or valued. No longer can we write mission statements that talk about our commitment to diversity and inclusion. It is time for these words to become radical action to deconstruct the curricula, affirmatively hire diverse faculty, and provide our students with the opportunity to experience success while valuing their individual experiences.

DISCUSSION QUESTIONS

- What barriers must we address in order to improve upon and increase the number of historically marginalized students in our art and design colleges?
- How can art schools address the uneven experiences and lack of access to arts curricula within the pre-K–12 educational landscape?
- What are alternative financial models we may consider sustaining small art and design colleges while also finding students in need?
- How might art and design institutions begin to actualize a process of decolonizing their course curricula throughout all art and design focus areas? (e.g., fine arts, fashion design, dance, graphic design, environmental design, etc.).

REFERENCES

Acuff, J. B. (2013). Discursive underground: Re-transcribing the history of art education using critical multicultural education. *Visual Inquiry: Learning & Teaching Art, 2*(3), 219–231. https://doi.org/10.1386/vi.2.3.219_1

AICAD. (2022, May 6). *What is AICAD? Mission and purpose*. https://www.aicad.org/about/#:~:text=MISSION%20AND%20PURPOSE&text=Founded%20in%201991%2C%20the%20mission,studying%20the%20arts%20and%20design

Cole, B. (1983). *The Renaissance artist at work: From Pisano to Titan*. Harper and Row.

Efland, A. D. (1990). *A history of art education: Intellectual and social currents in teaching the visual arts*. Teachers College Press.

Elpus, K. (2014). *Arts education as a pathway to college: College admittance, selectivity, and completion by arts and non-arts students*. https://www.americansforthearts.org/sites/default/files/artspathwaytocollege.pdf

Freedman, K. (2007). Artmaking/troublemaking: Creativity, policy, and leadership in art education. *Studies in Art Education, 48*(2), 204–217. https://www.jstor.org/stable/25475820

Houghton, N. (2016). Six into one: The contradictory art school curriculum and how it came about. *The International Journal of Art & Design Education, 35*(1), 107–120. https://doi.org/10.1111/jade.1203

Institute of International Education. (2020). *Open doors 2020 online: Report on international educational exchange*. https://www.iie.org/Research-and-Insights/Open-Doors

Langlois, J. (2020). Invisible hospitalities of the art school. *Public, 31*(61), 196–207. https://doi.org/https://doi.org/10.1386/public_00030_1\

National Association of Colleges of Art and Design. (2022). *NASAD Handbook 2021–22*. https://nasad.arts-accredit.org/wp-content/uploads/sites/3/2022/04/AD-2021-22-Handbook-Final-04-08-2022.pdf

National Center for Education Statistics. (2021). *Integrated Postsecondary Education Data System* (IPEDS). https://nces.ed.gov/ipeds/datacenter/InstitutionProfile.aspx

Parsad, B., & Spiegelman, M (2012). *Arts education in public elementary and secondary schools: 1999–2000 and 2009–10*. National Center for Education Statistics, Institute of Education Sciences, U.S. Department of Education. Washington, DC. http://nces.ed.gov/pubs2012/2012014rev.pdf

Rabkin, N., & Hedberg, E .C.(2011). *Arts education in America: What the declines mean for arts participation*. https://www.arts.gov/sites/default/files/2008-SPPA-ArtsLearning.pdf

Seltzer, R. (2019). As art schools show signs of stress, what can liberal arts colleges learn? *Inside Higher Education*. Retrieved February 7, 2019. https://www.insidehighered.com/print/news/2019/02/07/art-schools-show-signs-stress-what-can-liberal-arts-colleges-learn

White, R. D. (2012, December) Toy-making is serious business in Southern California. *LA Times*. https://www.latimes.com/business/la-xpm-2012-dec-22-la-fi-socal-enterprise-toys-20121223-story.html

CHAPTER 14

MEN'S COLLEGES IN THE UNITED STATES

A Tale of Three Cities

Terrell L. Strayhorn
Virginia Union University

Institutional diversity is a distinguishing feature of higher education in the United States (U.S.). Though not as formal and federally structured as other countries, the U.S. *system of higher education* is best characterized as a loosely-coupled confederation of over 4,300 colleges and universities (C&Us). Well over half of all postsecondary institutions in the U.S. are two-year community colleges with open access missions, awarding mostly associates (AA) degrees and technical certificates to students looking for workforce development, upskilling, and preparation to transfer to a 4-year institution (Cain, 1999; Cohen & Brawer, 1996). According to recent reports (Strayhorn, 2021), there are 103 historically Black colleges and universities (HBCUs) today, educating over 300,000 students collectively. That HBCUs represent just 3% of the entire enterprise yet educate over 20% of African Americans earning bachelor's degrees demonstrates how these "national treasures" outpunch their weight class and contribute to reducing inequity in broader society (Saunders & Nagle, 2018).

Over time, the system of higher education in the U.S. grew to include new different institutional types as a broader effort to accommodate new learners. For instance, the 1920s were marked by the admission of growing numbers of women at women's college such as Wellesley and Spelman

---

Institutional Diversity in American Postsecondary Education, pp. 177–191
Copyright © 2024 by Information Age Publishing
www.infoagepub.com
All rights of reproduction in any form reserved.

178 T. L. STRAYHORN

College, along with other teaching or "normal" schools (Stoecker & Pascarella, 1991; Thelin, 2004). Often overlooked in the evolutionary history of U.S. higher education are seminaries and schools for the deaf and hard of hearing, such as Galludet in Washington, DC (Gordon, 1997; Parker, 2015). Indeed, institutional diversity is a distinctive feature of U.S. higher education that marks it off from other countries around the globe and such variety reflects a deeper underlying philosophy of expanding college access for all students (Tierney & Hagedorn, 2002).

Not all higher education institutions (HEIs) however, can be easily classified according to their admissions criteria, degree offerings, or the predominant racial composition of campus, as *some HEIs* cut across these categories. For instance, there are 13 historically Black community colleges (HBCCs) in the U.S. that together enroll approximately 50,000 students annually (Elliott et al., 2019); with two exceptions, HBCCs are public institutions and almost half are located in a single state (Alabama). There are 10 HBCUs designated as research (R2) universities including Howard University, Southern University, Morgan State University, Tennessee State University, and Jackson State University, among others (Strayhorn, 2022).

As a final, and important, example there are three all-male[1] HEIs in the U.S.—Hampden Sydney College (Virginia), Morehouse College (Georgia), and Indiana's Wabash College[2] (in alpha order)—each distinct in its own way. For instance, Hampden-Sydney is the 10th oldest HEI in the U.S., whereas Morehouse College is a private, 4-year liberal arts college located in Atlanta, the state's capital city with nearly 500,000 people living within city limits. Though few in number nowadays, men's colleges represent an important segment of the U.S. higher education enterprise. Before delving into details about men's colleges in the U.S., historical foundations and evolution of this institutional type are discussed in the next section.

HISTORY

In many senses, *most* HEIs in the U.S. began as men's colleges. With the founding of Harvard College—now, *University*[3]—in 1636, higher education in the U.S. was established to educate and train the *sons* of wealthy White families as statesmen (i.e., politicians) and clergy (i.e., church leaders). Evidence of this social reality abounds. For instance, a *New England First Fruits* pamphlet printed in 1643 is one of the earliest known *written* summaries of Harvard College's mission and key aspects of its 17th century campus life. Readers will be struck by the narrowly circumscribed curriculum (e.g., politics, ethics) and almost-exclusive use of masculine pronouns, "men," and other such references.

Men's Colleges in the United States 179

Not only was Harvard College *founded for* the personal, political, and ministerial development of White, wealthy *men* for the Massachusetts Bay Colony, but the nation's oldest HEI was *named after* its first benefactor, a White Puritan clergy*man* John Harvard (Thelin, 2004). Indeed, "the founding of Harvard College ... form[s] the first chapter of higher education in the United States and a vital part of American social history (Morison, 1998, p. xii). Modeled largely after early universities in Europe, Harvard's curriculum, culture (i.e., customs, traditions), and organizational structure has had a profound influence on the development, expansion and evolution of the nation's higher education enterprise (Morison, 1998), especially at the last remaining men's colleges.

As the nation's first HEI, so to speak, it is important to note Harvard's close patterning after European models of admissions criteria, degree requirements, and curriculum, resembling Cambridge and Oxford. Though over half of Harvard's all-male graduates in the 17th century became ministers, Harvard never functioned as a theological school.[4] The general curriculum focused on ancient texts, humane letters (i.e., rhetoric, logic) from the Renaissance, articles of the Reformation, as well as ethics and politics (Schmidt, 1957). Interestingly, Latin was the language of instruction and Harvard's first students were expected to arrive *well-versed* in Latin grammar, which provided a strong foundation for following the prescribed plan of study in Greek and Hebrew (Morison, 1998). In lieu of problem-based learning, lecture, and groupwork, recitation was the standard mode of instruction (Blackburn & Conrad, 1986), although relatively little explicit attention was given to aligning teaching style (*pedagogy*) with the content of the curriculum early on.

The curriculum reflected aspects of the campus culture at the first all-male HEIs in the U.S. For example, Harvard's curriculum was structured to encourage unfettered competition as men wrestled in the classroom to outperform, outshine, and outlast their highly talented male peers. The development of certain fields, like engineering, as a profession in the 1880s helped define Lehigh University's male identity (Forcier, 2004).

Campus cultural and performing arts were developed to usher in a humanizing and civilizing force at Harvard and other early all-male colleges. For instance, culture, art, and music provided an alternative to the hard-drinking, misogynistic, anti-academic culture of fraternities that had become an expected reality for first-year students at Dartmouth (Forcier, 2004). Similar advances were made at schools like Lehigh and Boston College.

Stemming from a larger, growing, effort of C&Us to focus on the psychological well-being of students developed in response to wartime service, early men's colleges, like Harvard, established certain support services. For example, Dartmouth established its Office of Student Counseling in

1952 in an attempt to meet students' mental and physical health needs (Forcier, 2004).

Since the founding of Harvard to now, there has been a drastic change in men's colleges as they have almost disappeared, with three exceptions: Hampden-Sydney College, Morehouse College, and Wabash College. It was during the forty years following the 1920s that most men's colleges opened their doors to women for financial and social reasons (Whitney, 2000). For example, two of the forces driving the move toward co-education (hereafter, *co-ed*) were that the vast majority of males preferred being around women *and* colleges were able to increase their revenue via greater enrollment, which positioned them to be more academically competitive (Morison, 1998). Despite these positive aims, it is important to note that early men's colleges did little to prepare for women and early women students reported hostile, unwelcoming, and oppressive campus environments (Graham, 1978; Walsh & Walsh, 1982). Indeed, "coeducation did not necessarily bring educational equity for men and women. Physical access to an institution did not mean that women were represented in positions of power, that policies were changed to reflect a more diverse constituent, or even that they were nominally accepted as equals" (Poulson & Miller-Bernal, 2004, p. ix).

ORGANIZATIONAL STRUCTURE AND CULTURE

Hampden-Sydney College (H-SC)

H-SC is led by a President who serves as the chief executive officer (CEO) of the College. Overseeing the academic enterprise is the dean of faculty, who also serves as the Chief Academic Officer (CAO) for regional accreditation purposes. Other cabinet leaders include three Vice Presidents (VPs) for advancement, business affairs, and enrollment management, respectively; two directors, and two other deans (i.e., inclusive excellence, student life). In terms of organizational governance, the Board of Trustees (BOT) defines and periodically reviews the mission, appoints the president, and oversees the fiduciary responsibility of the College. The 33-member BOT is comprised of members with significant corporate, education, government, and global experience. There are also 11 trustee emeriti. The CAO oversees the academic enterprise. Each academic major is coordinated by a program chair who is a member of the full-time faculty. H-SC employs 111 faculty: 91% full-time instructional, 9% part-time, and mostly all have a PhD (or equivalent).

Morehouse College

Morehouse is led by a President who serves as the CEO of the College. Overseeing the academic enterprise is the provost and senior vice president (SVP) of academic affairs, who also serves as the CAO for regional accreditation purposes. Other cabinet leaders include two SVPs, five VPs, one assistant vice president and director of Title III, including the chief administrative officer, chief financial officer (CFO), and chief information officer (CIO). In terms of organizational governance, the Board of Trustees (BOT) oversees the fiduciary responsibility of the College. The BOT is composed of 6 officers, 27 trustees, 3 faculty trustees, 3 student trustees, and 6 emeritus members.

The CAO oversees the division of academic affairs, which, at Morehouse, is comprised of seven academic divisions, including Business Administration & Economics, Creative & Performing Arts, and Social Sciences & Cultural Studies, for example. Each academic major is coordinated by a program director who is a member of the full-time faculty. Morehouse employs 172 faculty: 94% full-time, 85% with PhDs, 15% research/non-instructional, plus 3 part-time graduate assistants.

Wabash College

Wabash is led by a President who serves as the CEO of the College. Overseeing the academic enterprise is the dean of the college, who also serves as the CAO for regional accreditation purposes; Wabash is accredited by the Higher Learning Commission (HLC). Other cabinet leaders include 8 executive leaders, such as chief of staff, dean of students, dean of advancement, and dean of enrollment management. In terms of organizational governance, a 41-member BOT oversees the fiduciary responsibility of the College. The CAO oversees the division of academic affairs, which offers 39 academic majors and minors. Each academic program is coordinated by a department chair; most department chairs are White men, at the time of this writing. Wabash employs 98 faculty: 92% full-time, 100% with PhDs (or equivalent), and 8% part-time.

STUDENT SUCCESS AND POPULATIONS

Men's colleges are presumed to provide a unique environment with several advantages for men that are less accessible or unavailable at co-ed colleges (Bankart, 1998). For instance, men's colleges are filled with role models, supportive culture, inspiring history, and to some extent, greater acceptance

182 T. L. STRAYHORN

of diversity. They may also act as a repository of ideas that critique the status quo, foster brotherhood, and prepare students for life and leadership.

Hampden-Sydney College

Remarkably, Hampden-Sydney College was founded *before* the United States existed—Virginia was still a colony under British rule. Today, Hampden-Sydney College is classified as a 4-year, private college whose highest degree awarded is the bachelors. Located in a rural setting within the Commonwealth of Virginia, Hampden-Sydney enrolls approximately 881 students[5] according to the *National Center for Education Statistics* and boasts a student-to-faculty ratio of 9 to 1. Virtually all students at Hampden-Sydney are enrolled full-time (99%), 73% hail from in-state, 3% are formally registered with the Office of Disability Services, and though 82% identify as White, 7% are Black/African American, 5% are Hispanic/Latinx, and 25 received post-9/11 GI Bill benefits during 2019–2020 academic year (AY)—reflecting the most recent data.

Affordability is a major issue in higher education and college costs can be prohibitive for economically disadvantaged students attending private, highly-selective institutions like Hampden-Sydney. For example, tuition and fees for the 2020–2021 AY were $48,100, representing a 2% hike in just one year. Almost all students receive some type of aid, ranging from federal work study (FWS), scholarship, loan, to Pell grants, as a few examples. The average Pell grant award is $4,440.

The University's tagline—"forming good *men* and good citizens since 1776"—mirrors its value proposition as a top-ranked liberal arts college offering over 50 academic majors and the 5th best college library, according to *The Princeton Review*. The most popular academic majors reflect the college's prevailing masculine culture, although there's some *local evidence* of critical shifts. For example, *Completions Data* show the largest numbers in science, technology, engineering, and math (STEM) fields generally (e.g., biology), business, history, economics, and political science. One faculty member shared with the author via email: "It can be pretty traditional in terms of what students study—mostly history, political science, and sciences, as many of our 'brothers' aspire to med [i.e., medical] school, law school, and graduate study. I have seen some improvements, though, where faculty are incorporating critical perspectives, feminist approaches, and race-conscious frameworks."

Beyond core academics, Hampden-Sydney provides students with a suite of special learning opportunities and support services. For instance, the institution offers Army *Reserved Officer Training Corps* (ROTC), study abroad, over 60 registered student organizations (RSOs), a Frisbee golf

Men's Colleges in the United States   183

course, and 10 NCAA Division III athletic teams. Forty percent of students are members of fraternities. Student services vary in scope and scale, including academic advising, career counseling, and job placement services for graduates. A campus administrator shared with the author: "Hampden-Sydney is committed to helping our guys navigate to top jobs, promising careers, and gainful employment ... it doesn't stop at graduation ...we're committed to their futures after college too."

In terms of student success, Hampden-Sydney remains highly-ranked across metrics of institutional effectiveness. For instance, its first-year retention rate for first-time, full-time students is 79% (fall 2020). Its 4-year graduation rate is 62%, while the 6-year graduation rate (i.e., completion within 150% of normal time) is north of 70%. Graduation rates vary significantly by race/ethnicity (in rank order): Asian (100%), Hispanic/Latinx (89%), White (73%), Multiracial (63%), Black/African American (54%), and American Indian/Alaskan Native (50%).

Morehouse College

The *only* men's college also designated as an HBCU, Morehouse College is classified as a 4-year, private college whose highest degree awarded is the bachelors. Located in the Atlanta University Center with its "sister academy" (Spelman College) and Clark Atlanta University, Morehouse enrolls approximately 2,152 students according to the *National Center for Education Statistics* and reports a student-to-faculty ratio of 15 to 1. Virtually all students at Morehouse are enrolled full-time (93%), 7% are part-time, 72% hail from *outside* Georgia, 17% are formally registered with the Office of Disability Services, and though 74% identify as Black/African American, 25% are Multiracial or Race/Ethnicity Unknown, and 72 received post-9/11 GI Bill benefits during 2019–2020 academic year (AY)—reflecting the most recent data.

Compared to the other two men's colleges, Morehouse's tuition and fees are less but still present affordability challenges to the populations it serves. For example, tuition and fees for the 2020–2021 AY were $29,468, representing a 2.2% increase in the 12-month period. The majority of students (82%) receive some type of aid, ranging from federal work study (FWS), scholarship, loan, to Pell grants, as a few examples. The average Pell grant award is $5,296, likely reflecting the fact that more Morehouse students are first-generation and Pell-eligible based on federal poverty guidelines.

The mission of Morehouse College is "to develop men with disciplined minds who will lead lives of leadership and service." The most popular academic majors reflect the college's history. For example, *Completions Data* show the largest numbers in science, technology, engineering, and math

(STEM) fields generally (e.g., biology), business administration, kinesiology/sports, psychology, economics, and political science. The college's tagline reads: "We are a brotherhood of men on a mission to lead lives of consequence."

Beyond core academics, Morehouse provides students with formal and informal academic and social support services. For instance, the institution offers Army and Navy *Reserved Officer Training Corps* (ROTC), study abroad, teacher certification, over 50 RSOs, and 8 NCAA Division II athletics teams within the Southern Intercollegiate Athletic Conference (SIAC). Student services vary in scope and scale, including academic advising, career counseling, and job placement services for graduates. Notable alumni include Martin Luther King, Jr. (civil rights leader), Samuel Jackson (actor), Spike Lee (producer), Herman Cain (politician), Byron Cage (gospel singer), David Satcher (16th U.S. Surgeon General), and Raphael Warnock (Senator), to name a few.

In terms of student success, Morehouse is considered one of the nation's top HBCUs, regardless of size and geography. For instance, its first-year retention rate for first-time, full-time students is 86% (fall 2020). Its 4-year graduation rate is 40%, while the 6-year graduation rate (i.e., completion within 150% of normal time) is 56%. Graduation rates vary significantly by race/ethnicity (in rank order): American Indian/Alaskan Native (100%), Hispanic/Latinx (88%), and Black/African American (55%). Other accolades are noteworthy: #1 producer of Black men who go on to earn doctorates and #1 HBCU producer of Rhodes Scholars. These indicators of distinction relate to the mystique of "The Morehouse Man," a symbolic representation of the "student turned graduate," as one administrator shared with the author by phone—"it refers to a Morehouse graduate, in full bloom, defined by academic, intellectual, and professional success … one committed to continuous improvement of themselves and their communities."

Wabash College

Wabash is classified as a 4-year, private college whose highest degree awarded is the bachelors. Situated in picturesque Crawfordsville, Indiana, Wabash enrolls approximately 868 students[6] according to the *National Center for Education Statistics* and boasts a student-to-faculty ratio of 9 to 1. All students at Wabash are enrolled full-time, 74% hail from in-state, 5% are formally registered with the Office of Disability Services, and though 76% identify as White, 4% are Black/African American, 9% are Hispanic/Latinx, and 3 received post-9/11 GI Bill benefits during 2019–2020 academic year (AY)—reflecting the most recent data.

Similar to other highly-selective private C&Us, Wabash is expensive and can present affordability issues for first-generation, low-income, and other minoritized populations (Harper, 2012). For example, tuition and fees for the 2020–2021 AY were $45,850, representing a 2.5% hike in one year. Almost all students receive some type of aid, ranging from federal work study (FWS), scholarship, loan, to Pell grants, as a few examples. The average Pell grant award is $4,508.

Known for its top-ranked (#3) internship program, Wabash offers 39-degree programs in fields ranging from STEM, political science, philosophy, ancient Greek, and history to drama, art, and Spanish/Iberian studies. The most popular academic majors include, according to *Completions Data*: rhetoric, history, religion, economics, and political science/government. Twenty-six academic programs at Wabash are ranked in the Top 15% in the nation, based on instructional attention, quality instruction, and faculty-student engagement. Part of the institution's mystique, "The Gentleman's Rule" governs student conduct: "The student is expected to conduct himself at all times, both on and off the campus, as a gentleman and a responsible citizen."

Beyond core academics, Wabash provides students multiple opportunities for educationally purposeful engagement (Kuh, 2001). For instance, the institution offers Army *Reserved Officer Training Corps* (ROTC), study abroad, teacher certification, and over 70 RSOs. Nearly two-thirds of the student body is engaged in athletics, theater, music, Glee Club, and more. Student services vary in scope but converge on success—Wabash boasts a nationally-recognized internship program, job placement initiative, and 9th-place national ranking for "Happiest and Successful Alumni," according to *Forbes* (2022) magazine. One student shared: "The alumni network has been the biggest benefit since coming to Wabash College. Not only has it helped me land two internships, it has also given me access to thousands of adults who would drop everything at a moment's notice to help me. It is one thing to talk about the brotherhood at Wabash; it is another to truly experience it."

In terms of student success, Wabash is consistently highly-ranked across metrics of institutional effectiveness. For instance, its first-year retention rate for first-time, full-time students is 84% (fall 2020). Its 4-year graduation rate is 72%, while the 6-year graduation rate (i.e., completion within 150% of normal time) is 75%. Graduation rates vary significantly by race/ethnicity (in rank order): American Indian/Alaskan Native (100%), White (76%), Asian (67%), Black/African American (67%), and Hispanic/Latinx (65%), to name a few. Six months after graduation, 100% of Wabash recent graduates were employed, enrolled in graduate school, or enlisted in military service. The median mid-career earning of Wabash alumni is $143,800. Table 14.1 presents a summary table, highlighting data from all three men's colleges.

Table 14.1

U.S. Men's Colleges: Institutional Characteristics

Characteristic	Hampden-Sydney	Morehouse	Wabash
Enrollment	881	2,152	868
Control	Private	Private	Private
Student-faculty ratio	9:1	15:1	9:1
Registered disability	3%	17%	5%
% Full-time Student(s)	99%	93%	100%
Retention Rate	79%	86%	84%
4-year Graduation Rate	62%	40%	72%
6-year Graduation Rate	71%	56%	75%
Cohort Default Rate	4.7%	8.3%	2.8%

PROFESSIONAL CONTEXTS

Wabash "prides itself on being one of the *best* [emphasis added] colleges in the nation for young men preparing for life and leadership," as one senior-level leader shared with the author via email. The College seeks faculty and staff who are committed to providing purposeful engagement with students, matched by high levels of challenge and support. Marketing materials emphasize that students benefit from high value, high reward, and high contact with full-time faculty and staff.

Skills and dispositions that seem essential for working at Wabash can be gleaned from the institution's website, HR materials, and recent job postings. For instance, thematic analysis of recent job announcements indicates a premium is placed on staff members' ability to develop meaningful transformative experiences that prepare students for life and leadership in a global world. Another *desired* qualification is genuine interest in working with *talented* students to achieve personal and professional goals.

Working at Morehouse involves a great deal of direct student contact and an abiding commitment to the development of a nurturing campus environment for young men. For instance, the College's human resources (HR) webpage notes that "employees serve the mission by supporting and mentoring men who pursue education here." Other factors point to the expectation that campus faculty and staff will provide mentorship, support, and high-touch learning environments built on mutual trust. Marketing materials emphasize that students benefit from "the unequivocal support of [Morehouse's] entire staff."

Skills and dispositions that seem essential for working at "the Black Harvard of the South," as it is sometimes dubbed, can be gleaned from the institution's website, HR materials, and recent job postings. For instance, thematic analysis of recent job announcements reveals the importance of a proven record working effectively with community members in education outreach/advocacy, commitment to activism and advocacy especially organizing around social justice, prior experience working with students of color, and some basic knowledge of Black history and culture. It would seem necessary to know the life, legacy, and achievements of pioneering Black leaders like Benjamin Mays (an alum) and Frederick Douglas, after whom the Academic Success Center is named.

Working at Hampden-Sydney requires evidence of subject-matter expertise, relevant experience, and a track record for success. For instance, the College's HR website displays dozens of "current faculty [and staff] openings." Applying for a job requires candidates to submit a job application, cover letter, resume (or curriculum vita [CV]), plus professional references. As another example, one job underscores the role serves in advising capacity to student groups like Brother 4 Brother and collaborates with athletics. Thus, working at Hampden-Sydney likely requires faculty and staff to wear multiple hats—that is, to manage multiple work roles simultaneously— operate on teams, stay student-focused, and go beyond the call of duty regularly. Table 14.2 presents a summary comparing the three HEIs.

Table 14.2

U.S. Men's Colleges: Faculty Characteristics

Characteristic	Hampden-Sydney	Morehouse	Wabash
Full-time Faculty	101	137	90
Part-time Faculty	10	10	8
Research/Public Service	0	26	0
Graduate Assistants	0	3	0
Total Faculty & GA	111	172	98

FUTURE CONSIDERATIONS AND DIRECTIONS

Using information from this chapter, I advocate for policy and program changes to maintain or enhance the diversity that is critical for the stability, sustainability, and future viability of higher education generally and men's colleges in the U.S. specifically. Deep examination of each institution's academic core revealed obvious connections to traditional liberal arts education, best characterized by coursework in history, philosophy, language, and, increasingly, arts and music. Though slower than some co-ed, research, and public colleges, the nation's three men's colleges have adopted coursework in emerging, new fields including gender studies, Black studies, Asian studies, cybersecurity, and national security, to name a few. Faculty at men's colleges also provided evidence (e.g., syllabi, hyperlinks) to the author demonstrating meaningful incorporation of diverse teaching modalities (e.g., hybrid), culturally responsive pedagogies, and critical frameworks such Black feminist thought. I urge work in this space to continue in ways that promote welcoming environments at men's colleges for all students, even if these national treasures *choose* to limit enrollment to men only in the foreseeable future.

As private colleges, the nation's three men's colleges are comparatively expensive ranging from $25,000 and up per year. This significantly limits the number of students who can afford to *access* the transformative experience proffered by each institution. If Morehouse produces *socially-conscious leaders* for today and tomorrow *and* Wabash equips students for gainful employment, then the high costs of attendance limits that opportunity to those who can afford to pay out-of-pocket or qualify for significant grants and scholarships (e.g., Merit Scholars). Future researchers and analysts are encouraged to consider these ideas when working with college men. They might also conduct additional studies about college access, affordability, and educational equity at men's colleges.

Writing this chapter stretched the author in unexpected ways. First, I presumed that there was much more written about men's colleges. I was surprised to find such a paucity of literature, explicitly focusing on the history, mission, curriculum, and culture of men's colleges. Consequently, I argue that *all* HEIs started as men's colleges with the advent of Harvard College in 1636. Yet, the need for additional research on students' campus experiences, environmental conditions, staff performance, and faculty productivity at men's colleges is significant. Thus, future researchers and analysts are encouraged to use large, national datasets like the *National Survey of Student Engagement* (NSSE) and *College Student Experiences Questionnaire* (CSEQ) to assess student involvement, faculty-student engagement, and correlates of satisfaction, grades, and sense of belonging for diverse groups at men's colleges. Additionally, qualitative methods such as interviews, ethnography, observations, and document analysis can be used effectively to interrogate men's academic and social socialization to the norms of "The Gentleman's Rule" or "The Morehouse Man."

DISCUSSION QUESTIONS

1. Discuss and trace the historical evolution of men's colleges in the United States, naming the critical touchpoints that likely influenced their development and expansion.

2. In what ways has Harvard's original curriculum, culture, and organizational structure influenced these elements at the institution where you study and/or work?

3. Thinking about the three men's colleges featured in this chapter, name *at least* one way they're similar and one way they're distinct.

4. In the next 10 to 15 years, one of these institutions will likely become co-ed by enrolling women. In your opinion, which one is *most likely* to do so and why? And which is *unlikely* to do so and why?

5. Google a working definition of the term, "masculinity," including toxic masculinity, transgressive masculinity, and hegemonic masculinity. Using these definitions, apply them to men's colleges in the U.S. and campus environments at Hampden-Sydney, Morehouse, and Wabash.

REFERENCES

Bankart, C. P. (1998). The role of the men's movement at the all-male college: Challenge and opportunity. *Men and Masculinities, 1*(1), 91–102. https://doi.org/https://doi.org/10.1177/1097184X98001001006

Blackburn, R. T., & Conrad, C. F. (1986). The new revisionists and the history of U.S. higher education. *Higher Education, 15*, 211–230.

Cain, M. (1999). *The community college in the twenty-first century: A systems approach.* University Press of America.

Cohen, A. M., & Brawer, F. B. (1996). *The American community college* (3rd ed.). Jossey-Bass.

Elliott, K. C., Warshaw, J. B., & deGregory, C. A. (2019). Historically Black community colleges: A descriptive profile and call for context-based future research. *Community College Journal of Research & Practice, 43*(10–11), 770–784.

Forbes. (2022). *Wabash College.* https://www.forbes.com/colleges/wabash-college/

Forcier, M. F. D. (2004). "Men of Dartmouth" and "The Lady Engineers": Coeducation at Dartmouth College and Lehigh University. In S. L. Poulson & L. Miller-Bernal (Eds.), *Going coed: Women's experiences in formerly men's colleges and universities, 1950-2000* (pp. 153–180). Vanderbilt University Press.

Gordon, L. (1997). From seminary to university: An overview of women's higher education, 1870–1920. In L. F. Goodchild & H. Wechsler (Eds.), *The history of higher education* (2nd ed., pp. 473–498). Simon & Schuster Custom Publishing.

190 T. L. STRAYHORN

Graham, P. A. (1978). Expansion and exclusion: A history of women in American higher education. *Signs: Journal of Women in Culture and Society, 3*(4), 759–773.

Harper, S. R. (2012). Race without racism: How higher education researchers minimize racist institutional norms. *The Review of Higher Education, 36*(1), 9–29.

Kuh, G. D. (2001). Assessing what really matters to student learning: Inside the National Survey of Student Engagement. *Change, 33*(3), 10–17, 66.

Morison, S. E. (1998). *The founding of Harvard College: With a new foreword by Hugh Hawkins.* Harvard University Press.

National Center for Education Statistics. (2022). *Integrated Postsecondary Education Data System* (IPEDS). https://nces.ed.gov/ipeds/datacenter/InstitutionProfile.aspx

Parker, P. (2015). The historical role of women in higher education. *Administrative Issues Journal, 5*(1), 3–14. https://doi.org/https://doi.org/10.5929/2015.5.1.1

Poulson, S. L., & Miller-Bernal, L. (2004). Preface. In S. L. Poulson & L. Miller-Bernal (Eds.), *Going coed: Women's experiences in formerly men's colleges and universities, 1950–2000* (pp. ix–xiii). Vanderbilt University Press.

Saunders, K. M., & Nagle, B. T. (2018). *HBCUs punching above their weight: A state-level analysis of historically Black college and university enrollment graduation.*

Schmidt, G. P. (1957). *The liberal arts college: A chapter in American cultural history.* Rutgers University Press.

Stoecker, J., & Pascarella, E. T. (1991). Women's colleges and women's career attainments revisited. *Journal of Higher Education, 62,* 394–406.

Strayhorn, T. L. (2021). *A pledge of allegiance to America's historically Black colleges and universities: Key priorities of the Biden-Harris education agenda.* Center for the Study of HBCUs, Virginia Union University.

Strayhorn, T. L. (2022). Lessons learned from institutional responses to COVID-19: Evidence-based insights from a qualitative study of historically Black community colleges. *Community College Journal of Research & Practice, 46*(1–2), 30–40. https://doi.org/https://doi.org/10.1080/10668926.2021.1975173

Thelin, J. R. (2004). *A history of American higher education.* Johns Hopkins University Press.

Tierney, W. G., & Hagedorn, L. S. (Eds.). (2002). *Increasing access to college: Extending possibilities for all students.* State University of New York Press.

Walsh, M. R., & Walsh, F. R. (1982). Integrating men's colleges at the turn of the century. *Historic Journal of Massachusetts, 10*(2), 4.

Whitney, M. E. (2000). Women and the university. In *Papers of Alice Jackson Stuart, 1913–2001.* Charlottesville, VA.

ENDNOTES

1. Though the term "all-male" is used frequently, the author wishes to point out this is a misnomer as none of the campuses mentioned are exclusively male or comprised of men; women and others work as faculty, administrators, and staff. For example, the first woman to serve on the faculty at Wabash was hired in a non-tenurable, part-time position in 1973 (Bankart, 1998).

2. It's important to note that Rose-Hulman Institute of Technology—the other men's college in Indiana—started enrolling women in fall 1995 (Bankart, 1998).
3. Harvard College became Harvard University in 1780.
4. Harvard Divinity School was founded in 1819.
5. Interestingly, the U.S. Department of Education Integrated Postsecondary Education System (IPEDs) indicates that 8 females applied for admission to Hampden-Sydney in fall 2020; though 13% were admitted, none enrolled.
6. Interestingly, the U.S. Department of Education Integrated Postsecondary Education System (IPEDs) indicates that three females applied for admission to Wabash in fall 2020; none were admitted.

CHAPTER 15

U.S. WOMEN COLLEGES AND UNIVERSITIES

Carrie Kortegast
Northern Illinois University

Gender has long been at the center of U.S. higher education system. Historically, institutions of higher education purposely excluded women from attending. As Thelin (2011) stated, "there is no record of a woman of the colonial period having received a degree" (p. 55). De facto, early American institutions of higher education were all exclusively men's institutions. While some institutions of higher education allowed admission to white women in the 1800s, it was the rise of women's colleges that provided further access and opportunity for women to pursue college-level work. In 1960, there were about 230 women's colleges (Women's College Consortium, 2021); however, as of 2022, there were 36 women's colleges as well as four men's colleges in the U.S. Importantly, the vast majority of institutions that were founded as single-sex institutions are now coed.

Women's colleges have an uncomfortable legacy as institutions that provided access to college-level education for some women, but not all women. Historically, access was primarily for White, Christian, and wealthier women. Contemporary women's colleges tend to enroll students that are "more racially and ethnically diverse population of students than any of the comparison institutions" (Sax et al., 2015), but still less than 1% of women attend a women's college (Snyder & Dillow, 2012). Given women's college history of exclusion, the perception of elitism is still attached to

---

Institutional Diversity in American Postsecondary Education, pp. 193–207
Copyright © 2024 by Information Age Publishing
www.infoagepub.com
All rights of reproduction in any form reserved.

194 C. KORTEGAST

women's colleges. This is despite contemporary women's college being more diverse regarding race, ethnicity, age, and socioeconomic status (Miller-Bernal, 2012), as well as more welcoming to LGBTQ students than their counterparts.

The following chapter will provide a short history of the evolution of women's colleges in the U.S. Next, the chapter will discuss organizational structures, institutional culture, and professional contexts for women's colleges. The chapter will end with a discussion of future considerations and directions regarding these institutions. Throughout this chapter, the term "women's colleges" is used to discuss single-sex postsecondary institutions that limit enrollment to women. Research discussing these institutions often refer to them as "single-sex institutions" and, historically, but dated, "female colleges and seminaries." When referring to all women and all men's colleges, as Renn (2014) noted, the "bifurcation of gender into two and only two distinct categories is itself problematic" (p. 2). With an increasing number of individuals identifying with genders outside of binary gender understandings of man/women and biological sex male/female, men's and women's colleges have had to contend with what it means to be a "single-sex" institution in the 21st century. Given this, I will use the term "women's colleges" despite being limiting. However, researchers' original terms will be used when discussing the literature.

HISTORY

Prior to the 1800s, access to postsecondary education was limited to men. Women were barred from admission to institutions that provided college-level education. The founding of Mount Holyoke Seminary in 1837 (later to be renamed Mount Holyoke College) is often cited as the first institution dedicated to providing college-level work to women (Thelin, 2011) and served as a model for the establishment of other institutions dedicated to postsecondary education for women (Solomon, 1985). Georgia Female College (now Wesleyan College) was the first to be chartered to award degrees to women in 1836, however, the first students were not enrolled until January 1839. However, "despite its name, this pioneer institution resembled a superior academy more than a male college, regularly admitting twelve-year olds" (Solomon, 1985, p. 24). Subsequently, other women's colleges, often called academy, female institutes, or seminaries, were established to support the education of women (Thelin, 2011). During the 1860s alone, more than forty women's institutions were chartered (Geiger, 2016). At the same time, more colleges and universities were accepting women, with nearly half admitting women by 1880 (Schuman, 2005).

Shortly after their founding, the curriculum and preparation at women's institutions varied from vocational training to finishing-school to more rigorous education in the liberal arts that modeled college-level education men received (Solomon, 1985; Thelin, 2011). Early arguments for postsecondary education for women was seen as important for the new nation in "raising virtuous citizens" (Solomon, 1985, p. 15). As Solomon (1985) noted, "the of the Christian wife, mother, and teacher gave repeated urgency to women's education" (p. 16). In the early years, 70% of Mount Holyoke graduates became teachers (Horowitz, 1984). Similarly, Spelman College, at the time Spelman Seminary, initially served as a normal school primarily focused on teacher training before becoming a liberal arts college (Lefever, 2005). On the whole, there were limited occupations available to women outside of teacher and motherhood.

By the 1890s, the majority of women enrolled in postsecondary education were attending women's colleges (Geiger, 2016). However, with the expansion of coeducational public colleges and universities particularly, in the Midwest and West, more women started attending coeducational institutions except in New England and in the South, where "single-gender education remained the norm" (Thelin, 2011, p. 97). In the South, the creation of women's colleges and support for women's education arose out of a concern of sending Southern women north for their education. As Thelin (2011) stated, "their logic was that it was better to build a women's college close to home that inculcated traditional religious and regional values than to risk having young Southern women attend a renegade Northern college" (p. 84). These seminaries and colleges provided access to postsecondary education for some women but also denied access for others, particularly low-income and women of color. The establishment of Spelman College and Bennett College (see Soloman, 1985 and Lefever, 2005 about founding) arose out desires to provide educational opportunities to African American women in the South. The education of Black women was seen as a pathway to "racial uplift" by both white missionaries and the Black community (Gasman, 2007, p. 764). While outside the scope of this chapter, there is a complicated and racist and sexist history regarding white missionaries establishing educational institutions for racially minoritized individuals in the U.S.

While women's colleges often served to education and reify gender norms of the time, they also worked to fracture those gender norms. As Thelin (2011) notes, these institutions "provided an unprecedented opportunity for both students and faculty to pursue advance studies and serious academics. One result of this was that an inordinate number of alumnae from women's colleges of the 1880s went on to pursue advanced studies in law, medicine, and Ph.D. programs" (p. 98). The 1860–1920 was marked by transitions towards the liberal education (Soloman, 1985) and expanded academic interests to better integrate math, social, physical, and natural sciences. This led to an increase in women in science. For instance, 41% of the women scientist featured in the *Men of Science* first three volumes, released in 1906, 1910, and 1921, graduated from a women's college (Soloman, 1985). As such, these institutions did provide the possibility to go beyond teaching, religion, and motherhood. Additionally, during this time, many women's institutions dropped the term seminary to adapt college. For instance, Mills Seminary became Mills College in 1885, Mary Baldwin Seminary became Mary Baldwin University in 1923, and Spelman Seminary became Spelman College in 1924. The change to college signaled the mission and focus on providing college-level courses and liberal arts curriculum for women.

These possibilities and "serious academics" led to the prestige by 1930 of the Seven Sisters institutions, a consortium of women's colleges made up of Wellesley, Radcliffe, Smith, Mount Holyoke, Vassar, Barnard, and Bryn Mawr. These seven institutions "had acquired a collective reputation as the alma maters of a talented, privileged elite of American women" (Thelin, 2011, p. 227). This legacy of prestige, academic rigor, and opportunity for women continues even today.

The 1960s and 1970s saw a national shift towards coeducation with many historical men's and women's colleges shifting towards coeducation (Langdon, 2001). The cultural changes brought about by the women's rights and the civil rights movements, coupled with a financial pressure of shrinking enrollments, resulted in the majority of single-sex colleges and universities to become coeducation. This included Ivy League institutions such as Harvard, Yale, Princeton, Brown, Dartmouth (Cornell and University of Pennsylvania were already coed) as well as one of the Seven Sisters institutions, Vassar. Columbia University was the last Ivy League school to become coeducational in 1983. This happened after a failed attempt to merge with Barnard (Belkin, 1983), in which Barnard voted to remain coeducation. Other women's colleges that decided to make the shift to becoming coeducational included Sarah Lawrence College (1968), Bennington College (1969), and Skidmore College (1971). Over the course of two decades, the number of women's colleges began to rapidly decrease. In 1960, there were 233 women's colleges, which dwindled to 116 institutions by the 1980s (Langdon, 2001).

In response to the shuttering of many of these institutions, efforts to revitalize and remind women of the role of women's colleges began in the 1980s (Langdon, 2001). Touting successful graduates, such as Hillary Rodham Clinton, Katherine Hepburn, Margaret Mead, and Julia Child, marketing campaigns in the 1990s and beyond attempted to create a "niche market and use their special institutional status to their benefit in recruiting students" (p. 9). Viewbooks communicated advantages of attending a women's college, such as leadership development, supportive academic environment, and active social life (Kamauf, 2018). In order to increase enrollment, women's colleges began looking internationally and targeting places, such as the Middle East, where attending a women's college would be of interest (Lewin, 2008; Renn, 2017). Following the 2016 presidential election, the top women's colleges saw an increase in applications and enrollment (Jaschik, 2018). Students noted being attracted to women's colleges' missions related to social justice, history of activism, and commitment to gender equity.

ORGANIZATIONAL STRUCTURE AND CULTURE

Women's colleges tend to have similar organizational structures to small colleges in that they tend to be fairly flat organizational charts. Like other small, liberal arts colleges, student affairs work tends to be service oriented, and student centered, with administrators often fulfilling multiple roles (Hirt, 2006). Renn (2014) noted that "women's colleges may simultaneously claim distinctness in contexts in which the majority of institutions are coeducational, and they may assert that they are like coeducational peer institutions in many of their structures and functions" (p. 121). While the largest women's colleges have graduate programs, for the most part, they are focused on undergraduate education, with many being residential, liberal arts colleges. Hirt (2006) stated "the mission of liberal arts colleges and universities in the 21st century reflects a continuing focus on a traditional curriculum designed to promote holistic education and to graduate productive members of society" (p. 23). Critics of liberal arts education have questioned their relevancy and call for reinvention in order to survive (Hirt, 2006). Women's colleges have weathered the calls and questions about their relevancy and pushes to reinvent themselves. While some have been able to reinvent themselves, others have faced difficult decisions regarding closing, merging, and/or going coed.

Like other small private small colleges, women's colleges tend to have small endowments and be tuition dependent. Solomon noted in her 1985 book: "Today only the few women's colleges that have large enough endowments and sufficient alumnae support can remain single-sex" and "have found themselves competing still more fiercely for the brightest students" (p. 207). This warning continues today as several women's colleges have been at risk for closure or consolidation with other institutions as "the majority of these colleges are not wealthy" (Miller-Bernal, 2011, p. 221). For instance, Bennett College was on the verge of closure as their accreditor Southern Association of Colleges and Schools Commission on Colleges (SACSCOC) moved to revoke their accreditation because of financial issues

198   C. KORTEGAST

(Seltzer, 2021). On September 14, 2021, the President of Mills College, Elizabeth L. Hillman, issued a statement announcing that Mills College would merge with Northeastern University to become Mills College at Northeastern University. With the change, she also announced that the campus would be gender inclusive. This move was largely seen as a way to provide financial stability to the college in moving forward. In July 2021, Judson College, one of the oldest women's colleges in the country, closed after only enrolling 145 students in the spring and years of poor financial health (Whitford, 2021a).

STUDENT SUCCESS AND POPULATIONS

In order to remain relevant as well as attract new students, many contemporary women's colleges have transformed their curriculum to meet these demands and pressures. In 2021, Salem College announced revising their curriculum to center leadership and health as a way to differentiate themselves (Whitford, 2021b). Similarly, Agnes Scott College has received national recognition from *U.S. News & World Report* (2021) as the *most innovative school* for their approach to liberal arts education. The College's signature program, SUMMIT, integrates liberal arts and science education with co-curricular experiences focused on leadership development and global learning (Agnes Scott College, n.d.). Each student is supported in their development with the support of SUMMIT advisor, peer advisor, major advisor, and career advisor. As then President Elizabeth Kiss stated, SUMMIT was the response to the question "Why Agnes Scott?" (Association of Governing Boards of Universities and Colleges [AGB], 2020). The result of this "big idea" has led to increase enrollment (Biemiller, 2016) and national recognition. Similarly, Sweet Briar College, which was on the brink of closure in 2015, charted a new path by reorganizing and renovating its curriculum, focusing on integrated courses, leadership, and sustainability (Berrett, 2017). While Sweet Briar has seen increased enrollment and alumnae giving (Alachnowicz, 2021), its long-term survival still remains a lingering question.

The less paternalistic culture at women's colleges tend to foster more opportunities for women to take on leadership roles and challenge traditional gender roles (Manning, 2000). Women at women's colleges tend to pursue traditionally male-dominated disciplines such as math, science, and engineering at greater rates than at coeducational institutions. Kinzie et al. (2007) found that women college students interacted more frequently with faculty as well as experienced high levels of academic challenge. They concluded that this could be "a reflection of 'taking women seriously,' in that woman are experiencing high expectations for student performance and are deeply engaged in intellectual and creative activities" (p. 159). Moreover, women's college students are more likely to believe that they will be in regular communication with their professors and be able to assist with faculty research (Sax et al., 2015). This environment might encourage students to devote significant time and energy towards their studies and meeting faculty expectations (Kinzie et al., 2007).

Questions about who can attend a women's college have increased, with more young people identifying as transgender, non-binary, and genderqueer. Admissions office, campus administrators, as well as alumnae offices, have had to engage in critical conversations about who is allowed to attend as well as how to honor alums that identify differently than their undergraduate records. However, "as colleges for *women*, they have also become ground zero for extended debates about the inclusion of transgender women (and students who transition to identify as transgender men, or who identify as non-binary) in 'women's spaces'" (Weber, 2016, pp. 29–30).

Most notably, this debate has played out in admissions policies. In summer 2014, Mills became the first women's college to open admissions to transgender women, closely followed by Mount Holyoke in September 2014. Mount Holyoke's policy was the most gender-inclusive as it included transmen, transwomen, and non-binary people; basically, everyone but cisgender-men (Weber, 2016). Other women's colleges, mostly in the Northeast and West coast, followed by updating admissions policies to include transwomen. However, women's colleges in the South have been slower to include and recognize transgender and non-binary students and applicants (Weber, 2016). Across the board, there has been little consistency regarding admissions policies with institutions using a variety of biology- and identity-based criteria (Nanney & Brunsma, 2017). Moreover, this has led to many administrators, particularly within student affairs, navigating how to support transgender students and navigate institutional policies (Marine, 2011).

Women's colleges tend to enroll a more diverse student population than their institutional coeducational counterparts. Sax et al. (2015) study examining the characteristics students attending women's colleges between 1971 and 2011 found that women's colleges have become more racially, ethnically, and socioeconomically diverse over time. For example, women's colleges become more racially and ethnically diverse, with women of color making up nearly 50% of attendees. Additionally, over time, there has been a shift from enrolling students from the highest family income brackets compared to women attending coeducational institutions to enrolling more lower income students.

Graduates of women's colleges are more likely to go on to earn advance degrees than women at coeducational institutions (Lennon & Day, 2012). Women's colleges have been more effective in producing women students

200 C. KORTEGAST

that go onto earn doctoral degrees than their coeducational counterparts an (Wolf-Wendel, 1998; Wolf-Wendel et al., 2000; Tidball, 1980) and hold leadership positions in education, law, government, and business. For instance, between 1996–2006, 150 Black women graduates of Spelman College when onto pursue PhD programs in science and engineering (Thomas, 2008). This was more than any other undergraduate institution aside from Howard University, a coeducation HBCU, that is significantly larger than Spelman. As the past president Johnnetta Cole (1994) of Spelman stated, "At Spelman there is no assumption that Black folks don't like math and women cannot do science" (p. 151). Women's college graduates' pursuit of advance degrees, particularly in STEM fields, has remained constraint when considering women as more opportunity to attend the most elite universities post-1970s.

Students at women's colleges tend to participate in educational experiences and practices that contribute to positive learning outcomes than coeducational peers (Kinzie et al., 2007; Renn, 2014). These outcomes include leadership development, self-confidence, interpersonal development, and engagement with diversity (Lennon & Day, 2012; Kinzie et al., 2007; Renn, 2104). As Smith (1989) stated,

> The environment of women's colleges challenges women to become all those things they are not asked to be in many "coeducational" environments … the environment of these colleges provides opportunities for varieties of leadership styles, for success and failure, and for nonstereotyped approaches to women and "their" issues. (p. 50)

Women's colleges have a long history of having a "positive effect on intellectual self-esteem" (Astin, 1977, p. 232) which continues to this present day.

Women's colleges also provide vast opportunities to students to engage in leadership on campus (Solomon, 1985). Women's college alumnae were more likely to gain leadership experiences and hold a student leadership role in a student organization, campus media, and student government than their peers at other institutional types (Lennon & Day, 2012). Renn (2014) found that women's college students often believed that attending a women's college made a difference in their leadership experiences and development (Lennon & Day, 2012; Renn, 2014). In Renn and Lytle (2010) study of women's college students from six different regions of the world, they concluded that "the single-sex context and exposure to peer and adult female role models sensitized—or heightened sensitivity to—women's issues and social justice, including global feminisms and worldwide oppression of girls and women" (pp. 226–227). Often students enter planning to engaged in leadership opportunities such as student government and community involvement (Sax et al., 2015) and expected to be leaders in society after graduation (Renn, 2014).

Understandings of feminism, gender, and sexuality have been at times contentious topics for women's colleges. They have been places where women have had opportunities to challenge and rethink gender norms. At the same time, they have been places where understandings of women and womanhood have been reinscribed. Women's colleges have been contentious spaces for lesbian, queer, and trans individuals, as they have been places of both support and harm. Terms such as "BDOC: Big Dyke of Campus," "LUG: Lesbian Until Graduation," and "BUG: Bisexual Until Graduation" have been used as both endearments and warnings. Many women's colleges have been seen as supportive places for individuals to explore their own sexuality, particularly for lesbian, bisexual, pansexual, and queer students. Trans students attending women's colleges have described their campus environment as overtly genderist, transphobic, and transmisogynistic (Farmer et al., 2020) and have experienced transgender oppression (Hart & Lester, 2011). At the same time, transgender students have also reported more positive experiences at women's colleges than at other types of institutions (Freitas, 2017).

PROFESSIONAL CONTEXTS

Studies have found that women have more opportunities to interact with people different than themselves at women's colleges than peers at coeducational institutions. This included women's college graduates reporting learning to related to people of different backgrounds and understanding historical and social contests of issues (Lennon & Day, 2012). Kinzie et al. (2007) found "that compared to coeducational colleges, women's colleges both encourage and provide more opportunities for students to interact with people of different economic, racial, and social backgrounds" (p. 159). As such, these institutions often provide opportunity to engage with individuals with different backgrounds.

As of 2022, there were 36 women's colleges in the U.S. The vast majority are small colleges and universities focused on undergraduate education with enrollments between 1,000–2,900 students (NCES, 2021). The largest, Texas Women's University (TWU), is a public university with an enrollment of over 15,000 students at both the undergraduate and graduate level (NCES, 2021). While 90% of students identify as women, TWU is coeducation and states they are "the nation's largest university primarily for women" (TWU, 2020). However, there are nine women's colleges that have less than 850 students enrolled (NCES, 2021).

Women's colleges are mission driven institutions dedicated to the education of women. Additionally, many women's colleges are also religiously

202   C. KORTEGAST

affiliated, predominately catholic (e.g., Saint Mary's College, Mount Mary University, College of Saint Mary). Currently, there are two Historically Black Women's Colleges, Spelman College and Bennett College. At the core, women's college "tak[e] women's education seriously" (Smith, 1989, p. 50). This is demonstrated through a commitment to providing an academic and educational environment that centers on the belief that women are capable of academic rigor, research, and engagement. Women's leadership is often modeled throughout the institution, with women serving as academic and administrative leadership, faculty, and in student leadership roles. The top administrative positions (e.g., President, Provost, Dean of Students) are often held by women identified people.

FUTURE CONSIDERATIONS AND DIRECTIONS

In the fall of 1994, I entered Mount Holyoke College as a first-year student attracted to the idea of becoming an "uncommon women" (Wasserstein, 1991) and cultivating my emerging identity as a feminist. My college experience felt special. I saw examples of women's leadership all around me from student organizations, faculty, alumnae, and institutional leadership. Women's education and aspirations were taken seriously. I was taken seriously. I experienced the joy of playing a sport, rugby, where there was a position for all body sizes, and it was okay to be strong. Traditions and history framed my experience. Traditions like the Laurel Parade during graduation weekend where we all wore white in honor of the suffragettes and sang "Bread and Roses" at Mary Lyon's grave. Postgraduation, most of my friends went onto graduate school and pursued careers in various industries, often ones that were considered "male dominated." Mary Lyon's charge to "go forward, attempt great things, accomplish great things" often serving as a guide and mantra for us.

As a higher education faculty member and a women's college alumna, I have often contemplated what is the role of women's colleges in today's higher education landscape? Moreover, what does it mean to be, as Mount Holyoke states, a gender diverse women's college? Topics related to mission, purpose, and future often dominate conversations about the future and need for women's colleges in the U.S. Moreover, women's colleges are navigating the tension of being organized as an institution around understandings of gender. At the same time, they are simultaneously working to fracture social understandings of gender. While the manifestation of this tension might be new, women's colleges have historically grappled with questions about "who women are" (Hart & Lester, 2011, p. 197).

The sustainability and survival of women's colleges is closely linked with perceptions of relevance and financial support. In Renn's (2014) book *Women's Colleges and Universities in a Global Context*, she outlines five overarching roles that women's colleges and universities play in the 21st century. The five roles are: (1) providing access, (2) supportive environments that foster women's success, (3) leadership development and preparing future leaders for government, business, and civil society, (4) gender empowerment for students, faculty, and communities, and (5) symbolic role in society. The relevance of women's colleges, as outlined by Renn (2014), is clear; however, the messaging on the benefits and outcomes of attending a women's college is often less broadly known. Advocates and leaders of women's colleges need to continue to espouse the benefits to students in attending a women's college, both in the quality of the educational experience they receive as well as the postgraduation outcomes.

The future of women's colleges is also dependent upon increasing financial support. As previously mentioned, Soloman (1985) warned about the need for strong endowments to stave off going coeducational. Today, the larger threat is closures. The most selective and well-funded women's colleges are aggressively trying to cross the billion-dollar endowment mark. While the risk to closure is not immediate, there is still an urgency regarding the long-term sustainability of the institution and the need to protect and enhance educational opportunities at women's colleges. However, at the majority of women's colleges, there is an urgent need to aggressively increase revenue streams via enrollment and fundraising efforts. Moreover, fundraising campaigns need to be coupled with education to alumnae and others about why giving is important and how it is used to support the college.

In thinking about the past and future of women's colleges, I often think about the Emily Dickenson (a Mount Holyoke alumna) poem "I dwell in Possibility." In it, she offers up poetry as a place of creativity and freedom. Women's colleges have been places of possibilities. As Renn (2014), a women's college graduate herself, writes:

> They symbolize possibilities for women in education and the workforce. They also convey contradictory messages about the purposes of women's education and embody a paradox that rests on their existence as organizations that are both progressive and conservative. In some regions [of the world], these symbolic roles and contradictions raise questions about why women do not have equal access. In other regions, they raise questions about women's experiences at coeducational institutions. (p. 5)

Gender equity in the U.S. has never been a promise made, but one in which many individuals have hoped for. Women's colleges have made it their mission to center and support women's academic, professional, and personal aspirations. They have often provided possibilities of expanding what women can do and be.

DISCUSSION QUESTIONS

1. What is the role of women's colleges in the contemporary landscape of U.S. higher education?
2. What can other institutions learn about supporting the education of women from women's colleges?
3. How are other types of institutions of higher education grappling with creating greater understandings of gender diversity of students?
4. How might sexism shape understandings of the role, purpose, and existence of women's colleges?

REFERENCES

Agnes Scott College (n.d.). *SUMMIT talking points.* https://www.agnesscott.edu/communications-and-marketing/toolbox/summit-talking-points.html#:~:text=Agnes%20Scott%20College%20is%20home,understanding%20of%20complex%20global%20dynamics. https://www.chronicle.com/article/elevator-pitch-for-a-womens-college-revamp-curriculum-attract-students/

Alachnowicz, M. (2021, July 24). After 2015 near-closure, Sweet Briar College tops 2021 fundraising, enrollment goals. *WDBJ7 News.* https://www.wdbj7.com/2021/07/24/after-2015-near-closure-sweet-briar-college-tops-2021-fundraising-enrollment-goals/

Association of Governing Boards of Universities and Colleges. (2020). Case study: Agnes Scott College. *Innovation in Higher Education.* https://agb.org/wp-content/uploads/2019/01/casestudy_innovation_agnesscott.pdf

Astin, A. W. (1977). *Four critical years.* Jossey-Bass.

Belkin, L. (1983, August 30). First coed class enters Columbia College. *New York Times.* https://www.nytimes.com/1983/08/30/nyregion/first-coed-class-enters-columbia-college.html

Berrett, D. (2017, December 18). Sweet Briar chooses a core curriculum. *The Chronicle of Higher Education.* https://www.chronicle.com/article/sweet-briar-chooses-a-core-curriculum/

Biemiller, L. (2016, January 6). Elevator pitch for a women's college: Revamp curriculum, attract students. *The Chronicle of Higher Education.* https://www.chronicle.com/article/elevator-pitch-for-a-womens-college-revamp-curriculum-attract-students/

Cole, J. B. B. (1994). *Conversations: Straight talk with America's sister president.* Doubleday.

Farmer, L. B., Robbins, C. K., Keith, J. L., & Mabry, C. J. (2020). Transgender and gender-expansive students' experiences of genderism at women's colleges and universities. *Journal of Diversity in Higher Education, 13*(2), 146–157. https://doi.org/10.1037/dhe0000129

Freitas, A. (2017). Beyond acceptance: Serving the needs of transgender students at women's colleges. *Humboldt Journal of Social Relations, 39,* 294–314. https://www.jstor.org/stable/10.2307/90007886

Hart, J., & Lester, J. (2011). Starring students: Gender performance at a women's college. *NASPA Journal About Women in Higher Education, 4*(2), 193–217. https://doi.org/10.2202/1940-7890.1081

Hirt, J. B. (2006). *Where you work matters: Student affairs administration at different types of institutions.* University Press of America.

Horowitz, H. L. (1984). *Alma mater: Design and experience in the women's colleges from their nineteenth-century beginnings to the 1930s.* University of Massachusetts Press.

Gasman, M. (2007). Swept under the rug? A historiography of gender and black colleges. *American Educational Research Journal, 44*(4), 760–805. https://doi.org/10.3102/0002831207308639

Geiger, R. L. (2016). The ten generations of American higher education. In M. N. Bastedo, P. G. Altbach, & P. J. Gumport (Eds.), *American Higher Education in the twenty-first century: Social, political, and economic challenges* (4th ed.). Johns Hopkins University Press.

Jaschik, S. (2018, August 13). A Trump bump in yields at women's colleges. *Inside Higher Education.* https://www.insidehighered.com/admissions/article/2018/08/13/womens-colleges-see-boost-yield-wake-2016-election

Kamauf, R. (2018). *Viewbook marketing of women's colleges* (Publication No. 10684311). [Doctoral dissertation]. ProQuest Dissertations & Theses Global. https://www.proquest.com/dissertations-theses/viewbook-marketing-womens-colleges/docview/1975373148/se-2?accountid=12846

Kinzie, J. L., Thomas, A. D., Palmer, M. M., Umbach, P. D., & Kuh, G. D. (2007). Women students at coeducational and women's colleges: How do their experiences compare? *Journal of College Student Development, 48*(2), 145–165. https://doi.org/10.1353/csd.2007.0015

Langdon, E. A. (2001). Women's colleges then and now: Access then, equity now. *Peabody Journal of Education, 76*(1), 5–30. https://doi.org/10.1207/S15327930PJE7601_02

Lefever, H. G. (2005). The early origins of Spelman College. *The Journal of Blacks in Higher Education, 47,* 60–63. https://doi.org/10.2307/25073174

Lennon, S., & Day, J. (2012). *What matter in college after college: A comparative alumnae research study prepared for the Women's College Coalition.* https://www.womenscolleges.org/sites/default/files/report/files/main/2012hardwickdaycomparativealumnaesurveymarch2012_0.pdf

Lewin, T. (2008, June 3). 'Sisters' colleges see a bounty in the Middle East. *New York Times.* http://www.nytimes.com/2008/06/03/education/03sisters.html?pagewanted=all&_r=0

Manning, K. (2000). *Rituals, ceremonies, and cultural meaning in higher education.* Bergin & Garvery.

Marine, S. B. (2011). "Our college is changing": Women's college student affairs administrators and transgender students. *Journal of Homosexuality, 58*(9), 1165–1186. https://doi.org/10.1080/00918369.2011.605730

206 C. KORTEGAST

Miller-Bernal, L. (2011). The role of women's colleges in the twenty-first century. In L. M. Stulberg & S. L. Weinberg (Eds.), *Diversity in American higher education: Toward a more comprehensive approach*. Routledge.

Nanney, M., & Brunsma, D. L. (2017). Moving beyond cis-terhood: Determining gender through transgender admittance policies at U.S. women's colleges. *Gender & Society, 31*(2), 145–170. https://doi.org/10.1177/0891243217690100

National Center for Education Statistics [NCES]. (2021). *Enrollment and degrees conferred in degree-granting women's colleges, by selected characteristics and institution: Fall 2020 and 2019–20*. U.S. Department of Education. Institute of Education Sciences, National Center for Education Statistics. https://nces.ed.gov/programs/digest/d21/tables/dt21_312.30.asp

Renn, K. A. (2014). *Women's colleges and universities in global contexts*. John Hopkins.

Renn, K. A. (2017). The role of women's colleges and universities in providing access to postsecondary education. *The Review of Higher Education, 41*(1), 91–112. https://doi.org/10.1353/rhe.2017.0034

Renn, K.. & Lytle, J. H. (2010). Student leaders at women's postsecondary institutions: A global perspective. *Journal of Student Affairs Research and Practice, 47*(2), 215–232. https://doi.org/10.2202/1949-6605.6074

Sax, L. J., Lozano, J. B., & Vandenboom, C. Q. (2015). *Who attends a women's college?: Identifying unique characteristics and patterns of change, 1971–2011*. https://www.womenscolleges.org/discover/reports/who-attends-womens-college

Schuman, S. (2005). *Old main: Small colleges in twenty-first century America*. John Hopkins University Press.

Seltzer, R. (2021, March 25). *Bennett College Outlines New Direction*. https://www.insidehighered.com/quicktakes/2021/03/25/bennett-college-outlines-new-direction

Smith, D. G. (1989). *The challenge of diversity: Involvement or alienation in the academy?* ASHE-ERIC Report No. 5. Washington DC: George Washington University, School of Education and Human Development.

Snyder, T. D., & Dillow, S. A. (2012). *Digest of Education Statistics, 2011* (NCES 2012–001). National Center for Education Statistics, Institute of Education Sciences, U.S. Department of Education. Washington, DC.

Solomon, B. M. (1985). *In the company of educated women*. Yale University Press.

Texas Women's College. (2020). *About TWU*. https://twu.edu/about-twu/

Tidball, M. E. (1980). Women's Colleges and Women Achievers. *Signs, 5*(3), 504–517. https://www.jstor.org/stable/3173590

Thelin, J. R. (2011). *A history of American higher education* (2nd ed.). Johns Hopkins University Press.

Thomas, C. R. (2008, December 17). Spel-bounding: All-female Spelman College ranks no. 2 in sending Black graduates on to Ph.Ds in science and math. *Diverse Issues in Higher Education*. https://www.diverseeducation.com/students/article/15088066/spel-bounding-all-female-spelman-college-ranks-no-2-in-sending-black-graduates-on-to-phds-in-science-and-math#:~:text=Atlanta's%20Spelman%20College%2C%20an%20all,by%20the%20National%20Science%20Foundation.

U.S. News & World Report. (2021). *Most innovative schools*. https://www.usnews.com/best-colleges/rankings/national-liberal-arts-colleges/innovative

Wasserstein, W. (1991). *The Heidi chronicles: Uncommon women and others & Isn't it romantic*. Vintage.

Weber, S. (2016). "Womanhood does not reside in documentation": Queer and feminist student activism for transgender women's inclusion at women's colleges. *Journal of Lesbian Studies, 20*(1), 29–45. http://dx.doi.org/10.1080/10894160.2015.1076238

Whitford, E. (2021a, February 25). Liberal arts meets women's leadership in health. *Inside Higher Education*. https://www.insidehighered.com/news/2021/02/25/salem-college-refocuses-its-curriculum-health-and-leadership

Whitford, E. (2021b, May 7). Judson college will close. *Inside Higher Education*. https://www.insidehighered.com/news/2021/05/07/judson-college-closing-amid-enrollment-and-debt-woes

Wolf-Wendel, L. E. (1998). Models of excellence: The baccalaureate origins of successful European American women, African American women, and Latinas. *The Journal of Higher Education, 69*(2), 141–186. https://www.jstor.org/stable/2649247

Wolf-Wendel, L. E., Baker, B. D., & Morphew, C. C. (2000). Dollars and $ense: Institutional resources and the baccalaureate origins of women doctorates. *The Journal of Higher Education, 71*(2), 165–186. https://www.jstor.org/stable/2649247

Women's College Consortium. (2021). *History*. https://www.womenscolleges.org/history

CHAPTER 16

FAITH-BASED HIGHER EDUCATION IN THE UNITED STATES

The History and Present Status of Religiously Associated Institutions

Dennis E. Gregory and Kim E. Bullington
Old Dominion University

While this is true for some religiously affiliated institutions many will also value these efforts and provide support to students, even those who disagree with the underlying faith of the institution or the dogma of a particular faith As noted in this chapter, with over 1,000 religiously affiliated institutions in the United States, the diversity of institutions is great and students can choose in an institution that supports their beliefs and supports their academic and social endeavors. The diversity of the denominational sector of American higher education is so important and so varied, as a sector it will continue to do well. Of course, much will depend on the future of legislation providing a free community college education which will cut the legs out from under many tuition-focused private denominational institutions. This chapter will explore the histories of faith-based (religious) private institutions and nuance the ways in which they are distinctive from other non-sacred private institutions.

Institutional Diversity in American Postsecondary Education, pp. 209–222
Copyright © 2024 by Information Age Publishing
www.infoagepub.com
All rights of reproduction in any form reserved.

HISTORY

American higher education began in 1636 with the founding of Harvard College in Massachusetts. Harvard and the other institutions founded before the American Revolution were established primarily by faith-based groups of colonists seeking to combine their religious faiths through theocratic governments in those colonies (Thelin, 2019). Many of the early colleges were founded to train ministers for their respective faiths (Jencks & Reisman, 1968). The levels of faith-based involvement varied with some, such as the College of William and Mary, which were supported more by the Virginia government than the church, but all had similar purposes and goals for their institutions including the preparation of clergy (Marsden, 1994). As a goal of glorifying God, Harvard College had a goal to

> Let every student be plainly instructed and earnestly pressed to consider well the main end of his life and studies is to know God and Jesus Christ, which is eternal life, and therefore to lay Christ in the bottom, as the only foundation of all sound knowledge and learning. (Eby, 1915, p. 67)

After the American Revolution, in what has been called the national period (Dorn, 2017), the new states found prestige in creating state universities, with Georgia and North Carolina both claiming to have established the first public university, the former being the first to receive its charter in 1785 (Coulter, 1951) and the latter being the enroll students in 1795 (Snider, 1992). Other states, such as New Hampshire, sought to take over existing private institutions as public institutions; this resulted in a decision by the United States Supreme Court in which Dartmouth College challenged the efforts to take over the institution (Hagan, 1931). In this case, the Court decided that charters established with the King of England and the establishment of these private institutions remained valid under the contract clause of the United States Constitution, thus prohibiting state governments from against the will of the college's trustees from taking over the institution and making it public (Hagan, 1931). This means that private colleges and universities, particularly those which are denominational and religiously-based, can maintain their existence and operate legally due to the contract clause of the United States Constitution. This case has resulted in the ability for the diversity of our higher education system in the United States to develop into the system we now enjoy!

There is a difference between religious-based and secular institutions. First, religion can have an effect on alternative worldviews, thus secular institutions are not limited to religious worldviews. Secular institutions also work on a model of *freedom from* (Ringenberg, 2016), meaning they are not constrained to the denomination's teachings and beliefs. Also, when comparing public and private institutions, public institutions are confined by the requirements of the Constitution as well as federal and state laws. Private institutions do not have to follow the Constitution, though they are regulated by many state laws and federal laws if they accept federal funds. There are 18 religiously based institutions that do not accept federal monies (Clancy, 2017):

Aletheia Christian College (ID)	Bethlehem College & Seminary (MN)
Boyce College (KY)	Christendom College (VA)
Faith Bible College (ME)	Grove City College (PN)
Gutenberg College (OR)	Hillsdale College (MI)
Mid-America Baptist Theological Seminary (TN)	New College Franklin (TN)
New Saint Andrews College (ID)	Patrick Henry College (VA)
Pensacola Christian College (FL)	Principia College (IL)
Sattler College (MA)	Southern Baptist Theological Seminary (KY)
Southwestern Baptist Theological Seminary (TX)	Wyoming Catholic College (WY)

In the Colonial period, religious leaders and their communities saw a need to educate future ministers "to advance learning and perpetuate it to posterity, dreading to leave an illiterate Ministry to the Churches when our present Ministers shall lie in the Dust" (New England's First Fruits, 1643, p. 242). As the Colonists expanded into the frontier, religiously-affiliated schools and colleges were created with missions to assure that the word of God was accessible for the children and young adults. The mission of religious education was often combined with evangelism. Disciples of Christ leader, Alexander Campbell said "Colleges and churches go hand in hand in the progress of Christian civilization (Campbell, 1854, as cited in Campbell, 1882, p. 83).

From 1739 to 1745, a Great Awakening was sparked by the belief that colonial denominations were being perverted by secularism as the colonists moved further away from their churches as Enlightenment, which emphasized science and logic, made its way to the Colonies. Ministers spread the message that it was time to return to religion. The main concepts were that all people were born sinners and needed to be saved from Hell by accepting God's grace through direct, personal, and emotional connections with God (Bumsted & Van de Wetering, 1976). Others found that the belief that the relationship with God was casual, opposed these ideas, and supported more formalized religion (Bonomi, 1986). The first Great Awakening is purported to have influenced the Revolutionary War, but it also led to the creation of colonial colleges like Princeton (1747), Brown (1764), Rutgers (1766) Dartmouth (1769) (Divine et al., 1984).

In addition to the Ivy League universities, denominational colleges were created by many religious groups as the higher education system in the U.S. also grew. Prior to the American Revolution, Moravian College, founded in 1742, was the sixth oldest college in the country. Another early Moravian institution was Salem College, founded in 1772 in Winston-Salem, North Carolina. Hampden-Sydney College, in Virginia, was founded in 1775 and was the first Presbyterian college in the U.S. Another early Presbyterian institution is Tusculum University in Tennessee, which was founded in 1794. Georgetown University in Washington, D.C which was established in 1789, was the first Catholic institution. The first three Quaker institutions to be developed were Haverford (1833), Guilford in North Carolina (1837) and Earlham in Indiana (1847). Transylvania University was the first denominational college established west of the Allegheny mountains in 1780. Transylvania is affiliated with the Presbyterian church. The oldest Methodist affiliated institution is Randolph Macon College in Ashland, Virginia, which was founded in 1830.

Religion can be affected by social change. Wesleyan College, established in Macon, GA in 1836, was the first to grant degrees to women. The Freedman's Aid Society sought to create institutions throughout the Southern states after the Civil War. Many of these church-based colleges were initially started as seminaries and, if successful, grew to college status, but many closed or broke ties with the churches that established them.

Protestant colleges showed varying patterns between 1860 and 1890 but grew overall from 158 to 265 institutions (Geiger, 2007). Between 1850 and 1890, Catholic colleges grew at a rate of 33 per decade but closed at a rate of 85% (Geiger, 2007). In the 1930s, there were 311 members of the National Conference of Church-Related Colleges (Geiger, 2016), which was subsumed as the National Commission on Christian Higher Education of the Association of American Colleges in the 1940s (U.S. Office of Education, 1942), which then became a part of the American Association of Colleges and Universities (2022).

Mission Schools and Higher Education of Native Americans

There was a historical need for Native American education, but it really was a battle of power in an effort to assimilate Native Americans into colonial culture through conversion to Christianity and cultural erasure (Lomawaima, 1995). Mission schools were opened like Moore's Charity School (Dartmouth), William and Mary, and Harvard, to name a few, in the 1600–1700s (Huff, 1997). Colleges like Ottawa University, founded in

Faith-Based Higher Education in the United States   213

1865, was established by the Baptists but only enrolled one student, leading to a lawsuit that was not resolved until 1960 for $406,166 (Reyhner & Eder, 2007). The Croatan Normal School (now Pembroke State University), founded in 1885 by the North Carolina General Assembly, and Bacone's Indian University (now Bacone College), founded in 1888 by the American Baptist Mission Society were more successful in attracting and educating Native Americans, but collectively they only "served a tiny fraction of Indians" (Reyhner & Eder, 2007, p. 696).

Junior/community colleges date back to the early 20th century; they were created in response to the needs of the communities they would eventually serve. Some of the purposes of the junior college were to take pressure off the rapidly growing colleges and universities by taking first- and second-year students and to prepare high school graduates for the rigors of higher education (Cohen & Brawer, 1989). Under the guise of "democracy's colleges" (Brint & Karabel, 1989, p. 10), Protestants viewed religiously-based junior colleges as an opportunity to provide more access to higher education as well as to elevate more Protestants into the middle class. So did the Methodists, Baptists, and Catholics, who played a large role in creating denominational colleges (Brint & Karabel, 1989).

In 1859, William Mitchell, a University of Georgia trustee, submitted a plan to focus on the third and fourth years of college because students were not academically prepared; this effort was never implemented (Witt et al., 1994). However, in 1984, the president of Baylor University, the Reverend J. M. Carroll, recommended, in an effort to save failing Baptist colleges in Texas and Louisiana, that those institutions take on the first two years of college education and Baylor would be responsible for the third and fourth years (Baker, 1994; Eels, 1931; Ratcliff, 1994).

Approximately 68% of the junior colleges created between 1900 and 1916 had a church affiliation (McDowell, 1919). In 1949, 180 of the 322 privately-owned junior colleges were affiliated with a church (Cohen & Brawer, 1989). Decatur Baptist College in Decatur, TX, was founded in 1891 (Bogue, 1950) after a move and name change to Dallas Baptist University and is still in existence today. William Rainey Harper, the first president of the University of Chicago, had a large role in the creation of the junior college, but as a big proponent of the German model recommended that local Baptist colleges restrict their curricula to general education (Nevarez & Wood, 2010).

Starting in 1875 in Mississippi through the sponsorship of the General Christian Missionary Society of the Disciples of Christ, the Southern Christian Institute (SCI) was created to "train common school teachers for country colored schools and to educate students in the Christian faith and mortality according to the Scriptures" (Southern Christian Institute Catalog, as cited in Burnley, 2008, p. 193). SCI merged with Tougaloo

College in 1954 (Williamson, 2005). Lane (1933) compiled a list of the 19 junior colleges for Blacks/African Americans from the 1933 Junior College Directory; of those 13 were private, denominational institutions and two were public/private partnerships. Organizations like the African Methodist Episcopal, American Missionary Association, Methodist Episcopalians, and the Disciples of Christ wanted to ensure that religious doctrine remained a focus in junior colleges that focused on educating Blacks/African Americans.

Ferrum College, formerly Ferrum Junior College, was founded as a mission school by The United Methodist Church Women for Appalachian youth in 1909 and began taking students in 1914 as Ferrum Training School. The school attracted students from the rural area surrounding the community of Ferrum from Franklin and the surrounding counties. And by 1926 grew to become a junior college. In 1971, Ferrum Junior College became Ferrum College and began to institute its two-plus-two program offering both associate and bachelor's degrees. In 1976, the first four-year diploma was awarded. Ferrum has now begun to offer its first graduate courses. While initially being sponsored by the United Methodist Church Women and maintaining its Methodist affiliation, its program is based more on a broader interpretation of Christian thinking and not Methodist dogma (Ferrum College, 2021; Hurt, 1977).

ORGANIZATION STRUCTURE AND CULTURE

Religiously-based and denominational nonprofit institutions vary in size and student populations. Among the largest of these have grown in recent years because of their focus in online education. The largest of these are Liberty University (Evangelical Christian), with a student body of approximately 93,000 students, the large majority of which are online, Brigham Young University—Provo (Latter Day Saints—Mormon) with a student population of approximately 36,000, DePaul University (Roman Catholic) with a student population of approximately 22,000, and Saint John's University (Roman Catholic) with a student population of approximately 20,000 students (National Center for Education Statistics, 2022). One common characteristic is that all private institutions, including those which are religiously affiliated, have boards of trustees or the like, most of which are selected by the boards themselves. However, some denominational organizations, for example, The United Methodist Women, may have influence and such groups may require representation. For public institutions, governing board positions are typically appointed by the governor; for religious colleges and universities, it is usually the affiliated religious organization (e.g., church council) or the college or university president who selects and approves trustees.

The smallest denominational colleges range from Mount Angel Seminary (127 students), and Allegheny Wesleyan College (67 students) and San Diego Christian College (512 students) and Christendom College (539 students). These small institutions "primarily identify as seminaries or Bible colleges" (Lindsay, 2020, n.p.). The size of an institution varies depending upon its purpose, location, denominational connection and many other variables, though most denominational colleges are relatively small in comparison to public state universities and university systems.

The variations also result in differing administrative organizations. While true, most generally have a governing board which is self-perpetuating (i.e., it chooses its own members), may have members from pre-determined denominational groups (e.g., The United Methodist Women), may include clergy and alumni, and are generally larger than those of public institutions. This is often true since members of governing boards are seen as prime donors to the institution. As with most institutions of higher education, there is also usually a president or chancellor, a chief academic officer, a chief student affairs officer, and—very importantly—chief development officers. Because private institutions in general, and denominational institutions in particular, are primarily supported by tuition and external funding from donors, alumni and other types of external funding, the role of the president and chief development officer have strong foci on raising funds to support the institution. Denominational institutions often have a chaplain who may serve as a primary institutional leader as well as serving to connect the institution to its denominational base. Depending on the size and complexity of the organization, many private denominational institutions employee internal legal counsel to help prevent legal difficulty and to work with funds raised by development personnel including wills and estates, property donations (Pusser & Loss, n.d.)

STUDENT SUCCESS AND POPULATIONS

Because this is so diverse group of institutions, it is impossible to define who the students are at these institutions. They vary so much by location, size, affiliation, institutional purpose, and diversity. Some are specifically designed to educate a particular population or religious group, while others are evangelical and appeal to those with more conservative religious beliefs. Suffice it to say that those seeking a particular faith-based educational setting have great diversity in those settings among the religious- and denominational-based institutions. These institutions range greatly in academic selectivity, size, location, and virtually any other characteristic one might choose. Private denominational institutions are often more expensive than their public counterparts, but many offer tuition discounts, large amounts of financial aid, or specifically appeal to persons from specific socioeconomic levels. Levels of academic success also vary widely across these institutions, depending on selectivity and the populations from which they draw their students. As noted earlier, several of these institutions have taken on large distance education programs and thus have variations within their student populations and success based upon which type of enrollment is chosen.

PROFESSIONAL CONTEXT

One of the authors of this chapter has extensive experience of working at private denominational institutions ranging in size from 800 students to 5000 students. The selectivity has varied from being very selective to the admission of a large majority of the applicants. The religious faith of those students attending these institutions has varied as well, with the students primarily attending due to geographic proximity rather than religious affiliation. One of these institutions is a member of a Power Five athletic conference, while the others were small and played Division III athletics. None of the institutions could be defined as highly religious, yet all three have chapels on campus, had a campus chaplain, and had some religious-focused courses and programs. The primary difference experienced by the author was not based upon religious affiliation but based upon wealth and prestige of the institution. While admittedly this experience was over twenty years ago, the author has maintained deep connections with these institutions and values the experience of being affiliated with them. At two of the institutions, staffing was constrained by the size of the institution and the capacity for fundraising and outside philanthropy, the flexibility of a private institution and the ability for the institution to grow and improve its status was palpable.

Working at a wealthy private denominational institution has great benefits but also has great challenges. A wealthy church-related institution has a great deal of flexibility in the type of student it seeks to enroll. Being less tuition driven allows greater selectivity and increased academic rigor. It also allows for less deferred maintenance and increased the possibility for increased capital improvement. Being a wealthy institution also allows salaries to be higher and thus higher quality faculty and staff may be attracted. Private institutions of all types have a great deal more flexibility in the enforcement of student conduct norms and other constitutional restraints placed on public institutions. Challenges on some employees may include increased pressure to operate the institution at growing levels of productivity and sometimes can result in pressure to please donors and parents who pay large amounts of tuition and give large gifts to the institution.

Attending such an institution as a student also provides great opportunities and future prospects, while studying at a small denominational institution also provides great opportunities to develop very close relationships with the small academic community within the institution. Studying at an institution which provides a learning and other types of environments which are related to a particular faith tradition may also provide support for students. The more resources that are available may also provide additional academic and student affairs support services and opportunities.

There are over 1,000 colleges and universities in the United States with a religious affiliation. These institutions are sponsored by many different faiths. These include, but are not limited to the Jewish faith, the Catholic faith, the Muslim faith, the Baptist church, the United Methodist Church, the Presbyterian church, the United Church of Christ, the Nazerine church, the Lutheran church, and many others. As a result, it is beyond the scope of this chapter to explore the diversity of cultures possessed by each institution within each of those sponsored by particular church groups.

If the reader wishes to study a particular institution or a faith group to explore the cultures of those institutions or groups, it is recommended they use the work of Edgar H. Schein (2016). Schein posits that the way to examine an institution's culture is to do so by looking at the institution as if it were a pyramid ranging from shallow factors at the top of the pyramid and deep factors at the bottom of the pyramid. At the shallowest level are, according to Schein, *artifacts* which are observable in an organization. These may be the physical indicators or policies that show what is important to the institution. The next level within which to study an institution's culture is deeper and includes *espoused values*. These may include vision and mission statements and illustrate organizational values and behaviors. At the deepest level of analysis is *underlying assumptions*. These are the below-the-surface assumptions held by leaders and employees (and in the spirit of colleges and universities—students) regarding workplace behaviors and how people should work together (Schein, 2016).

As noted above, because there is such wide variation among private denominational/religious institutions and because the size, wealth, and denominational connections vary so much, it is impossible to accurately describe the culture for this type of institution in general. For instance, the Catholic University of America is often seen as the *Pope's University* in the United States and is closely aligned to Catholic doctrine and religious beliefs. Other Catholic colleges and universities have been founded and operated by various orders of priests or nuns and have differing traditions and approaches to Catholic education. There are 28 Jesuit colleges, and they have a large range; some are major research universities, and some are small liberal arts institutions. The International Association of Jesuit Universities represents Jesuit institutions worldwide (Association of Jesuit

Colleges & Universities, n.d.). Notre Dame University, Boston College, and others have major athletic traditions and belong to Power Five athletic conferences, while others are single gender intuitions that are small and have limited or no athletic focus. Some institutions, like Liberty University, which is Baptist, and Wake Forest University, which evolved from a Baptist foundation but no longer is formally associated with the Southern Baptist Convention, differ greatly in their organization, focus, size, structure, and institutional culture. Wake Forest is a highly selective smaller institution with a law and medical school, while Liberty has developed a very strong distance education program, is less selective and has a much more conservative culture.

Among the best known of the 37 Jewish colleges and universities are Yeshiva University in New York City and Brandeis University in Waltham, Massachusetts. Both institutions are relatively small at under 10,000 students and Brandeis is highly selective. Because, among other things, Yeshiva is very urban, and Brandeis is in a small city. Both their cultures vary while providing broad academic programs and education based on Jewish traditions and educational approaches.

Historically Black Colleges and Universities (HBCUs) are defined as those founded before 1964 with the primary purpose of educating African American students. While many of these institutions are public, founded after the *Morrill Land Grant Act of 1890* (7 U.S.C. § 321 et seq.) many were also founded by and continue to be operated as denominational institutions. These include those founded by the African Methodist Episcopal Church, the Baptist Church, the Presbyterian Church, the American Baptist Churches USA, the United Methodist Church, the African Methodist Episcopal Zion Church, the United Church of Christ, the Christian Methodist Episcopal Church, the American Baptist Home Mission Society, the Seventh-Day Adventist Church, the Episcopal Church (United States), the American Missionary Association, the Catholic Church, and the Disciples Church (The Hundred-Seven, n.d.). Even today, religion plays a part in many HBCUs, and some remain markedly true to their religious founding, like Dillard University (Catholic), but many are religiously diverse and have welcomed other religions like Islam (Gasman & Nguyen, 2015). While tensions have existed due to religious beliefs and social issues (e.g., homosexuality, political ideologies), it is important that we do not make a distinction between HBCUs and non-HBCUs. "If this rationale were to be used to make sense of HBCU student populations, then other institutions with a Christian history such as the College of William and Mary (public) or Harvard University (private) would also be thought to enroll 'only Christian students'" (Gasman & Nguyen, 2015, p. 5).

The Association for Biblical Higher Education in Canada and the United States (ABHE) serves as an umbrella organization for more than

150 institutions of higher education focused on biblical education (ABHE, 2021). There are two national Christian higher education associations. The Association of Catholic Colleges and Universities (ACCU) founded in 1899 serves 247 Catholic institutions (AACU, 2021, n.p.). The Council for Christian Colleges and Universities (CCCU) is made up of 180 Christian institutions and operates on a global level (CCCU, 2021, n.p.), The Commission on Accrediting of the Association of Theological Schools (ATS) accredits more than 270 graduate schools of theology (ATS, 2021). The Transnational Association of Christian Colleges and Schools (TRACS) was founded in 1979 and serves 80 schools globally (TRACS, 2021). For the Jewish faith, the Association of Advanced Rabbinical and Talmudic Schools (AARTS) accredits 17 institutions (Council for Higher Education Accreditation, 2021).

FUTURE CONSIDERATIONS AND DIRECTIONS

The future of many denominational institutions seems secure, while others will continue to struggle due to the economic factors of maintaining such a small institution in today's economy, the need to grow tuition, the constant search for outside funding which was once the primary purview of private institutions but has become a growing trend at public community colleges and four-year institutions, and the constant search for students in a society which is questioning the value of a college degree. Persons with differing faith traditions than those which are predominant at a given intuition may face challenged of belief systems with little support for their faith. More conservative religious groups that sponsor institutions may seek to impose their belief systems on their students so that freedom of expression, personal beliefs about abortion rights, race and gender equality may also be challenged.

DISCUSSION QUESTIONS

1. When choosing an institution to attend or at which to work, what are the things that are most important to you? Is it the religious connection, the fact that it is an institution of faith, or is it size, rigor, wealth, or location? What difference do your own religious beliefs make in your evaluation of an institution which espouses the same beliefs? Differing beliefs? Many denominational institutions are small in enrollments, but may also, as a result, be limited in services. Does this make a difference?

2. HBCUs and other special purpose institutions have cultures quite different from *regular* institutions. For example, private HBCUs are often sponsored by religious groups. Does this make a difference when selecting a private or public institution?
3. How do private denominational institutions differ from private non-denominational institutions?

REFERENCES

American Association of Colleges and Universities. (2022). *About AAC&U*. https://www.aacu.org/about

Association for Biblical Higher Education. (2021). *About ABHE*. https://www.abhe.org/about-abhe/

Association of Catholic Colleges and Universities. (2021). *About ACCU*. https://www.accunet.org/About-ACCU

Association of Jesuit Colleges & Universities. (n.d.) *Jesuit colleges and universities*. https://www.ajcunet.edu/institutions

Association of Theological Schools. (2021). *About ATS*. https://www.ats.edu/about

Baker, G. A. (1994). *A handbook on the community college in America*. Greenwood Press.

Bogue, J. P. (1950). *The community college*. McGraw-Hill.

Bonomi, P. (1986). *Under the cope of heaven: Religion, society, and politics in Colonial America*. Oxford University Press.

Brint, S., & Karabel, J. (1989). *The diverted dream: Community colleges and the promise of educational opportunity in America, 1900–1985*. Oxford University Press.

Bumsted, J., & Van De Wetering, J. (1976). *What must I do to be saved?: The great awakening in colonial America*. The Dryden Press.

Burnley, L. A. (2008). *The cost of unity: African-American agency and education in the Christian ehurch, 1865–1914*. Mercer University Press.

Campbell, S. H. (1882). *Home life and reminiscences of Alexander Campbell by his wife, Selina Huntington Campbell*. John Burns. https://books.google.com/books?id=mGBCAAAAIAAJ

Clancy, D. (2017, December 2). *A list of colleges that don't take federal money*. https://deanclancy.com/a-list-of-colleges-that-dont-take-federal-money/

Cohen, A. M., & Brawer, F. B. (1989). *The American community college* (2nd ed.). Jossey-Bass.

Coulter, E. M. (1951). The University of Georgia – Old and new. *The Georgia Review, 5*(1), 12–21. https://jstor.org/stable/41385015

Council for Christian Colleges & Universities. (2021). *Our work and mission*. https://www.cccu.org/about/

Council for Higher Education Accreditation. (2021). *Association of advanced Rabbinical and Talmudic Schools*. https://www.chea.org/association-advanced-rabbinical-and-talmudic-schools-accreditation-commission

Divine, R., Breen, T. H., George, F., & Williams, R. H. (1984). *America: Past and present*. Scott, Foresman and Company.

Dorn, C. (2017). *For the common good: A new history of higher education in America*. Cornell University Press.

Eby, F. (1915). *Christianity and education*. Executive Board of the Baptist General Convention of Texas.

Eels, W. C. (1931). *The junior college*. Houghton Mifflin.

Ferrum College. (2021). *Ferrum history*. https://www.ferrum.edu/about/ferrum-history/

Gasman, M., & Nguyen, T-H. (2015). Myths dispelled: A historical account of diversity and inclusion at HBCUs. *New Directions for Higher Education, 2015*(170), 5–15.

Geiger, R. L. (2007). The era of multipurpose colleges in American higher education, 1850–1890. In H. S. Weschsler, L. F. Goodchild, & L. Eisenmann (Eds.), *The history of American higher education* (3rd ed., pp. 360–376). Pearson.

Geiger, R. L. (2016). *The history of American higher education: Learning and culture from the founding to World War II*. Princeton University Press.

Hagan, H. H. (1931). The Dartmouth College case. *Georgetown Law Journal, 19*(4). https://heinonline.org/HOL/P?h=hein.journals/glj19&i=435

Huff, D. J. (1997). *To live heroically: Institutional racism and American Indian education*. State University of New York Press.

Hurt, F. B. (1977). *A history of Ferrum College*. Stone Printing Company.

Jencks, C., & Riesman, D. (1968). *The American Revolution*. Doubleday.

Lane, D. A. (1933). The junior college movement among Negroes. *The Journal of Negro Education, 2*(3), 272–283. https://www.jstor.org/stable/2292199

Lindsay, S. (2020, December 14). *Complete list: The smallest college in the United States*. http://blog.prepscholar.com/the-smallest-colleges-in-the united-states.

Lomawaima, K. T. (1995). *Educating Native Americans*. In J. Banks (Ed.), *Handbook of research on multicultural education* (pp. 331–347). Macmillan.

Marsden, G. M. (1994). *The soul of the American university: From Protestant establishment to established nonbelief*. Oxford University Press.

McDowell, F. (1919). *The junior college*. U.S. Government Printing Office. https://files.eric.ed.gov/fulltext/ED541201.pdf

National Center for Education Statistics. (2022). CollegeNavigator. https://nces.ed.gov/collegenavigator/

Nevarez, C., & Wood, J. L. (2010). *Community college leadership and administration: Theory, practice, and change*. Peter Lang.

New England's First Fruits. (1643). Reprinted in *Collections of the Massachusetts Historical Society*, I (1792, 242).

Pusser, B., & Loss, C. P. (n.d.). *Colleges and organizational structure of universities: Governing boards, the president, faculty, administration and staff, students, future prospects*. https://education.stateuniversity.com/pages/1859/Colleges-Universities-Organizational-Structure.html

Ratcliff, J. L. (1994). Seven streams in the historical development of the modern American community college. In G. A. Baker, III, J. Dudziak, & P. Tyler (eds.), *A handbook on the community college in America: Its history, mission, and management* (pp. 3–16). Greenwood Press.

Reyhner, J., & Eder, J. (2007). Higher education of American Indians. In H. S. Weschsler, L. F. Goodchild, & L. Eisenmann (Eds.), *The history of American higher education* (3rd ed., pp. 694–702). Pearson.

Ringenberg, W. C. (2016). *The Christian college and the meaning of academic freedom.* Palgrave MacMillan.

Schein, E. H. (2016). *Organizational culture and leadership* (5th ed.). Wiley.

Snider, W. D. (1992). *Light on the hill: A history of the University of North Carolina at Chapel Hill.* The University of North Carolina Press.

The Hundred-Seven. (n.d.). *Spotlight on: HBCUs where faith matters.* www.the hundred-seven.org/religiouslife.html

Thelin, J. R. (2019). *A history of American higher education* (3rd ed.). Johns Hopkins University Press.

Transnational Association of Christian Colleges and Schools. (2021). *Home.* https://tracs.org/#

U.S. Office of Education. (1942). *Educational directory 1941–42.*

Williamson, J. A. (2005). "Quacks, quirks, agitators, and communists": Private Black colleges and the limits of institutional autonomy. In R. L. Geiger (Ed.), *History of higher education annal 2003–2004* (pp. 49–82). Routledge.

Witt, A. A. (1998). The federal investment in minority-serving institutions. *New Directions in Higher Education, 102*(1), 18–32.

CHAPTER 17

MILITARY AND MARITIME COLLEGES AND UNIVERSITIES

Julie Shank
George Mason University

Eric T. Olson
United States Military Academy

Emily Fisher Gray
Norwich University

Tamara S. McKenna
U.S. Coast Guard Academy

David Taliaferro
California State University Maritime Academy

David J. Mollahan
Marion Military Institute

Military and maritime colleges and universities are another special mission institutional type. For this chapter, we focus on institutions that grant associate's and baccalaureate level degrees, where all or the majority of students live together in a military style barracks, have a regimented daily structure involving physical fitness, focus on experiential learning, and develop leadership through peer governance. Attention to leadership supports

---

Institutional Diversity in American Postsecondary Education, pp. 223–237
Copyright © 2024 by Information Age Publishing
www.infoagepub.com
All rights of reproduction in any form reserved.

224 J. SHANK ET AL.

the heavy responsibilities that most graduates will undertake immediately, often in high-risk environments or with strategic implications. Intimately related to leadership are ethical behavior and professional conduct, undergirded by the academic rigor of the schools.

This chapter is focused not on ROTC programs at traditional universities, but on federal service academies, the junior and senior military colleges, and maritime colleges: institutions that offer higher education primarily or exclusively within a military setting, organize students into Corps of Cadets, and structure student life around military and professional training. The unique institutional cultures of military and maritime academies and colleges are closely tied to their founding principles.

HISTORY

In 1799, Alexander Hamilton proposed legislation to create several federally funded military schools focused on Engineering, Artillery, and Naval Training. Three years later, the United States Military Academy (USMA) was founded at West Point, NY on a strategic outpost on the Hudson River used by George Washington's Revolutionary War armies. Congress could not agree on the mission and funding of additional institutions so West Point remained the only federal military college until the founding of the United States Naval Academy (USNA) in 1845, when Congress recognized the need for specialized training for midshipmen and authorized a second military college sited in Annapolis, MD (Berube, 2020). In 1915, Congress consolidated several federal maritime programs into the United States Coast Guard Academy (USCGA) in New London, CT and President Franklin D. Roosevelt dedicated a separate United States Merchant Marine Academy (USMMA) at King's Point, NY in 1943. Soon after the establishment of the Air Force as a separate military branch in 1947, a fifth federal military college was added. The United States Air Force Academy (USAFA), established in 1955 in Colorado Springs, CO, is the only federal military academy situated away from the east coast.

The federal academies are among several options for military focused education in the United States. In 1819, a conviction that the nation needed more "citizen soldiers," as opposed to a professional military, led Capt. Alden Partridge to leave his post as Superintendent of the USMA and found the private American Literary, Scientific, and Military Academy, known since 1838 as Norwich University. Like the USMA, Partridge's academy offered students a practical education in science, engineering, history, and literature with the addition of hands-on military training to take place during hours students might otherwise engage in "useless amusement" ("Catalogue of the Officers and Cadets," 1821, pp. 9–10). He believed this would lead to the creation of a class of citizens engaged in civilian pursuits who were prepared to lead troops into battle if their state or country needed them. The Partridge model appealed to state legislatures, several of which set up their own military colleges to train officers for state militias. The state of Virginia created the Virginia Military Institute (VMI) in 1839, followed in 1842 by the South Carolina Military Academy (renamed The Citadel in 1910). Norwich, VMI, and The Citadel are non-federal, four-year senior military colleges that still organize most or all their students into a Corps of Cadets.

The United States depends on the maritime industry to achieve economic and defense strategic priorities. To that end, USMMA and six state maritime academies, State University of New York Maritime Academy (SUNY Maritime), Massachusetts Maritime Academy, Maine Maritime Academy, Texas A&M Maritime, California State University Maritime Academy, and Great Lakes Academy, focus on the education of licensed officers aboard U.S. flagged merchant marine vessels. Like the military service academies, these institutions are also mission focused, leverage close relationships with government, industry, and international partners to inform the development of their students, and receive federal funding and physical resources, including the training vessels. In the case of all cadets or midshipmen pursuing U.S. Coast Guard licensure, they must be provided an opportunity to take the licensing exam and, attend the academy for at least 3 years, and participate in a training cruise of at least 6 months duration ("Regulations and Minimum Standards for State," 1981).

There are also several two-year junior military colleges, including Valley Forge Military Academy, New Mexico Military Institute, Georgia Military College, Wentworth Military Academy in Missouri, and Marion Military Institute in Alabama. And the citizen-soldier model of the private or state military colleges lives on in the Reserve Officer Training Corps (ROTC) program, developed at Norwich University in 1916 by General Leonard Wood, then Chief of Staff of the Army (Lord, 2016, p. 22). The ROTC program allows students at many colleges and universities in the United States to receive military training as part of their studies. Most graduates of ROTC programs, including Corps of Cadets graduates of the non-federal senior military colleges, commission in one of the branches of the U.S. Armed Forces or in the National Guard, but many take their military education directly into the civilian world, often in public-service careers such as police officers, teachers, or civil service. By contrast, graduates of the federal military academies are all expected to be commissioned as officers and serve a minimum of five years in active-duty status, in the military branch for which they trained. USMMA graduates commit to fulfill a maritime service obligation, which can include service as a commissioned officer

226   J. SHANK ET AL.

or employment as a merchant marine officer sailing aboard U.S. flagged vessels.

Military leaders describe their missions in terms of "task and purpose," that is, the task to be accomplished and the purpose for which the task must be completed. The mission statements of military and maritime academies and colleges reveal the "task and purpose" and intended outcomes of military higher education. The mission statements of the federal service academies, junior and senior military colleges, and maritime academies are similar to that of the USMA, which reads:

> To educate, train, and inspire the Corps of Cadets so that each graduate is a commissioned leader of character committed to the values of Duty, Honor, Country and prepared for a career of professional excellence and service to Nation as an officer in the United States Army. (United States Military Academy West Point, n.d.-b)

Military colleges achieve their purpose—preparing students to serve the nation, predominantly through military service, though also through law enforcement, education, or other local, state, or federal service—through accomplishing not only the tasks of education and training in leadership but also inculcating values such as duty, honor, and patriotism. The purpose and values of each military college have remained constant since each school's founding, some as long as 200 years ago. Some of the tasks necessary to achieve those purposes have shifted over time, as tactics and technologies have evolved, and global challenges have emerged. Military officers today need to be educated to have the mental acuity and flexibility to respond to an ever-changing geopolitical context, and many will find themselves in situations where life and death decisions may hinge on complex and unique circumstances. But some tasks have changed little, such as physical training to build strength and endurance, and ethical development to ensure sound principles and moral reliability.

ORGANIZATIONAL STRUCTURES AND CULTURES

Many of the leaders and administrative personnel of military and maritime colleges and universities are recognizable by name and function, such as academic provosts and deans, chiefs of staff, heads of information or information technology divisions, admissions, communications and marketing, and chief financial officers, with counseling centers and medical staff. In some instances, academic and professional staff also wear uniforms and carry military rank, such as at Norwich and VMI.

Some titles, particularly the student affairs positions and that of the president, however, may not be as easily recognized. The President of a military college or university is often called a Superintendent. The Vice President for Student Affairs is known as the Commandant of Cadets (or Midshipmen). At a minimum, the office of the commandant is generally composed of a deputy and a staff section in charge of operations that schedules and manages a wide range of events, activities, and one of the unique features of a military college: military training. The office of the commandant is organized as a military staff, to include a deputy or chief of staff to supervise the function of the office, and operations section that plans and manages most of the daily routine followed by the student body, and special staff sections responsible for activities and programs that support the personnel, administrative, and logistical needs of the student.

Other members of the Commandant's staff administer important programs that support a positive and healthy living and learning environment such as the development and administration of rules and regulations, an honor code, the equal opportunity and sexual assault prevention and response programs, and the services of an impartial and confidential resource for student issues and grievances (the inspector general), which fulfill roles of housing and residence life, student conduct and Title IX. Honor codes, which are a revered part of the student experience and will be explained later, include academic integrity, but also include lying or deception of any form, and stealing. The housing and residence life staff provide direct supervision of the daily routine and functioning of the student body, oversight of leadership provided by student leaders.

Hands-on mentoring of the student leader development happens with the student military chain of command who are selected by the commandant and their staff, and, if the system includes it, an elected form of student government. The commandant is also responsible for critical elements of the leadership development process, most importantly the military education and training, physical development, and moral-ethical growth of the student.

The office of the commandant also plays a role in leadership development. The heart of leader development at these institutions is understanding and practicing military basics, which is the foundation upon which the larger and more expansive leadership and character learning initiatives begin. These basics are defined by the constant reinforcement of grooming standards, uniform wear, barracks room cleanliness, and adherence to military protocols, traditions, and general conduct and performance standards. The office of the commandant at a military institution may also include (or work closely with) a special center of excellence established at many military schools that has specific leadership and moral-ethical development responsibilities. For example, the A.J. Rane Center for Leadership (CFL) at Marion Military Institute is responsible to develop, coordinate, and integrate Corps-wide co- and extra-curricular activities that are designed to further develop leadership and character attributes through a more formal approach to leader development education (Marion Military Institute, n.d.).

STUDENT SUCCESS AND POPULATION

Achieving equilibrium between the four program areas in terms of how priorities are assigned, and resources allocated to each (especially student and faculty time) is perhaps the most important challenge that a military or maritime college's leadership must address. A critical responsibility of the leadership is to ensure that the academies are graduating officers whose pre-commissioning experience has equipped them to meet the needs of the service to which they will be assigned. Though many civilian universities include one or more of the program areas as part of their offerings, the specific mission of military and maritime colleges and universities shapes the characteristics and the nature of each, making the student experience unique.

The Academic Program

The academies are top-tier universities and leadership grants a high priority to academics. Students spend most of their time either in class or studying. But the distinctive design of the curricula, the intended outcome of the academic program, and the resulting experiences of the staff and faculty must be understood in light of the mission of the academies to develop military leaders. Curricula at military colleges include both disciplinary and professional elements, with more core courses, resulting in heavy course loads and more credits required for graduation.

The purpose of academic pursuit at the academies is distinctive. In most cases, the body of knowledge that a student amasses or the mastery of specific subject matter in a field of study is less important than the reasoning skills that are acquired through the process of learning. The premium is less on graduating chemists, mechanical engineers, or political scientists than on developing critical thinkers, problem solvers, and decision makers who can apply their skills in a wide range of situations, under the demanding conditions of combat or lifesaving missions.

Military Education and Training

As mentioned above, there is a time in the academic curriculum dedicated to learning the basics of the services in the armed forces in a classroom environment. Students at all military and maritime colleges and universities will spend time in military and professional training during the academic year. There are also off campus opportunities, between semesters or over the summer. Students may serve with active-duty units or formations of the armed forces with the merchant marine at sea. Additionally, military formations for accountability, parades and drill to instill discipline, and inspections of rooms and uniform wear and grooming standards are expectations for all who partake in the military aspect of a military or maritime college.

Perhaps the most pervasive element of the military program, with the farthest-reaching effect on culture and student life, is the military leadership experience at the academies. Students gain experience with military leadership, as both followers and leaders, through practice. Students lead their peers by holding them accountable to disciplinary and honor standards. The living environment is also structured to replicate some of the organizational constructs that students will experience in their chosen branch of service. The student body is administratively divided into units or formations, each of which is led by a student chain of command. Active-duty, reserve, and/or retired officers and/or non-commissioned officers are assigned to each unit to coach, mentor, and monitor and assist with the performance and the development of the student chain of command. These staff also assess members of the units—leaders and their subordinates—and the results of these assessments are included in the evaluation of overall performance that ultimately determines whether a student will graduate and be commissioned.

Physical Education and Performance

Given the nature of the military profession, it should come as no surprise that the military and many maritime colleges all maintain robust physical programs. Most core curricula contain some form of physical education courses that are offered. These courses are generally relevant to the physical demands and requirements that are placed on military women and men, such as military movement, swimming, combatives, and the like. Physical fitness testing at regular intervals is also required. Successful proficiency is required to commission. Many of the tests are the same as those taken by service members of the related branch of the armed forces.

Almost all students are required to participate in some form of competitive sport. All the military and maritime colleges field teams that compete in the various NCAA divisions, in some cases achieving top national rankings. Students may also opt to participate in a wide array of club sports that compete with other regional colleges and universities. Additionally, the service academies offer intramural sports programs for competition within the student body. More than recreation, sports cultivate mental toughness, a warrior ethos, and instill a "never quit" attitude.

As is the case with the other program areas, the purpose of the physical program goes beyond excellence in individual performance or team honors and awards. Ultimately, it is the value added to leadership development and teamwork that is the most important benefit. Physical fitness is essential for officers, both in terms of the ability to endure a wide range of extremely demanding environments and in setting the example for subordinates in military units. The requirement to take physical education courses, pass physical fitness tests, and participate in competitive sports supports these ends. The nature of competitive sports provides opportunities that cannot be duplicated in a conventional classroom or other extracurricular activities. Athletic competition is a critical component for developing leadership and teamwork skills. Competitive sports are also a proven way to maintain fitness, which is necessary both as a cadet and when in the military service. Athletics and physical fitness requirements contribute to developing grit and determination, which can be carried to excel on and off the field, while in school and beyond.

Moral-Ethical Development

Of the components that comprise the overall leadership development programs at the academies, moral-ethical development has been the most difficult to grasp. This is at least in part due to the fact that agreement on what constitutes ethical behavior and how expansive the reach of such development programs should be has shifted over time.

For most of the history of military and maritime colleges, the primary vehicle of moral-ethical development has been an honor code. All institutions have had some version of an honor code similar to that of the United States Military Academy, which states that "a cadet will not lie, cheat, or steal, or tolerate those who do" (United States Military Academy West Point, n.d.-a). The honor codes have been the most enduring feature of their respective moral-ethical development programs. However, the system that supports the code at each institution has changed over time. Historically, the sanction for violations of the honor code has been expulsion, effectively meaning that the purpose of the system was to "screen out" those who exhibited unethical behavior. Under this system, the process of development was essentially a byproduct, an assumption that fear of expulsion resulted in behavior modification, which through a process of quasi-cognitive dissonance might bring about positive character change or development.

Recently, there have been several fundamental changes in the administration of the moral-ethical development programs at service academies. One of the most controversial changes, especially amongst academy alumni, is a fundamental change in the philosophy underpinning the administration of the honor system. Most of the service academies that have historically embraced the one-sanction approach to violations of the honor code (that is, expulsion) as a means of "weeding out" dishonorable students now see benefits in taking a more developmental approach in their systems, mirroring the philosophy that underpins the other program areas. Depending on the nature and severity of the offense, various sanctions short of expulsion may be meted out, for example, specially designed mentorship programs during one or two semesters or short-term suspensions that entail time spent away from the academy in some sort of rehabilitative activity, which might even include service in an active-duty unit.

PROFESSIONAL CONTEXT

The mission, history, and culture of these institutions are inextricably linked to the leadership demanded by the environments that graduates enter. The mission and culture are centered on preparation for military and/or government service, and heavily influence the organization and professional context. Staff and faculty experiences may vary depending on whether they are military members or civilians, the size of the school, and engagement with students, but the residential and often cloistered nature that separates the students from friends, family, and the surrounding community influences the student experience. The mission, and therefore the student experience, is often based on four components of development: academic; physical (athletic); military or professional; and moral/ethical (United States Military Academy West Point, n.d.-b). The relationship of these elements is critical to student success.

The emphasis on service and martial values makes a military education different from that of other types of colleges and universities, many of which also aim to produce leaders. Service, in this context, is often viewed as service to the nation, with demanding missions often performed in extreme environments. Unlike traditional universities, military and maritime academies and colleges achieve their purpose of creating leaders ready to serve the nation through the balance of four program areas: rigorous academics, military training, physical exercise, and moral-ethical development. At the federal service academies, faculty are often expected to contribute in more than one of these areas. Many service academy faculty are experienced military officers who have obtained advanced degrees in a content area but are expected to contribute primarily to the overall military mission of the institution; scholarly activities are secondary.

In contrast, the civilian faculty of service academies, junior and senior military colleges, and maritime academies tend to be civilian scholars who are encouraged to publish academic work and engage with the scholarly community in addition to teaching and institutional service duties. Tactical and physical training at the non-federal military colleges is undertaken largely by officers of the various military branches assigned to the college for that purpose. Though personnel assignments and expectations differ between the federal military academies and the state military colleges, both types of institutions focus collective efforts toward a balance of academic pursuits with military and physical training. Working with the students who self-select to sacrifice and serve at a military or maritime college or university is a very rewarding experience. The campuses are well-maintained and significant funds go into their upkeep. There is tremendous institutional pride in the physical appearance of the campus grounds and buildings as well as fierce loyalty to each school itself. Alumni often fund through donations many buildings, activities, and programs that federal or state funding will not or cannot support.

FUTURE CONSIDERATIONS AND DIRECTIONS

Several ethical questions need focus and attention. Inclusion of the diverse makeup of the U.S. population is one area that military colleges and universities are grappling with. Different elements of this group of institutions lead and lag in the area of diversity. There is also debate over the need for a military focused higher education institution.

Equally significant in terms of the benefit to the various branches of the armed forces is the expansion of the scope of moral-ethical development programs at their academies. Beyond acting honorably in terms of what an honor code demands, there is an increased understanding that ethical behavior expected of a commissioned officer is also about a broader range of character traits and behaviors, the quality of one's service to the nation and its people, and faithful custodianship of the military profession itself. Learning and practicing ethical behavior now touch upon a wide range of subject areas, including respect for others, inclusiveness, tolerance, and other high priority matters for the armed forces today. In response, a wider range of moral-ethical development experiences have been incorporated into the academies' leadership development programs, and moral-ethical considerations are an integral part of the students' life.

Inclusiveness and cultural awareness are ethical imperatives. The greatest resource in today's military is its personnel. We need leaders who can think critically about where they and their people come from. The military needs to reflect the society that it will serve and defend. We may lose out on some of the best leaders who may shy away if we can't be inclusive of all populations. Graduates need to be prepared and supported to succeed in multiple environments, and a crucial element of this success will be a graduate's ability to lead diverse organizations.

Racial and gender integration was implemented unevenly across military and maritime colleges and universities. Racial integration began in the 1860s, right after the conclusion of the Civil War. Notably, USMA's first black graduate was in 1877 (Georgia Historical Society, 2017). Other service academies followed. Racial integration for other military colleges followed later, generally in the 1960s and 1970s. Recent efforts to recruit more underrepresented minority groups have been prioritized in every school's strategic plan. In the 1970s, all the maritime academies, service academies, and some senior and junior military colleges, such as Norwich University and Marion Military Institute (MMI) integrated women into their programs. Some senior and junior military colleges did not integrate women until the 1990s or 2000s. Ideally, the military service academies and colleges should reflect the demographics of the United States as a whole, but it has proved challenging to attract a varied racial and gender mix of institutions specializing in military or maritime education. In 2020, the federal service academies enrolled between 20% and 40% female students. Senior military colleges enroll between 13 and 28% female students. In contrast, in 2020, women made up 59.5% of college students across the United States (Carrasco, 2021). Current demographics are encouraging against larger, global statistics that show less than 5% of the international maritime workforce being female, however, more diversification is needed to meet future challenges.

The military has offered increasing opportunities for women and gender minorities, especially since the 2013 abolition of the U.S. military's limits on females serving in direct combat roles. The removal of gender limitations in the military has also attracted non-binary and transgender students to military colleges and academies. California State University Maritime Academy, a regimented university in the Cal State University system, has revised its cadet manual to make uniform and grooming standards more welcoming to non-binary students, and the other academies and colleges will likely follow if the U.S. Military moves in this direction. But military academies and colleges still have work to do before students of diverse racial and gender backgrounds and sexual orientations feel entirely welcome in institutions that were originally designed to serve the white, middle-class male population of potential military officers. Racial incidents like those publicized at the Air Force Academy in 2018 and concerns about sexual assault on all military and maritime campuses and during training experiences (gCaptain, 2021) are among the challenges facing military academies and colleges.

The relevance of military colleges service academies has also been questioned over time. Almost since the inception of military colleges and universities, detractors have argued against them. The first charge to abolish service academies was aimed at West Point in 1830 (Beauchamp, 2015). Most recently, in the wake of cheating scandals, another volley against service academies and military colleges was fired (Beauchamp, 2015; Fleming, 2015). The expense of the institutions has been touted as a reason for this as well. Supporters of service academies point to the diversity of commissioning programs supports a professionally trained officer corps, and the various sources, Service Academies, ROTC, and short officer training programs that last only a few months, allow a diversity of individuals to enter the military from various walks of life that support civil-military relations as well as provide opportunities for "citizen-soldiers" to round out the officer corps. Some of the benefits of military colleges include demanding standards, development of the whole person through the four pillars described above, and development of the resilient leaders of character (Association of Military Colleges and Schools of the United States, n.d.).

The military colleges discussed in this chapter provide future leaders of our country's sons and daughters who go into harm's way on the battlefield and to serve and protect our nation, our cities, and our communities, often as "citizen soldiers." To achieve this, the curricula are designed as a whole institution effort to develop students morally, mentally, physically, and professionally within a military culture. The students are immersed in an environment where they lead their peers, holding them accountable in honor and conduct. With long histories or short, these institutions can and must adapt to provide an inclusive environment that is supportive of the diverse student bodies needed to be leaders of the future is also an imperative, as they must lead in the diverse world that they will enter on graduation.

DISCUSSION QUESTIONS

1. Perhaps unsurprisingly, different constituencies question the need for service academies, and military or maritime colleges and universities. What can an immersive experience in a military

or maritime university offer that cannot be offered through another commissioning source, such as ROTC or Office Candidate School?

2. How do we make sure that the makeup of the student body at our military and maritime colleges is representative of the society that the graduates will ultimately serve, will meet the needs of our services, and retain the support of the American people? How should one address irregularities in retention and graduation rates across gender, racial, ethnic, and other lines? How do we assist incoming students who may be disadvantaged owing to disparities in education, social, or cultural background that may characterize the sector of society where they have been raised? How do we equip leaders to manage diversity in their life and work, such as leading a diverse workforce or operating in other cultures?

3. How does a university keep abreast of the latest changes (such as technological, social, public-private partnerships) and keep the military experience and curricula relevant to the needs of the nation, given that military and maritime officers are immediately placed in possible high-risk and high-impact environments? How should military and maritime colleges and universities balance program areas or make necessary adjustments to the allocation of time, resources, and focus between these areas while preserving their identity and purpose as well as preparing graduates with the tools they need to succeed immediately after graduation?

4. In modern society when only one half of one percent of the American population serve in the active-duty military at any given time and fewer and fewer are selecting or qualified to serve (Pew Research Center, 2011), how can military and maritime institutions continue to attract students committed to serving their country?

5. Military and maritime universities are slowly moving toward gender balance, though they still enroll a larger proportion of males. Along with increasing numbers of women, these institutions are successfully attracting transgender and non-binary students, possibly due to uniform requirements and leadership and career opportunities that de-emphasize gender. Sexual harassment and assault, a concern for all universities, can be particularly problematic in cadet hierarchies where students are leading each other, and patterns of gender discrimination can continue into

military service. How can these challenges be addressed within traditionally male-dominated military and maritime universities?

REFERENCES

Association of Military Colleges and Schools of the United States. (n.d.). *Benefits of military school*. AMCSUS. Retrieved November 15, 2021, from https://amcsus. org/benefits-of-military-school/

Beauchamp, S. (2015, January 25). Abolish West Point—And the other service academies, too. *Chicago Tribune*. https://www.chicagotribune.com/news/chi-abolish-west-point-and-the-other-service-academies-too-20150124-story. html

Berube, C. (2020). *USNA 175th anniversary: Significant eras, leaders, and the city of Annapolis* (No. 80). Retrieved November 1, 2021, from https://podcasts. google.com

Carrasco, M. (2021, September 8). Record numbers of men 'give up' on college. *Inside Higher Ed*. https://www.insidehighered.com/quicktakes/2021/09/08/ record-numbers-men-%E2%80%98give-%E2%80%99-college

Catalogue of the officers and cadets of the American Literary, Scientific and Military Academy. (1821). Norwich University.

Fleming, B. (2015, January 6). Let's abolish West Point: Military academies serve no one, squander millions of tax dollars. *Salon*. https://www.salon. com/2015/01/05/lets_abolish_west_point_military_academies_serve_no_one_ squander_millions_of_tax_dollars/

gCaptain. (2021, November 11). *USMMA midshipmen respond to congress members calling for sea year suspension: Read their letter to committee leaders*. https:// gcaptain.com/usmma-midshipmen-respond-to-congress-members-calling-for-sea-year-suspension/

Georgia Historical Society. (2017, March 20). *Marker Monday: The First Black Graduate of West Point. Georgia Historical Society*. https://georgiahistory.com/ marker-monday-the-first-black-graduate-of-west-point/

Lord, G. T. (2016, Fall). Captain Alden Partridge and the origins of ROTC: A reappraisal. *The Norwich Record*.

Marion Military Institute. (n.d.). *Anthony J. Rane Center for Leadership*. MMI. Retrieved November 13, 2021, from https://marionmilitary.edu/campus-life/ leadership-center/

Pew Research Center. (2011). *Chapter 6: A profile of the modern military*. http://www. pewsocialtrends.org/2011/10/05/chapter-6-a-profile-of-the-modern-military/

Regulations and Minimum Standards for State, Territorial or Regional Maritime Academies and Colleges, Pub. L. No. 96–453, 46 U.S. (1981). https://www. ecfr.gov/current/title-46/chapter-II/subchapter-H/part-310

United States Military Academy West Point. (n.d.-a). *Honor code*. Retrieved November 13, 2021, from https://www.westpoint.edu/military/simon-center-for-the-professional-military-ethic/honor

United States Military Academy West Point. (n.d.-b). *United States Military Academy West Point*. Retrieved November 13, 2021, from https://www.westpoint.edu/

Virginia Military Institute. (2021). *Board of visitors*. https://www.vmi.edu/about/governance/board-of-visitors/

CHAPTER 18

OCCUPATIONAL AND VOCATIONAL INSTITUTIONS

Kimberly R. Davis
Penn State University

The evolution and development of occupational and technical colleges, also known as career and technical education (CTE) in the United States, have depended on organizational support for institutions offering CTE programs; federal legislation and funding have been unifying forces for CTE nationwide (Gordon & Schultz, 2020). In the formative years of the United States, there were no coordinated national movements related to vocational education. However, individuals and groups who recognized the need for an eventual national program for vocational education began acting on a smaller scale (Barlow, 1976b). For example, in large cities with high concentrations of craftsmen, the manual labor movement exposed the need for vocational education efforts (Barlow, 1976b). This chapter will use the terms career and technical education (CTE) to focus on identifying the distinguishing features of this industry focused institution which are separate from the role of community colleges in professional education. Chapter 18 focuses on the role of community colleges and other two-year institutions. Rather, this chapter centers on the role of apprenticeships and other cooperative education as a distinguishing feature of CTE institutions and this chapter begins with their historical evolution.

HISTORY

Throughout the 1820s, local institutes such as the Franklin Institute (Philadelphia), Maryland Institute for the Promotion of the Mechanic Arts

---

Institutional Diversity in American Postsecondary Education, pp. 239–248
Copyright © 2024 by Information Age Publishing
www.infoagepub.com
All rights of reproduction in any form reserved.

240   K. R. DAVIS

(Baltimore), and the Ohio Mechanics' Institute (Cincinnati) were established to serve the population's vocational needs. (Barlow, 1976b). While the purposes and facilities were similar across the different institutes, their approaches and practices varied, as they were tailored to meet local needs and conditions (Barlow, 1976b).

Organized national efforts to promote industrial education began in the early 1900s. Recognizing that industrial education would impact the wealth of the nation and contribute to well-being throughout society, the National Society for the Promotion of Industrial Education (NSPIE) emerged after a meeting of approximately 250 industrialists and educators in November 1906 (Barlow, 1976c). The NSPIE focused on promoting interest in and educating about the value of industrial education, which was understood to mean vocational training between manual training and college-level engineering (Barlow, 1976c).

Throughout the 20th century, the field of vocational education continued to grow and change. As programs at high schools and community colleges began offering curricula that prepared students in their vocational programs for work or further education in a technical field, the terminology shifted from "vocational education" to "career and technical education" (Gordon & Schultz, 2020). In the late 1990s, members of the American Vocational Association (formerly NSPIE and the National Society for Vocational Education) recognized that vocational education had become more academic, challenging, and technical; to reflect the nature of the association's work, members voted in December 1998 to change the name to the Association for Career and Technical Education (ACTE), which is the name the organization maintains today (ACTE, 2002).

In 1914, Congress established the Commission on National Aid to Vocational Education, which was responsible for demonstrating the need for vocational education and federal funding to achieve its purposes (Barlow, 1976c). The commission provided evidence that support for vocational education should come from a national level rather than local, as vocational education would serve the nation and reach across state lines (Barlow, 1976c). Further, the commission recommended offering grants for training and paying the teachers who would be responsible for vocational education (Barlow, 1976c). The findings of the report informed the legislation that later became the Smith-Hughes Act.

Vocational education in the higher education setting grew quickly after the Smith-Hughes Act of 1917 provided federal financial aid for these programs (Barlow, 1976a). While vocational courses only represented 18% of course offerings in public junior colleges and 9% in private junior colleges in 1917–1918, by 1935, vocational offerings represented 25% of terminal courses in public junior colleges (Barlow, 1976a). During World War II, vocational and trade schools provided critical assistance in training for defense needs; through the Office of Education's National Defense Training Program, nearly 7,500,000 people were trained to fill vacancies in fields such as armament, aircraft, and shipbuilding (Barlow, 1976a).

Recognizing the importance of vocational schools during times of peace and war, efforts to maintain funding for these institutions continued after World War II (Barlow, 1976a). Following the war, new fields and industries emerged that required additional vocational knowledge, such as how to develop new skills and tools (Barlow, 1976a). In 1946, the George-Barden Act authorized the use of federal funds for aspects of vocational education, such as salaries and expenses of state directors and counselors (Barlow, 1976a). The act also provided "training and work experience programs for out-of-school youth" (p. 76), and funds to purchase or rent tools necessary for vocational instruction (Barlow, 1976a). This more flexible act, combined with the Smith-Hughes Act, provided over $36 million in funding for vocational education training across the nation (Barlow, 1976a).

Later, the Vocational Education Act (VEA) of 1963, expanded federal funding for vocational education at the secondary, postsecondary, and adult education levels from specific categories (e.g., agriculture, home economics, and practical nursing) to "preparing all groups in the community regardless of their vocational emphasis or attachment to the labor force" (Wolfe, 1978, p. 8). In 1968, amendments to the VEA specifically targeted funding for postsecondary education as well as disadvantaged or handicapped students (Wolfe, 1978). Finally, in 1976, additional amendments targeted sex discrimination and bias in vocational education programs as well as state-level issues with planning and evaluation (Wolfe, 1978). Statistics from the U.S. Office of Education showed that total enrollment in vocational education grew significantly following the VEA and its subsequent amendments. Nationwide, vocational enrollment grew from 3.6 million in 1958 to 7.5 million in 1968 and 13.6 million by 1974 (Barlow, 1976a). Specifically, in postsecondary and adult programs, enrollments in post-secondary and adult programs grew from 1.4 million and 3.4 million in FY 1973 to 2.2 and 4.1 million, respectively, in FY 1978 (Wolfe, 1978).

In 1984, the Carl D. Perkins Vocational Education Act replaced the VEA and aimed to increase the skills of the labor force and offer equal opportunities for adults pursuing vocational education (Gordon & Schultz, 2020). Whereas previous acts emphasized the expansion of vocational education, the Perkins Act focused on reaching at-risk populations (Gordon & Schultz, 2020). Subsequent legislation, such as the Carl D. Perkins Vocational and Applied Technology Act of 1990 (Perkins II Act), emphasized the combination of academic and vocational skills needed for work in a global society with rapid technological advances (Gordon & Schultz, 2020). The Carl D. Perkins Vocational and Technical Act of 1998 (Perkins III Act) brought new accountability measures, including performance measures related to "placement, retention, and completion of postsecondary education or placement in military service or employment" (Gordon & Schultz, 2020, p. 127). Later, the Carl D. Perkins Career and Technical Education Act of 2006 (Perkins IV) notably utilized the "career and technical education" terminology rather than "vocational education" (Gordon & Schultz, 2020). Most recently, the 2018 Strengthening Career and Technical Education for the 21st Century Act (Perkins V) emphasized areas such as program improvement, data-driven decision-making, flexibility, and accountability (Gordon & Schultz, 2020).

ORGANIZATION STRUCTURE AND CULTURE

While community colleges offer many CTE programs, there are also technical institutions that help students prepare for careers in specific areas by earning certificates, diplomas, or degrees in various "skilled trades, applied sciences and technologies" (Council on Occupational Education [COE], n.d.-b). The U.S. Department of Education recognizes the COE as "a national institutional accrediting agency for the accreditation of non-degree-granting and applied associate degree-granting postsecondary occupational education institutions" (Williams & Smarr, 2022, p. 2). These occupational programs may be traditional programs (delivered completely on campus), hybrid programs (less than 50% delivered via distance education), or distance education programs (50% or more delivered via distance education), but at least 25% of the institution's full-time equivalent students must be in traditional programs (COE, 2022-b). The COE defines occupational education program as "a sequence of instruction and related activities (e.g., laboratory activities and/or work-based activities) designed to provide educational and workplace competencies that lead to a credential" (COE, 2022-b, p. 80). The hands-on training and a comparable environment to a workplace at technical institutions help students to transition into the workplace or advance their existing careers. Further, instructional activities reflect "professional and practice-based competencies" (COE, 2022-b, p. 57) and integrate health and safety practices into the curriculum. COE member institutions encompass multiple institutional types, including apprenticeship institutes, federal agencies, job corps, military, public rehabilitation, and public and private degree and non-degree (COE, n.d.-b). The structure of these institutions varies.

With origins as far back as the early colonial period, apprenticeship has been recognized as "the oldest known type of vocational education in the United States" (Gordon & Schultz, 2020, p. 6). In exchange for work, the overseer typically agreed to offer the apprentice food, clothing, shelter, and religious training as well as skills necessary for the trade

Occupational and Vocational Institutions   243

(Gordon & Scholtz, 2020). Today, apprentices work under formal agreements but reside in their own homes, work traditional schedules, and earn wages; on average, beginning apprentices are 25 years old (Gordon & Scholtz, 2020). Registered Apprenticeship Programs are registered with the U.S. Department of Labor and must meet established standards from the Department of Labor (Purifoy & Davis, 2022). Apprentices are paid about half of what fully trained craftspeople earn, though wages increase every six months until the apprentice completes their training (Gordon & Scholtz, 2020). About two-thirds of apprenticeships today are in the construction and manufacturing trades, though apprentices may also work in electronics, service industries, public administration, or healthcare (Gordon & Scholtz, 2020). Contemporary apprenticeships combine earning and learning, wherein apprentices attend classes after work to learn the theoretical foundations of their crafts; further, they may learn mathematics skills, blueprint reading, or applied English (Gordon & Scholtz, 2020). However, apprenticeship institutes do not typically offer robust academic or student support services.

Federal agencies and military programs operate somewhat differently and may be considered occupational *training* programs rather than occupational *education* programs. Federal agencies and military institutions rarely offer their training to the public because they have additional qualifications for entry; for example, intelligence schools require their students to have government-issued security clearance (Purifoy & Davis, 2022). Whereas many occupational institutions partner with employers to place their graduates, federal agencies and the military typically employ their students after they complete their training. Further, completers of the military and federal agency programs often return to their schools later and teach future generations of students (Purifoy & Davis, 2022). Federal agencies and military programs also do not have the same responsibilities under Title IV and the Gainful Employment Act to document student loans (Purifoy & Davis, 2022).

Job Corps is a nationwide career training program that is fully funded by the federal government and has been operating for more than five decades; since 1964, more than 2 million individuals have been trained and educated through Job Corps (U.S. Department of Labor [DOL], n.d.). The program is open to people ages 16 through 24 and helps them "complete their high school education, trains them for meaningful careers, and assists them with obtaining employment" (U.S. DOL, n.d.). Students at Job Corps receive basic living benefits, including meals, a furnished room, clothing for career training, a living allowance, basic medical care, a childcare allotment, and books and supplies (Job Corps, n.d.). Further, Job Corps offers student services such as recreational activities and student organizations (Job Corps, n.d.). After Job Corps, graduates may choose

244 K. R. DAVIS

from multiple pathways, including entering the workforce or beginning an apprenticeship, pursuing higher education, or joining the military (U.S. DOL, n.d.).

Non-degree institutions offer programs and certifications but do not offer associate degrees, whereas degree institutions offer associate degrees in addition to other programs and certifications. These institutions may be public or private and may be general institutions (e.g., Concorde Career College, Futura Career Institute, J. F. Ingram State Technical College) or industry-specific (e.g., Georgia Institute of Cosmetology, Precision Welding Academy, U.S. Truck Driver Training School) (COE, n.d.-a). The most common services for students at these institutions are certification and career preparation and financial services. Specifically, many have financial services offices to assist with financial aid and help students pay for their programs. Degree and non-degree institutions may also offer preparation for students approaching their licensure examinations or career services for students and graduates who need resume assistance or interview preparation.

STUDENT SUCCESS AND POPULATIONS

The diversity of student populations has been especially important in postsecondary CTE, and federal funding programs have helped to maintain this diversity (Bragg, 2018). However, postsecondary CTE programs have been perceived as alternatives for students who were deemed unlikely to successfully pursue baccalaureate degrees (Bragg, 2018). The VEA of 1963 recognized that students with special needs could benefit from vocational education, and amendments to the VEA in 1968 and 1976 set aside funding specifically for students with disabilities, economically disadvantaged students, students with limited English proficiency, teen parents, and "students in programs considered nontraditional for their gender" (Bragg, 2018, p. 166). The association of CTE with special education has contributed to the marginalization of CTE students from college-bound students (Bragg, 2018). Although CTE aimed to provide students with the academic and vocational skills necessary to secure an entry-level job, inequitable outcomes for students from diverse racial and ethnic backgrounds became an unintended consequence of these efforts (Bragg, 2018).

In addition to high school graduates matriculating shortly after high school, adult learners represent a significant demographic in postsecondary CTE programs (Bragg, 2018). These adult learners often have experience in the labor market or previous college enrollment but enroll in postsecondary CTE programs to receive training and skills that will help them attain better or higher-wage jobs (Bragg, 2018). As a result of their past educational and professional experiences, many adult learners favor curricula that are clearly aligned with the labor market and provide training and credentials that are relevant to jobs in their fields (Bragg, 2018).

Despite demographic challenges and other inequities, there are several clear benefits for students pursuing technical education and their families. On average, graduates of technical colleges hold less debt than the average graduates of 4-year institutions, and they demonstrate high rates of placement into jobs (COE, n.d.-b). Skilled workers who complete technical education programs also have opportunities to move into managerial positions with even more competitive salaries (COE, n.d.-b).

PROFESSIONAL CONTEXT

Institutions accredited by the COE must meet specific requirements to serve their students and the institution. For example, Standard Five for COE accreditation, Learning Resources, requires institutions to provide and maintain the objectives for each program, and all learning resources should be readily available for student and faculty use, including meeting the applicable safety standards (COE, 2022-a). Similarly, Standard Eight (Human Resources) provides guidelines for all employees, including faculty, administrative and supervisory personnel, instructional support staff, and non-instructional support staff/services. Satisfying Standard Eight requires a sufficient number of employees "to fulfill the mission and operate the programs of the institution" (COE, 2022-a, p. 76) and ensuring that administrative and supervisory personnel have the education and experience to properly perform their duties.

Most relevant to student affairs practitioners is Standard Ten, Student Success and Activities. Standard Ten encompasses many areas traditionally associated with student affairs, such as academic advisement, counseling, financial assistance, orientation, retention, grievances, records, and admissions (COE, 2022-a). Students need support navigating the admissions process, including financing their education. Once admitted, students will require orientation and academic advising to become acquainted with the institution and understand their path forward. As with other higher education institutions, occupational and apprenticeship institutions seek to retain their students and must make informed efforts to develop practices that contribute to student persistence and success. Federal agencies and military programs are not evaluated on student personnel services (Purifoy & Davis, 2022).

Many occupational and apprenticeship programs emphasize outcomes related to career preparation and placement; academic advising services help students determine which occupational education programs they would like to pursue (COE, 2022-a). A criterion of accreditation is that institutions provide career placement services for students who complete their programs and conduct follow-up studies with program completers and their employees (COE, 2022-a, p. 80). These services yield valuable information that the institutions can use to inform their future practice and service to students.

FUTURE CONSIDERATIONS AND DIRECTIONS

Programs at occupational and apprenticeship institutions continue to train students for careers that meet the needs of a changing nation and world. Looking to the future, these institutions must especially consider how technology and distance learning contribute to their service to students and the achievement of their institutional missions. As technology and learning methods continue to evolve, occupational and apprenticeship institutions should embrace platforms that are accessible to students and allow learners to complete programs that will lead to career advancement.

Regardless of the program delivery and learning format, occupational and apprenticeship institutions must also continue to explore opportunities for collaboration and socialization. Institutions can share strategies for recruitment and retention efforts, including promoting their institutions at local job fairs, establishing easily identifiable branding, sharing student testimonials, and increasing their social media presence (Burcaw & Aasheim, 2022). Further, institutions can network among themselves and share opportunities for short-term or sustained funding through grants (Burcaw & Aasheim, 2022).

Within their local communities, occupational and apprenticeship institutions must also increase their public presence and support each other in spaces outside of the institution (Burcaw & Aasheim, 2022). By communicating with representatives from these institutions can increase awareness of their programs and help the community understand how a safe and efficient workforce positively impacts the community (Burcaw & Aasheim, 2022). In addition to messaging through institutional social media accounts, institutions could benefit from involvement with community constituencies, including editorials and articles in the local newspaper (Burcaw & Aasheim, 2022). Occupational and apprenticeship institutions might glean ideas from other institutional types for how to most effectively promote the opportunities they afford to students and the community.

Historically, career and technical education programs have served diverse student populations (Bragg, 2018). Moving forward, occupational and apprenticeship institutions must understand and discuss how diversity impacts the workplace (Burcaw & Aasheim, 2022). Additionally, representatives from these institutions can communicate the value of a diverse workforce (Burcaw & Aasheim, 2022). As they promote diversity, however, personnel from occupational and apprenticeship institutions should also talk with minority students and employers to gain insight into the climate and landscape students encounter (Burcaw & Aasheim, 2022). Personnel from these institutions might need additional training and support to correct issues such as discrimination, racism, sexism, xenophobia, or homophobia (Burcaw & Aasheim, 2022).

REFLECTION QUESTIONS

1. Historically, vocational education received criticism for not addressing the needs of different learners and being unconcerned with social problems. How have occupational and apprenticeship institutions overcome this criticism? In what areas do they still need to improve?
2. What are some strategies that occupational and apprenticeship institutions might use to address CTE stigma?
3. Federal agencies and military programs are currently accredited by COE. How do these programs differ from other types of occupational and apprenticeship institutions? How are they the same?
4. What are some challenges that occupational and apprenticeship institutions face that are different from other types of higher education institutions? What are some shared challenges?
5. If you were writing a newspaper article or editorial about occupational and apprenticeship institutions, what topic would you choose, and why? What would you highlight in the article?

REFERENCES

Association for Career and Technical Education. (2002). *An association is reborn.* Techniques. https://www.acteonline.org/wp-content/uploads/2018/02/Association-Reborn.pdf

Barlow, M. L. (1976a). 200 years of vocational education: 1776–1976; Coming of age, 1926–1976. *American Vocational Journal, 51*(5), 63–88.

Barlow, M. L. (1976b). 200 years of vocational education: 1776–1976; Independent action, 1826–1876. *American Vocational Journal, 51*(5), 31–40.

Barlow, M. L. (1976c). 200 years of vocational education: 1776–1976; The vocational age emerges, 1876–1926. *American Vocational Journal, 51*(5), 45–58.

Bragg, D. D. (2018). Career and technical education: Old debates and persistent challenges. In J. S. Levin & S. T. Kater (Eds.), *Understanding community colleges* (2nd ed., pp. 158–180). Routledge.

Burcaw, J., & Aasheim, T. (2022). *Interactive discussion on accreditation* [PowerPoint slides]. Council on Occupational Education. https://council.org/wp-content/uploads/2022/11/Thursday-Nov-10-Apprenticeship-Special-Topic-FTIUM-COE-Interactive-Workshop.pdf

Council on Occupational Education. (2022-a). *Handbook of accreditation for public and non-public institutions.* https://council.org/wp-content/uploads/2022/06/2022-Generic-HB-5-11-2022-w-Covers-B.pdf

Council on Occupational Education. (2022-b). *Policies and rules of the commission: 2022 edition.* https://council.org/wp-content/uploads/2022/07/2022-PR-Manual-7-19-2022-FINAL-w-Covers-FINAL.pdf

Council on Occupational Education. (n.d.-a). *Member directory.* https://council.org/membership/

Council on Occupational Education. (n.d.-b). *Technical education—FAQs.* https://council.org/technical-education-frequently-asked-questions/

Gordon, H. R. D., & Schultz, D. (2020). *The history and growth of career and technical education in America* (5th ed.). Waveland.

Job Corps. (n.d.). *Live: Explore Job Corps benefits and find a local center.* https://www.jobcorps.gov/live

Purifoy, T., & Davis, L. (2022). *Accreditation visiting team member certification part 1* [PowerPoint slides]. Council on Occupational Education. https://council.org/wp-content/uploads/2022/11/Wednesday-Nov-9-Accreditation-Visiting-Team-MEMBER-Certification_Part-1_Annual-Meeting-2022_FINALc.pdf

U.S. Department of Labor. (n.d.). *What is Job Corps?* https://www.dol.gov/agencies/eta/jobcorps

Williams, K., & Smarr, K. (2022). *The COE approved program list (public, non-public, apprenticeships, and job corps)* [PowerPoint slides]. Council on Occupational Education. https://council.org/wp-content/uploads/2022/11/Wednesday-Nov-9-COE-Approved-Programs-List_Final_AM_November-2022_Final.pdf

Wolfe, M. L. (1978, August 1). *The vocational education act of 1963, as amended: A background paper* (Report No. CRS-78-166-EPW: LC-1043-U.S.). U.S. Department of Health Education & Welfare, National Institute of Education.

ABOUT THE AUTHORS

Stephanie Aguilar-Smith is an assistant professor of Counseling and Higher Education at the University of North Texas. Broadly, her research focuses on advancing educational equity and justice, particularly at Hispanic-Serving Institutions.

Yolanda M. Barnes, PhD (she/her) is an adjunct lecturer of higher education leadership and policy studies at the University of Houston. She has experienced urban serving institutions from a variety of vantage points, first as a student affairs professional, then a doctoral student, and now as an adjunct faculty member. Dr. Barnes' scholarly interests focus on looking at the ways in which federal and state policies unintentionally create college access barriers for underserved student populations.

Ginny Jones Boss, PhD (she/her) is an associate professor of College Student Affairs Administration and Leadership at the University of Georgia. She has attended and worked at four different research universities. Dr. Boss's research and practice are aimed at amplifying the ways scholars of color, particularly women and students, are interfacing with and transforming higher education through their active engagement on their campuses. Most of her work and scholarship takes place in research university contexts.

Kim E. Bullington, PhD (she/her/) is the Programs Manager for the Department of Engineering Management and Systems Engineering at Old Dominion University. She is also an Adjunct Assistant Professor in the Educational Foundations and Leadership Department at Old Dominion.

250   ABOUT the AUTHORS

Vincent D. Carales is an associate professor of Higher Education at the University of Houston. He has over 20 years of higher education experience working in financial aid and as a student loan consultant. Dr. Carales's research focuses on understanding the experiences and educational outcomes of first generation, Latina/o, low-income and community college students.

Terry Chavis (he/him) (Lumbee) is a PhD student at the University of North Carolina at Greensboro. He is a descendant of Indigenous "People of the Darkwater" in rural, southeast North Carolina who were forced into assimilation and survived through sharecropping and tobacco farming. His research interests focus on the decolonization of higher education through culturally responsive pedagogy and centering the stories and experiences of students on our campuses, especially Indigenous students.

Ashley B. Clayton, PhD, MBA is the Jo Ellen Levy Yates Endowed Associate Professor in the Higher Education Administration program at Louisiana State University. Her research focuses on college access and success, and she is currently at her fourth land-grant institution.

Kimberly R. Davis is a data analyst for the Timothy J. Piazza Center for Fraternity and Sorority Research and Reform at Penn State University. Additionally, she is a postdoctoral fellow in the 2022–23 cohort of the NC State University Postsecondary Career and Technical Education (CTE) Research Fellows, sponsored by ECMC Foundation. Before earning her PhD, she worked in various student affairs functional areas, including housing and residence life, fraternity and sorority life, student conduct, and Title IX.

Roger Davis, Jr. (he/him) is a PhD candidate in the Department of Higher Education at the University of Mississippi. His research focuses on examining the shaped experiences of minoritized stakeholders in higher education, with an emphasis on the experiences of rural Black and first-generation students from the Mississippi Delta, as well as the recruitment and retention of Black students, faculty, and administrators.

Tiffany J. Davis, PhD (she/her) is associate dean for student belonging and success and clinical professor of higher education within the College of Education at the University of Houston, a large, urban serving institution. Her scholarship addresses two major strands: socialization and professional pathways for the higher education profession and issues related to equity and inclusion.

Dong Manh Dinh, EdD (he/him), is a Director for FIRST@DU, which supports and celebrates first-generation students at the University of Denver. His research is focused on addressing invisibility of services and programs for AA&NHPI populations on college campuses.

Erin E. Doran (she/her) is an associate professor of Higher Education at University of Texas at El Paso. Between 2009 and 2016, she was an adjunct instructor of U.S. History at Northeast Lakeview College, a community college in the San Antonio metro. Her research focuses on Latina/o/x community college students, the faculty who teach them, and Hispanic-Serving Institutions (HSIs).

Becket C. Duncan is a PhD candidate in the Higher Education program at the University of Denver. He works as a Research Analyst in the Division of Student Affairs at the University of Colorado Boulder. His research focuses on regional public universities, geospatial mapping and data analysis, university-community relationships, and residential housing near institutions of higher education.

Kristine Jan Cruz Espinoza is a Pinay PhD student in the Higher Education program at the University of Nevada, Las Vegas. Her research interests revolve around race-based higher education policies, focusing on Minority-Serving Institutions and racial data classification. Before doctoral studies, she worked as the Student Affairs Officer at the UCLA Asian American Studies Department.

Emily Fisher Gray, PhD is a Professor of History at Norwich University, the Military College of Vermont. She has 20 years of experience teaching civilian students and military cadets about Early Modern Germany, with a special emphasis on active learning pedagogy. At Norwich, she has served in administrative roles with international education, faculty governance, and Diversity, Equity, and Inclusion.

Dennis Gregory, EdD (he/ him) is Associate Professor of Higher Education at Old Dominion University in Norfolk, VA. His recent areas of research include higher education law, with focus on freedom of speech and academic freedom and comparative and international higher education.

Demeturie Toso-Lafaele Gogue, PhD (he/him/his), is a Sāmoan and CHamoru Assistant Professor of Higher Education in the Department of Leadership in Education at the University of Massachusetts Boston. His research explores how higher education institutions operate as racialized

252 ABOUT the AUTHORS

organizations and its impact on students' experiences, diversity initiatives, and institutional processes and practices.

Ayana T. Hardaway, PhD, is a sponsored research administrator and scholar-practitioner in higher education. Her research explores Black girls and women in P–20 educational and social contexts, college student development and success, and critical qualitative methods.

Aaron W. Hughey is a University Distinguished Professor at Western Kentucky University in the Department of Counseling and Student Affairs, where he has coordinated the master's degree program in student affairs in higher education for over 30 years. Before joining the faculty, he spent 10 years as an administrator, primarily in Housing and Residence Life.

Brandy Jones, MSEd, is a scholar-practitioner and researcher in higher education. Her research primarily focuses on Black women in higher education. She also studies the experiences of Black college students and investigates organizational culture within higher education.

Jennifer M. Johnson PhD, is an associate professor of Higher Education at Temple University. She is an active scholar-practitioner in the field of college access and success. Her scholarship explores students' experiences and outcomes at the intersection of race, gender, and class across diverse institutional contexts.

Sabrina Klein is a PhD candidate in the Higher Education & Organizational Change division at the University of California, Los Angeles. Her research centers rurality and college access; particularly on rural students, rural communities, rural-serving higher education institutions, and the role of regional labor markets.

Andrew Koricich is the executive director of the Alliance for Research on Regional Colleges and associate professor of higher education at Appalachian State University. His research interests focus on rural issues in postsecondary education, with a particular emphasis on rural and rural-serving institutions.

Carrie Kortegast, PhD, is an associate professor of higher education and student affairs at Northern Illinois University. She has written on the experiences of student affairs professionals at small colleges and the experiences of LGBTQ individuals in higher education.

About the Authors   253

Victoria C. Lloyd, MEd (she/her) is an education research analyst for the Louisiana Department of Education and a doctoral student studying Higher Education with a focus on state finance at Louisiana State University. She grew up in a city served by a land-grant university and is currently completing her education at the same one. Her research aims to identify and address barriers to college access.

Carolyn H. Livingston, PhD (she/her) is the Vice President for Student Life and Dean of Students at Carleton College. Best known for its academic excellence and warm, welcoming campus community, Carleton is a small, residential private liberal arts college in the historic river town of Northfield, Minnesota. Prior to coming to Carleton, Livingston was Senior Associate Vice President for Student Life and Title IX Coordinator for Students at Emory University and held positions at the University of Virginia. Livingston has published articles and presented papers on assessment and evaluation, persistence and graduation for first-generation and low-income students, and staffing practices in higher education. She holds both a doctorate and a master's degree from the University of Virginia and a bachelor's degree from N.C. State University.

Tamara S. McKenna is the Associate Athletics Director at the U.S. Coast Guard Academy. Prior to this role, she served as the Associate Director of Admissions. She has an MBA from George Mason University, and her undergraduate degree is from USCGA.

David J. Mollahan is the 16th President of Marion Military Institute. Prior to his retirement, he served as the Humanities and Social Sciences Division Director and Senior Marine at the U.S. Naval Academy, completing a 30-year career as Marine Corps officer.

Nicholas E. Negrete (he/him) serves as the Vice President for Student Affairs and Campus Diversity & Inclusion at Otis College of Art and Design. Prior to this role, he served as, Vice President for Diversity, Equity, Inclusion and Belonging and Dean of Student Affairs at Otis College, in addition to serving in a variety of roles at public land-grant colleges and universities in both California and the Northeast. His areas of specialization include building diverse and inclusive practices, assessment and student retention, supporting students in crises, and developing faculty's competence and confidence related to supporting students in distress.

Mike Hoa Nguyen, PhD (he/him), is Assistant Professor of Education at New York University and Principal Investigator of the Minority-Serving Institutions Data Project. His research critically examines the benefits and

254 ABOUT the AUTHORS

consequences of racialized public policy instruments in expanding and/or constraining educational systems, with a specific focus on how these dynamics shape access, learning, opportunity, and success within and beyond schools for Students of Color.

Eric T. Olson is a graduate of and was an assistant professor of international relations and economics at the United States Military Academy. He later returned to the Academy to serve as the Commandant of Cadets (Dean of Students). He subsequently reached the rank of major general in the U.S. Army before retiring from active duty in 2006.

Christa J. Porter, PhD (she/her) is an assistant professor of Higher Education Administration at and faculty affiliate within the Division of Diversity, Equity, and Inclusion at Kent State University. She examines policies and practices that influence the development and trajectory of Black women in higher education at diverse institutional types; college student development (at the intersections of identities); and research and praxis in higher education and student affairs. Prior to becoming a faculty member, she served as a student affairs administrator at various institutional types, including two small colleges, Agnes Scott College and Emory University.

Tara Leigh Sands (she/her) is an EdD student at the University of Rochester in Educational Leadership and works at Rowan College at Burlington County in New Jersey. She is an advocate for Indigenous Peoples and knowledge. She is an active volunteer in NASPA: Student Affairs Administrators in Higher Education Indigenous Peoples Knowledge Community.

Sharron Scott, EdD, is a higher education research manager, educator, and scholar-practitioner. Her research agenda promotes college access, equity, and the persistence of traditionally underrepresented populations. Her recent publications about the Ivy League experience include: "Investigating Ivy: Black Undergraduate Students at Selective Universities"; "Ivy Issues: An Exploration of Black Students' Racialized Interactions on Ivy League Campuses" and "Beyond Bothered: Exploring Identity, Stressors, and Challenges of Black Women Ivy Collegians."

Julie Shank PhD is currently the Deputy Commandant for Operations, Plans, and Training at Virginia Military Institute and a PhD candidate in the Education program at George Mason University. She is a retired Naval officer, and a proud graduate and former Brigade Operations Officer of the United States Naval Academy.

Terrell L. Strayhorn, PhD (he/him), is Professor of Education and Psychology at Virginia Union University, where he also serves as Associate Provost, Interim Dean in the School of Arts & Sciences, and Director of Research in the Center for the Study of Historically Black Colleges and Universities (HBCUs). He has worked in a variety of institutional types including predominantly White, land-grant research universities and private, urban, historically Black colleges, where he has served in various roles, including Provost/Chief Academic Officer. Author of over 13 books and 200+ academic publications, Strayhorn's scholarly interests focus on student success, racial equity, and the factors, environments, and institutional qualities that condition sense of belonging in higher education for faculty, staff, and students.

David Taliaferro is the Commandant of Cadets at California State University Maritime Academy, bringing leadership experience as a maritime professional, military officer, and higher education administrator. Most recently, he served as the Director of Leadership and Ethics at the United States Merchant Marine Academy in Kings Point, New York. He is currently a doctoral candidate in the Adult Learning and Leadership program at Columbia University.

Yoi Tanaka, MA (she/her) is the Vice President of Admissions at Otis College of Art and Design. Prior to this role, she was the Vice President of Admissions Art Center College of Design in Pasadena, Associate Dean of Admissions and Records at Santa Ana College and Director of Admissions at the School of Visual Arts in New York. She holds a Master's in Visual Arts Administration and has focused on accessibility, diversity, equity and inclusion in admissions and enrollment management in art and design education.

Stephanie J. Tisdale is a PhD candidate at Temple University in the Policy and Organizational Studies Program with a concentration in Higher Education.

Rikka J. Venturanza PhD is a lecturer in the Asian American Studies Department at the California State University, Northridge. Her research agenda aims to advance equity and inclusion initiatives for immigrant-origin, immigration-impacted, racially minoritized college student populations. Prior to her appointment, Rikka developed, implemented, and coordinated student-centered programs and lectured on ethnic studies courses at public four- and two-year AANAPISIs in California.

256 ABOUT the AUTHORS

Janelle L. West, EdD, is the Interim Dean of Graduate & Continuing Studies at Widener University and former Visiting Scholar at the University of Pennsylvania. Her research investigates college choice and enrollment patterns at historically Black colleges and universities (HBCUs) and the experiences of Black women in higher education.

April Brannon Yazza (she/they) (Diné and Shiwi) is an EdD student at the University of New Mexico and is of the Red Running into the Water People clan born for the Zuni People. Her paternal father is of the Zuni People and her maternal father is of the Black Streak Wood which influence her dedication to focus on Indigenous student identity development through reflective practices that are rooted in cultural values, kinship, and genius.

Casey Yocum is the Coordinator of Collaboration for the Virginia Community College System Office; she is also a doctoral student at Virginia Commonwealth University. She has a BS in Deaf Studies from Towson University and an MSEd from Southern Illinois University Edwardsville; her thesis focused on the experiences of deaf students on college campuses.

Eboni M. Zamani-Gallaher, PhD (she/her), currently serves as the Renée and Richard Goldman Interim Dean of the University of Pittsburgh School of Education. Previously, Zamani-Gallaher served as the Associate Dean for Equity, Justice, and Strategic Partnerships in the School of Education. An accomplished scholar, her work focuses on equitable participation in higher education; transfer, access, and retention policies; minoritized student populations in marginalized institutional contexts; and racial equity and campus climate in postsecondary education pathways.